ALBERT BERMEL

Molière's

Theatrical

Bounty

A NEW VIEW OF THE PLAYS

Southern Illinois University Press   *Carbondale and Edwardsville*

Edited by Teresa White
Production supervised by Natalia Nadraga
93   92   91   90   4   3   2   1

Library of Congress Cataloging-in-Publication Data

Bermel, Albert.
   Molière's theatrical bounty: a new view of the plays / Albert
Bermel.
        p.   cm.
      Bibliography: p.
      Includes index.
      1. Molière, 1622–1673—Criticism and interpretation.   I. Title.
PQ1860.B29   1990
842'.4—dc 19   89-5982
ISBN 0-8093-1550-5   CIP
ISBN 0-8093-1551-3   (pbk.)

Frontispiece: The Misanthrope, *1987. The Guthrie Theater, Minneapolis, MN. Artistic director: Garland Wright. Translator: Richard Wilbur. Director: Garland Wright. Set designer: Joel Fontaine. Costume designer: Jack Edwards. Lighting designer: Peter Maradudin. Caroline Lagerfelt as Célimène; Daniel Davis as Alceste. Photograph by Joe Giannetti.*

The paper used in this publication meets the minimum requirements of American National Standard for Information Sciences—Permanence of Paper for Printed Library Materials, ANSI Z39.48-1984. ♾

FOR JOYCE

For sharing

Contents

Illustrations ix

Preface xi

Introduction: Taking Off from Aristotle 1

PART ONE   PRELIMINARIES 17

The Jealous Husband 19

The Flying Doctor 22

The Botcher, or The Setbacks 25

Loving Spite 30

Two Precious Maidens Ridiculed 34

Sganarelle, or The Imaginary Cuckold 39

Don Garcie of Navarre, or The Jealous Prince 44

The School for Husbands 49

PART TWO   DIVERSIONS 55

The Nuisances 57

The Forced Marriage 62

The Princess of Elis 65

Doctor Love 70

Mélicerte 75

Comic Pastorale 77

The Sicilian, or Love the Painter 78

Monsieur de Pourceaugnac 80

The Magnificent Lovers 84

Psyche 87

PART THREE   FULFILLMENTS 91

1. Masters of the House

The School for Wives 93

The Criticism of The School for Wives 103

The Rehearsal at Versailles 107

George Dandin, or The Confounded Husband   115
The Miser   147
Tartuffe, or The Impostor   158
The Bourgeois Gentleman   173
The Imaginary Invalid   182
2. Mistresses of the House
Amphitryon   193
The Seductive Countess   203
The Learned Ladies   205
3. Loners
Don Juan   219
The Misanthrope   235
The Doctor in Spite of Himself   251
The Scams of Scapin   257

Conclusion: Molière's Afterlife   265
Molière's Characters   271
Bibliography   275
Index   279

Illustrations

Frontispiece

The Misanthrope

Following page 124

The Flying Doctor

Sganarelle, or The Imaginary Cuckold

The Forced Marriage

The Doctor in Spite of Himself

Malpractice, or Love's the Best Doctor

Malpractice, or Love's the Best Doctor

The Miser

The Miser

The Miser

The Miser

The Miser

The Miser

Tartuffe

Tartuffe

Tartuffe

Tartuffe

Tartuffe

The Imaginary Invalid

The Learned Ladies

Scapin

Scapin

Don Juan

The Misanthrope

The Misanthrope

The Misanthrope

Preface

In this book I describe in more detail than is usual the incidents that make up the action onstage and the events that complement them with offstage contributions from the story. Readers familiar with the plays will, I hope, recognize that these are not routine summaries but attempts to redefine those incidents. In *The Criticism of the School for Wives* and *The Rehearsal at Versailles*, Molière shows his own irritation with misunderstandings of what he meant that go back to faulty readings of what *has taken place* between the characters. He allows ample room for disagreement about the incidents, before we get to the meanings, and readers who dissent from my versions of those incidents will at least notice exactly where we begin to part company. There is an additional reason for recapitulating at least some of the action of each play and that is the repetition of names. Dorante, Valère, Cléante (Cléonte), Géronte, Dorimène, Gorgibus, Angélique, Oronte, Clitandre, Léandre, Mariane, and, most often, Sganarelle, recur as different roles, that is, as new implements of Molière's plotting. It seems to me desirable to remind readers of their special functions in each instance.

The book's three main divisions have been arrived at for the sake of convenience; they do not offer my granitic taxonomy of Molière's collected works. It is possible to slice the totality in different ways for critical purposes. As with any breakdown, this one includes many overlapping or marginal cases. The title of part I, "Preliminaries," should not be taken to imply that the earlier writings are inferior theatre. They accomplish admirably what Molière seems to have set out to do, and I see no value in comparing them unfavorably with plays written under other circumstances and for other audiences when Molière was an older, and therefore different, man and author. Their characters, situations, and themes may supply him with material he will reshape in his later plays, for he plundered his own work as unapologetically as he did other writers'; but one of his most fascinating qualities is his gift for transforming old material into new by an artistic process akin to the assembling of found objects into collages. *The Flying Doctor* succeeds in its own right, but it also leads to *The Doctor in Spite of Himself* and *The Imaginary Invalid.* From the early farcical romp *The Jealous Husband,* he retains the farce while adding a pathos that verges on tragedy when he opens it up into

George Dandin. Two Precious Maidens Ridiculed is one of his most relentless satires and also a precursor of *The Learned Ladies.*

The "Diversions," part II, those spectacular *divertissements* for the king, should, according to my breakdown, include *George Dandin* and *The Bourgeois Gentleman,* but those plays have acquired a life of their own without the original accompaniments of ballet, music, and machinery; and I have preferred to treat them as drama. In a preface to the published version of *Doctor Love,* Molière explains that he wrote, rehearsed, and staged it (with fantastic sets and costumes and complex machinery) in five days. Even though these entertainments may have diverted the author from other purposes, as well as the king from love and business, he seems to have had a good time creating them, despite the pressures; and most of them would probably still hold a stage astonishingly well—if impresarios today mounted them as prodigally as the seventeenth century did.

As for "Fulfillments" (part III), the complicated and ambiguous plays examined under this heading need a separate chapter each, which could have been tripled or quadrupled in length and still not have come wholly to grips with the work, even if it hewed to the intricacies of the plotting and the evolution of the characters. This part's three subdivisions—"Masters of the House," "Mistresses of the House," and "Loners"—constitute the heart of the book and most of its novelties (if any; one never knows what the rest of the world is thinking and rushing into print). Once again, the contents of each subdivision must allow for overlapping. Harpagon and George Dandin may well qualify as loners, in addition to being masters of the house, but I hope that the slot I have selected for each play will justify itself in the separate chapters.

Within each part, the plays are dealt with in chronological order, although I see no purpose in arguing whether they "progress" or "retrogress," improve on what has gone before, or repudiate it, or fail to live up to it. Criticism that scrapes through the history of an author's output in search of a steady accumulation of quality, usually leading to a ranking of the plays from "disappointments" to "probable" or "undoubted masterpieces," uses comparison as a quirky measuring tool or artistic thermometer rather than as an aid to exploring each successive piece of work. Even though the chapters recognize the repeated application of certain themes and characterizations and dramatic structures, I wanted to come at each play as a piece of individual artistry, because that is how it will most often be read and how it will invariably be approached in the playhouse.

Since the chapters take issue here and there with previous criticism of Molière—if they did not, there would be no point in adding to it—I want to say emphatically that I am beholden to all of it that I have found for stimulus, provocation, information, and good reading, but most deeply to those writings that approach Molière's plays not simply as literature but as dramatic literature: in particular, W. G. Moore's pioneering *Molière: A New Criticism;* René Bray's *Molière: homme de théâtre*; Marcel Gutwirth's spirited *Molière, ou l'invention comique;* W. D. Howarth's *Molière: A Playwright and His Audience;* John Palmer's biography, that melodious counterpointing of historical reporting and critical judgments; and Jacques Guicharnaud's wide and, at the same time, microscopic study of three plays *(Tartuffe, Don Juan,* and *The Misanthrope),* and their shadings into the remainder of Molière's writings, in *Molière: une aventure théâtrale.* For most of the textual references I have gone gratefully to the later Bibliothèque de la Pléiade edition of Molière's *Oeuvres complètes,* edited by Georges Couton. My translations of extracts from the plays and French critics are sometimes fairly free, but in no case, I hope, so as to misrepresent the original.

More personal obligations are owing to Robert S. Phillips and Teresa White, model editors; to Eric Bentley, who offered many suggestions, every one of which I gratefully incorporated, and who read the manuscript with his uncommonly sympathetic understanding; to Helen Merrill—agent, sage counselor, friend; to John Carroll, the benefactor who made possible (as the public television commercials say) the book's index; to my wife and sons; and to the generations of undergraduates at Lehman College and Ph.D. candidates at the Graduate Center of the City University of New York, who, in the past seventeen years, have shared in rediscoveries of Molière's plays as we asked what they meant to yesterday's theatre and may mean to tomorrow's.

Introduction: Taking Off from Aristotle

Structure

These two exchanges come from *The Doctor in Spite of Himself:*

SGANARELLE . . . Aristotle hit it when he said, "Marry a woman; live with a demon."

MARTINE Listen to the clever man with his bonehead of an Aristotle! (I, 1)

GÉRONTE . . . The cause, please. Why did [my daughter] lose her voice?

SGANARELLE All our leading authorities will instruct you that she has an impediment to the mobility of her tongue.

GÉRONTE Then what's your professional diagnosis of this impediment to the mobility of her tongue?

SGANARELLE On that very point Aristotle says . . . some really fine things.

GÉRONTE I can imagine.

SGANARELLE Ah, there was a great man!

GÉRONTE Must have been.

SGANARELLE A *great* man. *(Displaying the length of his forearm)* Greater than even I am by that much . . . (II, 4)

If we tried to sum up Molière-on-Aristotle from these lines—a rash venture—we might conclude 1) that the playwright paid tribute to the philosopher by having his shrewd hero praise him; 2) that the playwright seasoned the praise with irony by pulling it from the mouth of a fake medical scholar; 3) that the playwright offered a sop to those scholars among his contemporaries who continually cited the philosopher; 4) that the playwright mocked these "leading authorities" who had turned the philosopher into a rule maker and used the revered name to bolster their diagnoses and postdiagnostic party conversation; 5) that the playwright was having it every which way. My own preference is for a combination of 1 and 4, although Sganarelle does

I

not quote Aristotle accurately or directly. But much as we only speculate on Molière's views of Aristotle—if he had solidified views—so we can only speculate on what he would have made of an Aristotelian analysis of his theatre, especially if, by a further straining of the imagination, we picture him alive today.[1] He would probably not dissent from the six component parts of a tragedy discerned by the father of criticism, because no subsequent critic has improved on the breakdown into plot, character, language, thought, design, and music, in descending order of significance. Nor would the playwright object in all likelihood to having Aristotle's analysis of tragedy applied to his own plays, which, even when they hover on the brink of tragedy, bravely—almost perversely—keep their hold on comedy. He would also appreciate that, after 2,300 years of use and abuse, Aristotle's guidance remains serviceable for many kinds of theatrical analyses, particularly since the components have weathered refinement and extensions, so that language incorporates style, thought includes themes and ideas, design includes not only scenery, costumes, and masks but also lighting and sound effects, and music includes recordings.[2]

But today's imaginary Molière would be bound to point out that Aristotle has also become an unwitting guide to forms of entertainment other than the

1. Molière's characters also mention Aristotle in other plays (e.g., *The Jealous Husband, The Forced Marriage, The Criticism of The School for Wives*), in each case, apparently more to satirize the intolerance of the philosopher's seventeenth-century exegetes than to poke fun at the great man himself. An edict passed by the national legislature in Paris one year after Molière's birth decreed a death sentence for criticism of Aristotle or Aristotelians. It seems unlikely that the edict was generally enforced, in other words, that Molière risked death every time he dropped Aristotle's name disrespectfully; but his distaste for neo- and quasi-Aristotelian arguments may date back to the early 1640s when he heard, or knew of, lectures by Pierre Gassendi (1592–1655), the Epicurean and anti-Aristotelian philosopher.

2. The *Poetics* is a slim document when compared with the *Natyashastra*, drawn up some centuries later (its exact date is uncertain) by Bharata Muni. As Balwant Gargi explains in his *Theatre in India*, the *Natyashastra* "gives all conceivable details of makeup and costumes, has exhaustive notes on direction and production, deals with the theory of aesthetics, and analyzes various sentiments and their portrayal. Difficult body postures; movements of the neck, the breast and the eyeballs; and styles of gait, color, jewelry, etc., are elaborately described." A handbook—virtually a bible—for the playwright, director, and actor, the *Natyashastra* includes, among its plenitude of information, instructions on how to feel an emotion *(bhava)* and how to transmit it to a spectator *(rasa)*.

tragic drama: his six components also inhere in those forms of narration that the *Poetics* could not have foreseen, in particular, short and long prose fiction, operas, narrative dance, feature films and their derivative, television plays. Much criticism of Molière, as of other playwrights, leaves a reader dissatisfied, because it might as well be tackling films or novels as plays. For this reason, our author could plead that, among its other services, criticism of his theatre should deal with his plays as creations for a stage. Such criticism will need to pose pointedly theatrical questions about any scene. Who is onstage and for how long? With whom? For what purposes? With what results? Who is withdrawn or kept absent from the stage, and why? Which characters are mentioned in this and other scenes but never appear onstage or among the dramatis personae? What effects do the characters who do appear have on their surroundings, and how do their surroundings influence them?

In film, directors and critics have recognized the artistry associated with framing, the enclosure during any shot of selected characters and parts of a set, as well as the successive angles of vision. In theatre, framing is less rigorous, untrammeled by the imposition of a lens. It allows spectators more freedom to swing and focus their eyes and attention within the boundaries of the playing area. In addition, film criticism deals with accomplished artifacts, finished work, whereas theatre criticism deals with the possibilities of a text; even reviews of a particular production imply chances seized or lost. A film critic may take issue with a director's taste or judgment, but only—and sometimes unfairly—by opposing it to his own notions of what the film under review might have been. A theatre critic can, in theory at least, take issue with a director's interpretation by referring it back to the given dialogue and stage directions or to interpretations of the same material by previous directors. Despite these differences, plays do undergo framing, scene by scene and moment by moment, and taking account of it calls for a criticism that emphasizes the interdependence of plot, character, design, and the remaining components, combining them in a conspective view of the written play's requirements and opportunities. Such a view cannot say what *ought to* happen on the stage. But it can open up the range of possible enactment.

Molière's drama has already spawned a large critical literature in French and a more limited one in English. But as his plays' popularity grows on this side of the Atlantic, critics and theatre artists alike have come to realize that the enigmatic nature of most of his work leaves significant choices open for interpretation. My purpose here is to illuminate these choices for directors, actors, and designers—not to provide hard-and-fast answers but rather to notice why and how these choices exist. In delving into Molière's theatricality, play by play, I assume that an analysis that holds true for tragedy holds broadly true for comedy and the other genres.

Because of the range of choices, I am following Aristotle in not attempting to appraise each play's dramatic effectiveness, how well it "works." Perhaps the philosopher omitted this component because he knew it would need to be infinitely, automatically adjustable to allow for taste, that is, for whim and prejudice. The dramatic effectiveness of any performance proceeds from so many variables—the performers' preparations and their skills on each occasion, the composition of the audience, its moods and tractability, the premises where it is given, and so on—that it seems to be less a component of a play than a grab bag of fortuitous circumstances. Yet, many theatre practitioners still feel they have an instinct, a gut reaction, inspired by a reading of the text, for what will or will not "work." That thousands of plays have "worked" in some circumstances and not in others does not deter them from the belief in—virtually the theology of—the "works/won't work" distinction. In other words, this pragmatic intuition itself does not work. Its shortcomings amply justify the recent investigations of the impact of specific performances on specific audiences by means of "reception" or "response" criticism.

Plot and Plotting

Aristotle defined plot *(mythos)* in the *Poetics* as "the arrangement of the incidents" (Butcher's translation, 1894) or "the structuring of the events" (Else's translation, 1967) and accounted it "the soul of tragedy" and "the goal of tragedy." Since the Renaissance, and possibly before, critics and historians have taken the word *plot* to allude variously to a play's story (the "plot summary"), its shape, framework, craftsmanship, conflicts, motives, sequence, suspense, or its causation, its dramatic logic. In usage, *plot* sometimes becomes a popular simile for cunning or planning. After acquiring outlines so blurred as to be imperceptible, the term has grown either meaningless or so crammed with meaning that it needs merciless pruning. Does it apply to structure? Yes, for what else can the "arrangement" or "structuring" (i.e., the organization) refer to? Does it apply to substance or content? Not quite; it appears not to cover the incidents or events themselves (which make up the substance or content), only their arrangement; and it happens that Aristotle does not dissect substance or content or roughly what John Crowe Ransom calls "texture." Yet, a play does not exist without content, any more than it exists without structure. In some writings, "plot" stands for *narrative,* although Aristotle's text makes clear that he is writing about the *organization* of the narrative, not the narrative itself.

In this book I use the word *plotting*, which sounds more active (and a bit more conspiratorial) than plot. It has slightly different implications from the traditional ones. Plotting refers to the playwright's framing of scenes, the deployment in each one of selected characters. The analogy here is with a lighting plot: the designation of certain lights, colors, and intensities, scene by scene. Some of the characters will occupy the stage at given moments, while the playwright keeps others out of sight and perhaps out of mind:

* When Orgon returns home he is greeted by his maid and brother-in-law, not by his wife or the shady priest he has sheltered and very nearly adopted, although the wife and parasitic guest are the principal subjects of the scene (*Tartuffe*, I, 4) that follows. Molière has withheld them, as well as the rest of Orgon's household, from the *plotting*.

* The first and last speeches of *George Dandin* are uttered by the central character in isolation; they amount to complaints about his plight. The *plotting* invites us to assume that what the character tells us in confidence about his plight in the first speech is the truth, since no other character refutes him; by the time the last scene rolls around, we have seen and heard enough from the other characters to suspect his version of the truth and to see that his mournful plight is, in large part, due to self-deception.

* In the *plotting* of the first two acts of *The Bourgeois Gentleman*, we meet Monsieur Jourdain's four teachers in a certain sequence that clarifies the play's meanings, in addition to enhancing its humor.

* The name of Anselme is mentioned a number of times during the first act of *The Miser*, but because of the *plotting* the character does not appear until the fifth act, when he behaves like a *deus ex machina*, a money-bearing arm of fate, which straightens out almost all the complications.

A playwright's deployment of the characters—their visible presence, presence in hiding, absence, arrivals, departures, false exits, the sequence in which he presents them and dismisses them—these constitute the plotting. If this writing technique has been isolated and identified before, either it has not been named or the name has not caught on.[3] Rather than coming up with a new and strange word for it, I have adapted the familiar one as a hubristic guess that what I understand by the term pretty well corresponds to what Aristotle could have understood. Plotting as a dramatic device applies to

3. I used *plotting* in this sense in an earlier book about the modern theatre, *Contradictory Characters* (1973). See esp. 21–23.

comedy as well as to tragedy and the other genres, but it can also apply to cinema and prose fiction. In a play, it determines which characters during a given sequence are on or off the stage; in a film, which characters are on or off the screen; in a novel or short story, which characters are on or off the page.

A play's main plot consists of the scenes in which the principal characters take part, although disagreements may well raise their provocative heads over which characters are principals (Orgon or Tartuffe?). Subplots consist of scenes between the secondary characters or between them and the principals, and here again disagreements may erupt and lead to squabbles over billing. (Is Valère a principal in *The Miser?* Is Cléante?) This distinction between main plot and subplots is limitedly helpful but loose and subject to the discretion and ambitions of directors, felicities of casting, and other stage variables and personal caprices.

Plotting also shapes the presentation of a play's conflicts. Toward the end of the first act of *The School for Wives*, Arnolphe is congratulating himself on his astuteness in having adopted the young ward whom he intends to marry and has shut up in a house with two servants guarding her. Then a friend strolls by, a youth named Horace, who innocently mentions that he has been courting the girl—he does not realize she is Arnolphe's ward. The act ends with Arnolphe shaken and bewildered, an effect calculated to unleash the conflict and immediately sharpen it because of the timing of Horace's appearance and Molière's pinpointing of these two characters for the encounter. In a similar kind of plotting, the first person George Dandin meets onstage is a chattering go-between employed by his wife's lover, a simpleton who tells Dandin about the wife's affair and agitates this already agitated husband further, bringing the conflict into play before Dandin—or we—have seen the lover or Dandin's four other antagonists: his in-laws, his wife, and her maid. In both these cases, the opponent and an opponent's substitute remain unaware that they are addressing the subject of their conversation and salting the dialogue with dramatic irony. The conflicts in *Don Juan* intensify through the play's five acts as the Don measures himself against a string of opponents, each of them more liable to break through his defenses than the ones before, culminating in the Statue, who will finally destroy him. The author keeps the conflicts simmering by attaching him throughout the play to his weakest opposition, the servant-companion Sganarelle, who would, if he could, act as Juan's conscience.

The Revue Format

The structure of Molière's plays observes the neoclassical pattern. A character's entrance, or occasionally an exit, marks a new scene. A principal character will usually feature in the final scene of an act to delineate the main plot more strongly. The plotting, as I have defined it, determines the structure, besides underlying the substance. But as a parallel pattern to this one, Molière introduced into his theatre a format not unlike that of a modern vaudeville, revue, or cabaret, with its succession of independent turns: comic routines, songs, monologues, conjuring, dancing, acrobatics, animal marvels. As producer, he wanted to provide the strongest opportunities for his actors, and so for many scenes he composed solos, duets, trios, and a few quartets. These, in addition to advancing the story, suited the personal talents of such early members of his company as Jodelet and Gros-René, latecomers like Mlle Beauval, and long-term members—Mlle de Brie, Madeleine Béjart, La Grange, Du Croisy, and, above all, himself. This alternative structure, derived in part from the commedia dell'arte, resembles the epic form used two and a half centuries later by Piscator and Brecht and by scores of their successors, but although it is cloaked in the formal division into neoclassical scenes, one can detect its subtle presence even in his more ambitious dramatic poems.

In practice the revue format usually resulted in typecasting. Madeleine Béjart played a series of quick-witted maidservants; Catherine de Brie and Thérèse du Parc and Armande Molière, beautiful heroines—Armande also did very young heroines, especially acerbic daughters; Jeanne-Olivier Beauval, gigglers; Charles La Grange, noblemen and sons; André Hubert, farcical or pedantic twerps.[4] As a rule, we associate typecasting with Hollywood-type casting, selecting actors to rework roles in which they have previously had successes. With Molière, as in all likelihood with Shakespeare and with Preston Sturges on the Paramount lot, we have roles written for certain performers and, in some cases, purposely extending their range: La Grange takes on Don Juan; Hubert does Amphitryon and several transvestite parts; Molière re-creates himself as a miser of over sixty and fluctuates between servants and masters, courtiers and peasants, playing several roles in *The Nuisances* and one role *as* several roles in *Scapin.*[5]

4. For an extended treatment of the known and probable casting of Molière's actors, see Herzel. Useful summaries appear in Bray, 222–43, and Howarth, 307–10.
5. René Bray writes: "When Molière is composing a play he has a predetermined interpretation in mind; he knows to whom he will confide each role, especially the

Action and Story

If plotting belongs strictly to the organization of a play, the definition put forward here leaves unrecognized the substance or content, the incidents or events themselves. I propose two names for the substance. The incidents that take place onstage, thanks to the plotting or disposition of the characters, together constitute the *action*. But there is also what might be called negative plotting, and this includes the incidents that took place before the start of the action plus the ones that take place between acts or scenes plus those that happen offstage (which the audience may not witness but will learn about later) at the same time as the scenes enacted onstage. All of this unstaged material combines with the action to constitute the *story*.

Thus, the story of *Don Juan* begins long before the action and encompasses it. It takes in the Don's earlier disputes with his father and with rivals, his stealing Doña Elvire from a convent, and his early employment of Sganarelle. The rescue of Don Juan and Sganarelle from drowning, which occurs out of sight between the first and second acts, also belongs to the story. These events, although not performed onstage in the action, are reported to us during the action. The action, then, fulfills two functions: it displays itself, and it recounts or implies the remaining portions of the story. These portions (story minus action) roughly equal what drama textbooks used to call exposition. But that word generally meant introductory information that launched a play. The textbooks fondly applied it to an opening scene of a drawing-room comedy in which servants dusted or laid a table while they confided family secrets to each other and the audience. Ibsen dated this use of the word by continuing to plant bits of story through a play's last act—sometimes into its closing lines.

The reporting of offstage events goes back to the beginnings of recorded Western theatre, to the Greek-messenger speeches reporting death, murder, battles, and other catastrophes that the playwrights thought inappropriate for

significant ones *(ceux qui comptent);* and he arranges his play to give work to the greatest possible number of colleagues. This may seem like an unworthy consideration to those who forget the requirements of the acting profession. They will rebel against the idea that a *Misanthrope* can have come into being to satisfy the otherwise legitimate ambitions of three actors. But I refuse to abstract Molière from the profession he has taken on, and prefer to relocate him amid the array of technical constraints and obligations in which his genius reveals itself even more strongly than in the unreality of a writer's study" (Bray, 200; my translation).

public observation.[6] Such reporting is a legacy of the art form that preceded the drama, the epic story, told orally, and in a few cases written, before plays came into being with their multiple characters who could speak for themselves. The Greek-messenger speech had its advantages, the main ones being that it freed the play from the limitations of its stage setting, pushed the story forward rapidly, and gave the storyteller entrusted with it an opportunity for bravura playing. Shakespeare employs it often, for instance, to rush the opening scene of *Henry IV, Part I* into movement after its languorous first monologue, when Westmoreland tells the king of the horrors that followed the battle between Owen Glendower and Mortimer.

As we consider the meanings of incidents in a play written since the era of Greek tragedy, the story, the exposition of nonenacted material, takes on importance. Because the author has chosen to have it reported, rather than witnessed, we can seldom take it at face value as we can the impersonal Greek-messenger speeches that relate the deaths of Agamemnon, Ajax, or Hippolytus. Before determining whether and how much of the speech is true, we must gauge the reliability of the reporter(s). Westmoreland speaks of "A thousand of [Mortimer's] people butchered, / Upon whose dead corpses there was such misuse, / Such beastly shameless transformation / By those Welshwomen done, as may not be / Without much shame retold or spoken of." Yet, the only Welsh woman the audience sees in the play is Glendower's gentle daughter, who sings a love song. We must suspect that Westmoreland is indulging in the wartime (and cold wartime) habit of casting the enemy as the devil. The task of getting at the truth behind reported events becomes even more complicated when two or more separate reports of the same circumstance differ in essentials or in details (the *Rashomon* effect, a favorite device of Pirandello); and one might say that the enigmatic character of much theatre, ancient and modern, proceeds from a spectator's doubts about whom to believe and to what extent. Commercial courtroom thrillers end by reconciling the conflicting accounts. The authors of more enduring theatre contrive

6. As a striking modern equivalent of the messenger speech, Giraudoux in his *Electra* has a prophetic figure called The Beggar describe in the past tense Orestes' killing of his mother and stepfather while it is happening and even gallop verbally ahead of the moment of death:

BEGGAR . . . But as [Aegisthus] died, he cried a name I shall not repeat.

AEGISTHUS *(his voice coming from offstage)* Electra—

BEGGAR I went too fast. He's just catching up with me.

From *Jean Giraudoux: Three Plays,* tr. Phyllis La Farge with Peter H. Judd (New York: Hill and Wang, 1964), 246.

no such reconciliation but leave the sorting out to the audience, much as a courtroom drama in life leaves the sorting of evidence, for better or for worse, to the jury.

Characters and Roles

Since the action of a play offers us more "substantial" substance than the expository portions that make up the rest of the story, we rely on the action for our appreciation of the conflicts. Given the plotting, which tells us what figures are brought together for the conflicts, the conflicts themselves depend on the personification of temperaments, wishes, and fears we call characterization. The conflicts in Molière's and most other plays arise from differences in sex, class, ambition, and personality, and I will say something about all of these. But a few general comments on conflicts between men and women may be in order here.

Much previous criticism treats the female roles in the plays that do not have a dominant female character as incidental, if not ornamental. I regard these roles as being integral. Sganarelle in *The Doctor in Spite of Himself* does not choose to become a doctor; his wife traps him into the transformation. Célimène, Agnès, Elmire, the Angélique of *George Dandin*, Élise and Frosine in *The Miser,* and others are equally roles of prime consequence for the staging of each work. We have still not recovered from the excesses of biographical critiques, according to which, the parts taken by Molière and his wife reflect *mutatis mutandis* the storminess of their marriage.[7] Even if there are convincing reasons for accepting the reflection, I find no reason for

---

7. A typical example: "In 1662 Molière committed the tragic mistake of marrying Armande Béjart, sister of the troupe's Madeleine Béjart, and a heartless flirt who was twenty-one years his junior. The same year he composed one of his most important comedies, *L'Ecole des Femmes (The School for Wives),* a study of marital incompatibility" (from Bernard D. N. Grebanier's introduction to his translation of *The Misanthrope* [Great Neck, NY: Barron's, 1959]). But what about the playwright's earlier studies of marital incompatibility, some written long before he married and including his first surviving play?

going further than the assumption that he had powerful differences with this particular woman and no reason at all for deducing that Molière was misogynistic. On the contrary, his women characters—including the ones originally played by his wife—make powerful cases for themselves, which cannot be overlooked or dismissed. Meanwhile, the playwright does not spare the men. We might even conclude that the worst enemy, the ultimate and unbeatable opponent of Arnolphe, Orgon, Dandin, Alceste, Harpagon, or Don Juan, is himself, and that the woman he loves or lives with understands this sadly comic condition better than he does.

To a performer or director, it seems self-evident that the characters in any play interact with one another. In criticism, the interactions, frequently delicate ones, have not enjoyed much recognition, which is to say that the consequences of those interactions have seldom been taken into enough account. The love, enmity, rivalry, domineering, obedience, defiance, and other relationships change as the action drives forward. They are dynamic. So are the characters. Instead of being fixed, self-contained psychological entities, the characters bruise and soothe one another, bring one another out: they respond to, and are themselves altered by, the words, moods, activities, and the supposed opinions of others. This interplay lies at the heart of all drama of distinction, not only Molière's, and it preoccupies my analysis in the coming pages, leading as it does to changes in the personalities of the characters *and changes in our perceptions of them.* Out of these changes comes a greater breadth of enactment for the performers.

We inevitably scrutinize figures in these or any plays as though they were people we have come to know, if incompletely. But it may be worth restating the obvious. Characters are no more (and certainly no less) than dramatic entities. Roles. If we lay them out for dissection at different points on a sympathy-antipathy axis—reacting to them with the same likes and dislikes we helplessly feel for real people—we are liable to misjudge the purposes for which they were created. Their "lives," bounded by the attitudes, speeches, and situations decreed by the playwright and grounded in the decisions of directors and the personalities lent them by actors, are more confined and, at the same time, more malleable, condensed, and highly charged than actual lives. What determines them as identities? Not their past or their genes but the ways in which the plotting is taken into account. The very selectivity of the plotting—these scenes in this sequence featuring these characters in these places—makes them more graphically snobbish, avaricious, hypochondriacal, hypocritical, deceptive, gullible, strenuously logical, generous, bashful, and continually surprising than real people are.

Thought

Aplay's action cannot help incorporating social commentary, which may be regarded as a subdivision of Aristotle's *thought*. Whether or not the author puts in descriptions of surroundings, architecture, interior decor, clothing, and other artifacts (in the dialogue or the stage directions), certain assumptions and issues fashionable in his time are bound to emerge. Much documentation has been expended on the extent to which Molière practiced satire, and exactly whom and what he aimed it at. Does he go so far as to make fun of his royal patron in his portraits of overbearing fathers or in his sycophantic obeisances to the king and court in *The Rehearsal at Versailles, The Criticism of the School for Wives*, and the last act of *Tartuffe?* He certainly seems to.[8] Mikhail Bulgakov in his play *A Cabal of Hypocrites* suggested that Louis XIV's despotic and eccentric demands and the prudish spite of many leading Church contemporaries made life oppressive for the purveyor of royal entertainments, by way of distant analogy with Stalin's and his acolytes' censorship of Bulgakov and other Soviet artists considered counterrevolutionary (and Stalin's tyranny, one might add, toward his official composer, Dmitry Shostakovich). Some or all of Molière's later plays do look like subtle forms of retaliation. The Jupiter of *Amphitryon* goes further; it is an almost brash caricature of Louis. Sources from life have also been proposed for such characterizations as Tartuffe, Arnolphe, Alceste, and Argan. Some of them may have incorporated self-portraiture and self-flagellation of which there is doubt-less an infusion in his (and all) drama.[9] But do we need to ask exactly

8. Molière's relationships with the young king and with Pierre Corneille have come in for great quantities of commentary, including at least one book that posits Corneille as the author of at least some of Molière's writings. What has been called "the Molière-Louis-Corneille question" is a complex matter that will be only touched on here and there in the text that follows this Introduction.
9. The related and vexing question of whether certain figures in the plays serve as the author's mouthpieces, or *raisonneurs*, is alluded to in the chapter on *The School for Wives*.

who the original targets were in order to appreciate the plays? I've chosen not to enter the lists of identifiers, partly out of a feeling of being disqualified through being unqualified, but more out of impatience with deterministic biographical criticism. To historians, it may matter whether Tartuffe was modeled on some particular *faux dévot* or on somebody not in the Church, or that Trissotin and Vadius in *The Learned Ladies* refer to the Abbé Cotin and to Gilles Ménage. But the elucidation of an original target bears hardly at all on how the play will be performed in our time or the future.

Molière did, however, repeatedly oppose the will of his protagonists not only to the will of other characters but also to the rules, manners, and conventions that governed institutions—the court, the medical profession, the Church, the law, society as a whole. And such opposition does bear heavily on our stagings, for individuals today, from admirable rebels and self-appointed consciences for humanity to criminals, continue to set their faces and principles against systems and conventional ideas. If modernizing directors now and then use Molière to "make a statement" about late twentieth-century conformists and nonconformers, they invite rebuke only when it turns into an overstatement that makes the playwright appear naïve. The plays overflow with social criticism. A production that fails to give that criticism its due is defective.

But the strongest and some of the dramatist's most artful criticism comes about in the plays because of his ability to stare into the face of evil and recognize it for what it is in its most insidious forms, temptation and trickery. In the role of Mascarille, *The Botcher* releases the first in Molière's succession of villain-heroes, some of them aiding their masters or a worthy cause, but all of them obeying an inner call to excel in the arts of doing wrong, even for the right reasons. As they issue a challenge to God, their peers, and circumstances to try stopping them, so they challenge their seventeenth-century audiences—and us—to see them for what they repeatedly tell us they are, swindlers *(fourbes)*. Instead of presenting them as mere lovable rogues, actors need to let us see their iron, their flint, their pitilessness, the harm and threats that they embody.[10]

As a group, most of Molière's knaves have this much in common: that they are dangerous and unscrupulous reincarnations of the medieval Vice.

---

10. For a contrasting reading of Mascarille—as a likable personality—see Jasinski, *Molière*, 36–37. ("An artist in his own way, he is not far from practicing art for the sake of art.")

I suggest this not to adopt a tone of disapproval or for the sake of moral edification—this playwright has suffered enough, during his lifetime and after, from the excesses of moralists—but to emphasize that giving these charm-radiating malefactors their due license onstage means helping audiences to understand why Molière was in his time—and remains—a controversial playwright, not simply a popular one. The less tolerant members of the Gallican church quickly spotted him as the enemy. Their conviction of original sin, at birth, before one has had the chance to do wrong, together with the possibility of salvation only through contrition, received jolt after jolt from these villains, whose antisocial acts go praised and unpunished.[11] The playwright covers his tracks by showing their immense expenditures of energy and acumen as wasted and futile, since fate will ultimately take over and the action be forced to yield to the working out of that portion of the story that preceded it.

Not only Church officials and their followers but also the medical, legal, and other scholarly professions had cause to range themselves against Molière, since he treated them as so much social excrescence, successors to the parasites of Plautus, and oblivious to their ineffectuality. Delectable as they may have been to Molière's audiences and still are to us in those scenes depicting their love of their own tongues, inability to speak intelligibly to others, and the harm they wreak, his hammering away at these pedantic pretenders gave offense and stirred up lasting grudges.

Molière's stated and often-quoted intent "to please" needs evaluating anew so that we do not let it cloak the spirit of rebellion that animated him and his creations.

Abstract Opposites

The playwright's Thought activates the critic's thoughts. Dramatic criticism has begged, borrowed, or stolen from literary theory one type of thematic analysis that has proved dead-ended for the drama. This arises from perceived "tensions" between pairs of abstract opposites. Masks and faces. Madness and sanity. Illusion (or appearance or fantasy or dreams or even pipe dreams) and truth (or reality). Emotion (or passion) and reason (or will). Necessity (or fate) and freedom. Despair (or cynicism) and hope (or idealism).

---

11. One of these characters who *is* punished, Tartuffe, turns out to be a false priest who preaches like a true ordained one.

Blindness and seeing. Animality (or callousness) and humanity—a particularly offensive distinction, this. Love and money. Materialism (or physicality or lust or greed) and spirituality (or chastity or altruism or love). Pretense (hypocrisy) and sincerity (candor). Suspicion and trust. The list may have no end. Such pairs of opposites, often referred to as "dualities" or less often as "dyads," may clarify the themes in a novel or poem, but they shed little light on any play text, which is a finished work only when considered as literature, as a work to read. In their application to a play considered as theatre, they amount to an alternative and weaker method of discerning conflicts between the motives of the characters, that is, as a belt route that skirts the dramatic substance. The only consequence I can conceive of for them in a production would be in the design—clashing styles or colors superimposed on each other or separating an acting area into two.[12]

Design

A degree of abstraction has already crept into late twentieth-century designs for Molière, but from the fine arts rather than from literary criticism. The setting the author decrees for each play will frequently seem to have—to borrow a popular term—an environmental impact on the characters, and usually not a beneficent one. They can then be affected by the neutrality of the street scene in *The School for Wives* or *Scapin;* the psychological constrictions imposed by the one room in Philaminte's or Harpagon's or Argan's home; the ambiguities that result from five acts of *The Misanthrope* laid in the house not of Alceste but of Célimène; the alterations to Monsieur Jourdain's drawing room; the different locations required for the separate acts of *Don Juan.* The designs, like many of the *mise en scènes,* are as a rule much less cautious and a great deal more affecting than the reviews that barely acknowledge them and the longer, more studied criticism that takes design as an Aristotelian "fact," but pursues it no further.

The rise to prominence, and even notoriety, of *auteur*-directors in the theatre, which occurred more than fifty years before the *Cahiers du Cinéma* critics spotted and named them in motion pictures, has forced criticism to

12. The pairs of opposites may not make sense as inspiration for the design of any Molière play, because in no play (except possibly *The School for Husbands*) is there a simple contrast of conceptual opposites, as there is in, for example, the chastity (or innocence or spiritual health) and guilt (or vengefulness or illness) in the *Hippolytus.*

reckon with design as itself a mode of interpretation.[13] We could watch many striking contemporary productions of classics, familiar and unfamiliar, while wearing earplugs and, nevertheless, leave the playhouse with a pretty clear idea of what the director, supported by design colleagues, has told us about each text. Design has become a director's wedge that can split open the entire trunk of an old play. Sometimes the wedge is driven in with a sledgehammer; at other times a couple of light taps, cunningly applied, afford us a radically new view of the play's recesses. We now have design as thought, design as character, design as language, design as (mood-charging) music. Molière reborn might recognize that we have very nearly reverted to the Baroque theatre of Italy and France.

13. I refer to the practitioners of the New Stagecraft, Appia and Craig, followed by Meyerhold, Reinhardt, Copeau, Jessner, Baty, Artaud, and at least a score of play reinventers of the past thirty years.

PART ONE

Preliminaries

The Jealous Husband

(*La Jalousie du Barbouillé*, Date Uncertain)

The name Le Barbouillé, which Molière confers on the unheroic hero of his first play,[1] has multiple connotations; it could mean the smeared, soiled, or bedaubed man, looking literally like someone dragged out of a wet ditch or swamp. "Mud all over" would be too polite an English equivalent and would not quite figuratively hint at his marital condition. "In the shit" is more like it, for the play's through line follows his frustrations in coping with what he views as the shortcomings of his wife: her gadding about, enjoying her young life, and not being available to minister to his desires. Theatre historians in France have pointed out that his name has other connections with his role, which the actor may have played with his face smeared or bearded with flour *(une barbe enfarinée)* or with charcoal to imitate the leather masks worn by certain commedia dell'arte performers or with a wine-colored complexion to denote his drinking.[2]

Whatever the form or hue of the facial overlay, it would have been stylized to match the setting and acting; and a production today will surely benefit from a treatment that is unabashedly theatrical—at one point, he appeals to another character to ask the audience whether or not he has had anything to drink. The original set consisted most likely of an outdoor space, a square, with one or perhaps two streets feeding into it, and a background of three practicable doorways leading into the homes of Le Barbouillé, his father-in-law, Gorgibus, and his neighbor, the Scholar. The mixed provenance of this little farce in thirteen scenes reminds us that Molière was one of the great codifiers of several traditions in the drama. He drew most of the characters from medieval and Renaissance French theatre, the set from adaptations of the Roman stages of Terence and possibly Plautus. To the commedia dell'arte, he owed not only the masks but also the character of the Scholar, a *dottore* from the University of Bologna or Padua, who, with his self-obsession and outpouring of philosophical jargon, is riding for a fall.

---

1. Other early plays, now vanished, that Molière may have written or adapted from various sources include *The Fine Blockhead, The Woodcutter, Gorgibus in the Sack,* and several doctor plays: *The Doctor in Love, The Pedantic Doctor,* and *The Three Rival Doctors.*

2. Couton 1: 1183. Jasinski, *Molière,* 19. Jasinski goes on to remark (22) that Le Barbouillé is "haunted by inconstancy and feminine perfidy. Molière is already Molière."

The plotting of the play's first half works partly by accretion as the characters introduce themselves. Scene 1: Le Barbouillé comes out of his house to deliver a monologue of a dozen lines; made "the unhappiest of men" by his straying wife, he ponders how he can punish her. Scene 2 adds the Scholar, who provides not one grain of sage or any other kind of advice for the jealous husband, and is pursued offstage still begging Le Barbouillé's questions. In scene 3, three new characters—the wife, Angélique, her sympathetic maid-companion, Cathau, and her admirer, Valère—offer a contrasting view of her; unhappy with her older, unappetizing, and heavy-drinking spouse, she cannot wait to succumb to Valère's entreaties. Scene 4: Le Barbouillé returns to raise the number of figures onstage to four, until Valère withdraws. Scene 5: the three remaining characters are brought up to five by the arrival of Angélique's father, Gorgibus, and his friend, Villebrequin. Scene 6: the Scholar comes back—there are now six characters present—to torment the others with his pedantry until Le Barbouillé drags him out of sight by the heels, still orating; and general uproar and confusion climactically end the first two-thirds of the play. The final third (scs. 7–13) settles down to the conflict between the marriage partners and its questionable resolution. She sneaks off to a party *(un bal)* for a tryst with Valère, banking on her husband's staying out at a bar; but although the dance is over when she gets there, she comes back after he does; and he locks her out of the house (scs. 8–10). In the following scene (11), she begs her husband to let her back in the house; he refuses; she pretends to stab herself; he comes outside to check; she slips inside and locks the door on him. Hearing them quarrel, Gorgibus emerges from his house and persuades them to kiss and make up (sc. 12). He and Villebrequin decline, in the closing scene, to take up the Scholar's proposal to read them a lengthy chapter from Aristotle on the nature of peace. Instead, they celebrate by going out to dinner with the (temporarily) reconciled couple.

The play was not found until more than a half century after Molière's death. Attribution specialists do not agree on how much he may have altered an existing manuscript or oral version, other than formalizing the dialogue. It could have been brought to him during his years of touring the provinces (1645–58) by Du Parc, who acted with Molière on and off for some sixteen years. There is no record of the text or performances of it under the present title, but a play called *The Jealousy of Fat-René* did have a number of performances in Paris in the early 1660s. Fat- (or *Gros-)* René was the name Du Parc went by when he acted in farces; in other parts he was known more respectfully as Monsieur du Parc. It looks as though the action, which dates back to a husband-and-wife incident in the *Decameron,* served as a vehicle for him or any other current member of the troupe able to extract laughs from the part of an oppressed husband.[3] At some time (perhaps initially, perhaps later), this domestic fracas was stirred into a scenario that called for an actor who specialized in scholars and their rigmarole. The synthesis, which appears informal, and which some critics have found "primitive," actually has a structure that holds up firmly onstage and interweaves the two big roles so that the Scholar's patter infuriates Le Barbouillé, who does not listen passively but performs a "slow burn" or, in keeping with the final syllables of his name, a slow boil. The rage he feels—and vents as he hauls the Scholar away feet first—prepares plausibly enough for his vexation during the subsequent scene with Angélique.

That young woman does not engage in adultery or even near-adultery in the action. When we first see her, she has just met Valère for the first time; to deepen the acquaintance, she goes to the party but arrives after it has broken up. She is no innocent, though. When her father comes on the scene, she lies to him, swearing that she has not been out of the house and that Le Barbouillé is drunk. This is not quite the Angélique who will "confound" her husband in almost exactly the same fashion when Molière feels possessive enough about the play in 1668 to shift its scene 11, slightly altered and enriched, into the third act of *George Dandin* and to throw away the reconciliation. If she has more or less the same grudges as her successor about her propulsion into a marriage she did not want, she does not voice most of them; she has no dominating parents, as the later Angélique does; and unlike Angélique II, she does not come from a higher level in the class structure than her husband. She lives in a farce, whereas *George Dandin* will acquire the lineaments of a tragifarce.

On the other side of the marriage equation, Le Barbouillé feels jealous, and with reason, but he is not a cuckold—yet. Perhaps his rage at the prospect of her mild flirtation's ripening into a more substantial relationship with Valère, or some other attractive young man, dries out his tongue: in the last scene he speaks not one word.

The Jealous Husband has little story to support its action. We see onstage everything we need to know about the dramatic situation. Angélique's journeys to and from the party constitute the only unenacted episode. As a result,

3. Du Parc's offstage name was René Berthelot. Gros-René, Gros-Guillaume, and other popular stars gave their stage names to a number of farces, as did many film favorites to silent farces shot between 1914 and 1926 and written for the likes of Chaplin, Mack Swain ("Ambrose"), and Mabel Normand.

the action moves forward with no ambiguity as Le Barbouillé proves to his dissatisfaction that he has a loveless marriage. This main plot might seem temporarily derailed by the Scholar's speeches, but they are less a subplot than sidetrackings that contribute to the suspense. The triangular conflict thus takes place not really between the husband, wife, and lover, since Valère has only two quick walk-ons, but between the husband, wife, and distracting Scholar. It is the Scholar, too, who lends the straightforward farce some touches of studied, literary comedy. His harangues, meticulously worked out in their rhetorical rhythms and balance, give the sense of having been polished over many years with an utter indifference to whoever his onstage audience happens to be, and they create a symmetry in the casting—a counterpart to Le Barbouillé, another figure embedded in his own isolation.

The Flying Doctor
(*Le Médecin volant*, Date Uncertain)

In the rushing action of *The Flying Doctor*, a tributary plot grows strong enough to overwhelm the play's main current and to become the real source of laughter. The generating plot: Valère and Lucile are in love; her father, Gorgibus, wants her to marry an older man, Villebrequin;[4] she fakes illness in order to put off the marriage; Valère enlists his servant, Sganarelle, to play a doctor who will recommend that Lucile enjoy plentiful fresh air by moving to a pavilion in the garden, where Valère can visit her in secret. The commanding subplot: Sganarelle dresses in a medico's cloak and hat and plausibly carries out the impersonation; but at one point Gorgibus comes upon him without his doctor's garb, and he has to improvise a swift excuse, that he is the doctor's cast-off twin brother, Narcissus; from then on he must embody two roles and appear simultaneously in different places.

The scenes that follow this doubling of the main character (12–15) consist of the most intricate plotting Molière would contrive. Sganarelle appears as

4. Villebrequin is a lengthening of Villequin, the offstage name of the actor De Brie, who presumably played the Villebrequin in *The Jealous Husband* and in some earlier and later plays, including *The Imaginary Cuckold*, so that his name may have meant something to regular spectators. In *The Flying Doctor* Villebrequin is mentioned in the story but does not appear in the action. De Brie was not, it seems, much of a talent, and played only tiny roles. Molière probably kept him in the troupe in order to retain the services of his wife, the charming and versatile Catherine de Brie.

Narcissus inside the house at an upstairs window; leaps out to don his cloak and hat and become the phony doctor; drops the cloak and hat to scale the wall to the window; leaps out of the window again—and at last gratifies the desire of Gorgibus to see the two brothers together at the window by embracing the cloak and hat in a convincing demonstration of fraternal love. Molière has added what might be called a Hitchcock touch to sharpen the suspense: the servant Gros-René has noticed Sganarelle's cloak and hat on the ground and will pick them up, so that the ruse of "stealing" the personality of a doctor can go on for only so long.[5] The question becomes not whether Sganarelle will be found out but when—for how long he can sustain his act.

As the working-out of an intrigue, *The Flying Doctor* sets up a pattern that the playwright will adhere to, with a variety of twists, in most of his subsequent plays. A plan is hatched to bring together a pair of lovers, especially if an unwanted marriage threatens their union. Sometimes there is more than one plan (*The Botcher* has no fewer than ten) or two pairs of lovers (*The Botcher* again, *Loving Spite, The Miser, The Bourgeois Gentleman, Scapin*). Sometimes the plan or plans succeed through fluke or foolishness or misunderstandings (*The School for Wives, The Learned Ladies, The Seductive Countess, Tartuffe, The Imaginary Cuckold*, and, again, *The Botcher, The Miser*, and *Scapin*); sometimes the planning fails (*The Misanthrope, The Botcher*) or is abandoned (*Don Juan* and, yet again, *The Miser*). In one case (*George Dandin*), a plan intended to *dissolve* a marriage fails; in another case (*The Forced Marriage*) a weak intention—rather than anything as decisive or coherent as a plan—cannot avert a marriage that is clearly going to prove calamitous. Molière saw early in his writing career that an intrigue gives the action of a play a clear purpose, an impulsion that overpowers the audience's doubts about believability, and that even when an intrigue goes awry, the *échec* can be turned to comic account.

The intrigue begins in *The Flying Doctor* with Lucile's cousin, Sabine. She is not a servant, but as a role, she anticipates the succession of nimble-witted maidservants who chastise the young lovers for their own good and afford them aid and comfort beyond the call of loyalty. When Sabine proposes the false-doctor plan to Valère and suggests Sganarelle for the part, Valère speaks of his valet contemptuously; and when Sganarelle appears, he acts up to the

5. The pun on *volant* in the title means that Sganarelle is both a flying doctor and a thieving doctor. There had been at least one earlier *Flying/Thieving Doctor* in Italy, and others followed in both Italy and France, some of them postdating Molière's to trade on the latter's popularity. For details see Couton 1: 29–30, including several of his footnotes, which provide further references.

impression his master has conveyed that he is unresourceful: "I wouldn't know how to start . . . I don't have the brains for it. I'm not subtle enough; I'm not even bright." But for the reward of ten pistoles his master is holding out to him, "Once I'm a doctor, where do I go?" (sc. 2.) A few minutes later Sabine introduces her uncle to "the cleverest doctor in the world" (sc. 4), and Sganarelle heads full tilt into his career as a physician. He begins by jabbering in foreign languages, and continues by imbibing a sample of the patient's urine, from which he diagnoses an inflammation in the intestines—and then asks for another sample. The urine, as we see in shadow play, is white wine poured by Sabine and Lucile into a professional-looking beaker, and it provokes an aside from the taster: "If every patient pisses like this, I want to be a doctor for the rest of my life." [6] He manages to weather an encounter with a lawyer who is intent on plumbing the depth of this renowned doctor's scholarly capacity; luckily, the lawyer is another of those pedants who indulge in one-sided dialogue, and Sganarelle, by listening and saying little, comes out of the ordeal undetected. By the time his exploits have led him into defenestrations and walking up walls and engaging in two-voiced conversations with his imaginary brother, the impression of incompetence that he and Valère conveyed at first has melted away, and an audience cannot but admire his verbal and physical bravura: he can spout medicalese, he can speak in tongues, he can fly. A transformation! Here again, Molière is establishing a pattern he will frequently revert to: characterization and plotting accomplished by the cumulative correcting of first impressions.[7]

In other respects, too, this little farce will supply inspiration for the later drama of Molière. Sganarelle will beget six more characters with the same name but differing pedigrees. He will be the first in a succession of servants who have superior brains to those of their masters, although the class distinctions in *The Flying Doctor* are only lightly adumbrated. There will be more false doctors, as well as a few false doctors who can lay claim to authentic, recognized credentials, and more female patients who are not so much sick as lovesick, curable instantly with the right prescription—the right husband.

6. The testing and tasting of urine were not uncommon in the seventeenth century, although some physicians and textbooks called this forerunner of urinalysis "charlatanism" and its practitioners "scoundrels" and "impostors" (see Couton 1:1188).

7. In several of his plays, Molière takes the opposite tack and *reinforces* the first impressions of his leading characters, most notably when Scapin first appears and brags about his courage and abilities and when George Dandin walks into and out of the play as an inveterate loser.

Finally, the intrigue pattern will always invoke a danger, the risk that at any moment somebody will see through the mask of the impersonator and snatch it off.

The Botcher, or The Setbacks
(*L'Étourdi ou les Contretemps*, 1658)

Molière's third play has suffered, even in France, from some neglect, which is strange in view of its early success with audiences in Lyon and Paris and its welcome in England when modified and softened into Dryden's *Sir Martin Mar-All* (1677).[8] Since the Baker and Miller translation *(The Blunderer*, 1739), it has not found its way into English again, in part no doubt because Molière wrote it in mock-heroic rhyming couplets, not easy to translate, and in part because its tepid reputation (due to unfavorable and, at times, unfair comparison with the literary qualities of the later verse plays) has been hard to live down. Neglect breeds neglect. But this seminal farce-comedy has poetry that is supple, rapid, witty; a sparkling action; two leading roles that good actors can "run" with (one of them, the valet Mascarille's, is the longest by line count in Molière's drama); a wealth of encounters that can register vivaciously with spectators; and a dark underside.

In addition, the playwright's variations on the main plot—he prodigally sets up no fewer than ten of them—keep delivering surprises. This plot arises from the determination of an overanxious young man named Lélie to free and marry a beautiful slave named Célie before his rival, Léandre, can do the same. To this difficult task, he assigns the fertile and doggedly inventive Mascarille. Nothing new so far. The staple comic situation goes back to Plautus, if not beyond him to the Greek New Comedy; and we know from the beginning that the love match will take place, if only because of the lovers' rhyming names,[9] just as we know that Célie will prove to be of acceptable

8. Pepys went to see *Sir Martin Mar-All; or, The Feign'd Innocence*, freely adapted by Dryden from a literal translation by the Duke of Newcastle, at least ten times, and repeatedly told his diary it was the most mirthful play he had seen and "undoubtedly the best comedy ever was wrote" (John Dryden: *Dramatic Works*, ed. Montague Summers, vol. 2 [1932; reprint, New York: Gordian, 1968], 77–78).

9. Lélie (Lelio) and Célie (Celia) were standardized lovers from Italian comedy; Léandre (Leandro) was another. Some of the remaining characters in the play also bear French modifications of Italian names; they include Pandolfe, Anselme, Hippolyte (Ippolita), and Trufaldin, whose Italian forebear Truffaldino was not an old

lineage, not a slave (except of the plotting). But there is a catch, a novelty:[10]
Lélie cannot hold back, cannot wait; he must interfere in—and botch—every
attempt by Mascarille to win Célie for him.

Thus, after Mascarille strikes up an innocent conversation with Célie
while her master, Trufaldin, is listening, and after he has allayed Trufaldin's suspicions, Lélie appears and gives the game away (I, 4). After
Mascarille "dips" a purse containing gold—enough to purchase Célie—
out of an old man's cloak and drops it to the ground, Lélie picks it up
and hands it back (I, 6). After Mascarille persuades Lélie's father, Pandolfe,
to buy Célie and bundle her out of town to remove her from temptation
(Mascarille actually intends to have Lélie follow her), Lélie rescues her
from what he thinks is an abduction and brings her back (I, 9). Mascarille
next pretends to have quarreled with his master and to transfer his
allegiance to Léandre, to whom he confides that Célie is promiscuous,
every man's sweetheart ("But don't believe me; go ahead as planned./
Take up this easy punk; give her your hand./ The whole town will be
thankful, as it should,/ For you'll be marrying the public good"); Lélie
then reveals that he did not quarrel with Mascarille and he indignantly
clears Célie's reputation (III, 4). And so it continues.

Molière has plotted each scene and its counterscene so that the two
characters are separated. The valet does not let the master know of his
intentions, for fear of seeing them bungled in advance, and so they will get
botched, instead, when halfway realized.

Mascarille thereupon revises his methods: he will let Lélie in on each
stratagem and even enlist him as a performer. But the revision will bring him
no more success. He tries, for example, to worm himself into the confidence
of Célie's master by introducing Lélie as a merchant from Armenia who has
traveled from Turkey with a message from Trufaldin's long-lost son. But the
"Armenian" forgets his cues, misapprehends the hissed promptings from his
valet, and is thoroughly distracted by the presence of his yearned-for Célie.
Trufaldin wants to know where he saw the son. Lélie, whose geography is
no stronger than his tactical sense, mistakes Italy for the outposts of the

---

Pantalone figure, as in Molière, but a zany servant, an equivalent of Arlecchino
and sometimes a lowbrow lover. In Gozzi's Venetian plays, written a century later,
Truffaldino is usually paired off with Smeraldina.

10. The novelty begins not with Molière but with Beltrame (Niccolò Barbieri), whose
L'Inavertito supplied the outline and some of the complications for *The Botcher.* But
the play has a mixture of sources, which are summarized in Gutwirth 25–26.

Turkish Empire and replies, "Turin." Mascarille tries to cover up by quickly advising that the gentleman meant to say "Tunis":

> Armenians have a strange ineptitude
> Of speech that strikes us French as being crude.
> They change each word that has a *nis* for *rin,*
> And when they mean *Tunis,* they say *Turin.* (IV, 2)

The explanation does not smooth matters over, possibly because Trufaldin has swiftly assembled in his head, and even more swiftly dismissed from that vessel, the few words that have a *nis* in them; but even more possibly because Lélie has been conspicuously making sheep's eyes at his slave.

Mascarille will try four more schemes and each time Lélie will puncture them. On paper the action may appear repetitious, but onstage the suspense grows more acute as spectators no longer wonder whether Lélie will keep botching—they know by now that he will. Rather, they wait to see which notion Mascarille will come up with next and how exactly Lélie will again spike his own chances. By the final scenes, Mascarille's efforts have gone for naught. Fate in the form of the traditional ending steps in; reveals Célie to be Trufaldin's long-lost daughter; diverts Léandre to Hippolyte, a damsel to whom Lélie was formerly and restlessly engaged; and restores Trufaldin's long-lost son, who came late into the action and looked like another rival for Célie's hand—there is a swiftly averted glance here at incestuous attraction.

A couple of times Mascarille has referred to Lélie's imp, which persists in ruining his plans, and with which he must keep jousting. By this time he knows his master's deficiencies. He ought, if he is as shrewd as he seems, to give up or else to take measures to frustrate the imp before the next candle (or, in some cases, a whole chandelier) flames up in his imagination. Why, a spectator may ask, does Mascarille not acknowledge that the odds lie against him? Why does he not back out? Why? Because the botcher of the title is, in effect, not simply Lélie but the self-defeating partnership. There are imps on both sides of it. If the imp of infatuation drives Lélie, his valet is galvanized by the imp of ambition, which whispers temptations to him whenever he permits himself to think of putting an end to the apparently doomed quest for Célie. His imp will not allow him to turn away from a challenge, which it interprets as his longing for fame eternal. It confides that "after this rare exploit" he will "be painted as a hero, laurels on [his] head, and below the portrait an inscription in gold" and in Latin: "Long live Mascarille, the emperor of crooks" (II, 8). But the contest between imps is actually a war between a demon and an angel, for in the action, Mascarille's dishonesty is gashed, over and over, by the perverse integrity of his master. There is good abroad in the world, in the form of Lélie's aggressive imp, his conscience, that beneficent power that fortuitously clogs up the lines of evil. Could it be prescient, aware that Mascarille's ten crafty tactics will go for nothing, that Célie is *destined* for Lélie? This play has an ethical base. Its obstructionist is a good man, while its entertaining conniver is a bad one.

Some writers have traced distinctions between the three Mascarille personae (the ones in this play, *Loving Spite,* and *Two Precious Maidens Ridiculed),* who wore masks in the original productions, and the seven, probably unmasked Sganarelles; the Mascarilles evolve into the type of *fourbe* or knave, while the Sganarelles become victims or dupes.[11] But the distinctions, refinements of character, social rank, mission, and hindrance, hold just as cogently *among* the Mascarilles and *among* the Sganarelles. During his career the author drew liberally from his early characterizations to assemble the later ones, but not as schematically as the two lines of descent would imply. Tartuffe, Don Juan, the Sganarelle of *The Doctor in Spite of Himself,* and Scapin are the products of artistic miscegenation; they borrow bits and pieces of personality from the Sganarelle of *The Flying Doctor* and the Mascarille of *The Botcher,* as well as from other would-be manipulators of events or "playwrights within the plays."

As Mascarille's foil, in at least two senses of that word, Lélie has a role that in size and scope far exceeds the usual boundaries of the *jeune premier.* By turns he grows roisterous (in the first scene he defies Léandre, who happens not to be present, to "carry off" Célie); extravagant in his self-congratulations at having hatched better plans than Mascarille's; lugubrious in mourning for his father, who is not dead; crestfallen and, in places, filled with self-loathing to learn that he has committed yet another blunder; and indignant that Mascarille does not let him in on forthcoming schemes. He even reveals flashes of ingenuity between his long spells of ingenuousness, as when he composes a letter to Trufaldin, claiming to be a Spanish marquis who fathered Célie and will shortly come to collect her; unhappily for him, the letter arrives just in time to scotch a masterly trick by Mascarille that would have put Célie into their hands. The exigencies of the plotting compel him to undergo a beating from Mascarille (IV, 6) and thereby be reduced to the status of a slave,

11. See, e.g., Howarth, esp. 87–105.

a role reversal Molière will revert to in *Scapin*. [12] Marcel Gutwirth remarks that Célie "deserves something better than Lélie,"[13] and if we look at the two of them from within the action—that is, as people, rather than roles—this may be true, since she is a sharp-witted youngster. But Lélie has a stage life that furnishes ample opportunities for a versatile comedian who is much more than another comedian's "feed," and for accomplishing his characterization in melodious comic verse.

Nor has the author slighted the other, smaller parts. In the trio of fathers (Célie's, Lélie's, and Hippolyte's) he has fashioned three shuffling but distinctively enlivened Pantalone figures. Anselme at one point happens to meet Pandolfe who, according to Mascarille, has died. The skit on a ghost scene (II, 4) includes lines spoken by Anselme that have a farcical and almost twentieth-century disrespect for mortality:

> I beg you now to disappear
> And pray that gracious heaven will hear
> My wish: that you find perfect health
> And joy in your distinguished death.

But the last, sardonic word remains with Mascarille. Although he has evinced no sexual appetite during the action, something in him (his imp or his better self?) suddenly hungers for a mate. Just as suddenly, and in very few words, fate once again obliges. Even so, he cannot resist a dig at the perils of matrimony:

MASCARILLE You're all provided for. I must appeal:
　　　　　　　Is there no girl to suit poor Mascarille?
　　　　　　　Standing here, two by two together, you
　　　　　　　Are giving me the itch for marriage too.
ANSELME　　 I have one for you.
MASCARILLE　 Come, and may heaven inspired
　　　　　　　Bless us with children we ourselves have sired! (V, 11)

12. Mascarille is the earliest sketch for Scapin as a developed role, and not by accident. The full title of the 1629 Beltrame play into which Molière dipped heavily is *The Blockhead, or Scappino Disconcerted and Mezzetino Tormented.*
13. Gutwirth, 36.

Loving Spite
(*Dépit Amoureux*, 1658?)

The opening act of Molière's second full-length play in verse ends on a baffling note. Éraste loves Lucile. In all likelihood, she loves him in return, because she sends him a note inviting him to put his proposal to her father and to meet her that very evening. But Éraste has a rival, Valère, who appears confident to the point of cockiness about *his* future with Lucile. We soon hear why. Éraste learns from what seems to be a reliable source, Valère's servant, that Lucile has secretly married his rival. Could the servant be lying? Is Lucile leading both of her suitors on, or only one, and if so, which and for what reason?

The second act explains what has happened by digging back into the story. Lucile has a sister with the bisexual name of Ascagne, who felt sorry for Valère while he was making unrewarded advances to Lucile; Ascagne's sympathy metamorphosed into love; she presented herself as Lucile one night; he proposed; she accepted and became his wife then and there. Lucile and Valère know nothing of Ascagne's deception. Lucile rightly believes herself single. Valère wrongly believes himself her husband. But there is a further complication. Ascagne goes about disguised as a man. Nobody but her confidante knows she is a woman, not even her father, Albert.[14] Before Ascagne was born, a rich somebody left a large inheritance to Albert and his offspring, provided the new child was a male. If it proved to be a female, the inheritance would ricochet to another gentleman named Polidore, who happens to be the father of—Valère. Albert, not wishing to surrender the wealth, swapped his baby girl for a flower seller's (presumably illegitimate) baby boy. But in a sequence of quick moves, the boy died, and Ascagne was taken back by her mother, who dressed and reared her as a son, to keep up the pretense. Ascagne has remained outwardly and unhappily a son ever since. The mother is dead, and Albert feels guilty when he thinks (mistakenly) that he has raised a son who is not his own child for the sake of the inheritance.

---

14. French critics mostly find that the "principal source" of *Loving Spite* is Nicolo Secchi's *L'Interesse* (*Covetousness* or *Greed*, 1585) in which the heroine, like Ascagne, wears male attire; and other possible sources are cited by Lancaster and Michaut. Molière could also have been aware of the many English plays by Shakespeare and others in which a young woman (played by a young male actor) gets into male disguise for protection or the better to pursue some intrigue.

But by now he has gone too deeply into the inheritance to give it up and confess.

The probability threshold may seem unduly low here. Could Ascagne have hidden her true sex for all these years from her father, sister, and friends? Is it likely that Valère would have wedded someone he knew during the daytime as a young man, even if we make allowances for the poor lighting in those benighted days? Well, probability, like beauty, lies in the vision of the beholder, and for seventeenth-century spectators the darkening—the blinding—effect of night's cloak and its murky advantages belonged to an acceptable dramatic convention, which persisted for another couple of centuries until the advent of realism and electricity. (In 1788, Count Almaviva in *The Marriage of Figaro* imagines he is enjoying a nocturnal tryst in the unlit garden with Suzanne when he is making love to his wife.) In the same spirit of respect for conventional, rather than logical, plausibility, Valère finds in the last act that Ascagne is a woman, and the woman he married. After two seconds of surprise, he embraces this unexpected onslaught of fate as he "feels seized with wonder, love, and pleasure at the same time."

The inner structure of this play's five acts departs drastically from that of the one before. *The Botcher* amounts to a string of intrigues, each initiated by Mascarille and each swiftly stymied by Lélie. A Mascarille appears in *Loving Spite*, too, as Valère's man, but he sows no deliberate intrigues, only confusion when he reports that his master has married Lucile. And he is in some ways the opposite of the first Mascarille: cautious, placid, and self-protective, a fresh role for this half-masked figure.[15] No intrigues at all get under way in the action. But two deceptions, rather than intrigues, continue from the prefatory story: the one begun by Albert over the inheritance and the one perpetuated by Ascagne over her identity. This comedy, then, arises from another dramaturgical tradition, but a venerable one—the carefully wrought tangle of misinformation and misunderstandings. Its characters exert little will power; they are all, even Ascagne and Albert, the pawns of given circumstances, buffeted by the winds of chance, keeping from being thrown off-balance by reacting rather than by asserting themselves. In such a situation, motives and personalities count for less than the overall pattern of the plotting.

---

15. Molière may have revamped the Mascarille role not only because it performs a function different from the one in *The Botcher* but also because he did not play it, choosing instead to undertake the part of Albert. However, he gives Mascarille one of his own characteristics, which he sometimes turned to dramatic account, a cough, explicitly mentioned in V, 2.

But that pattern would start the envy of a draughtsman. Until the last two scenes (V, 7 and 8), which are in the nature of a celebratory gathering for the climax, the author seldom brings or keeps onstage more than three characters at once, and much of the time he makes do with two. One might argue that this arrangement of roles aligns the action with the standards of plotting expected in a neoclassical drama, and that the playing area, delimited severely by spectators sitting on the stage, would have suffered from gridlock in the blocking if the playwright-director had not been sparing with his actors; and both of these considerations have some validity. But the plotting has a more positive aspect; Molière uses it to meter out the flow of dramatic material, sometimes letting only a trickle escape in order to hold back a revelation from the roles who are present. As the most notable example, Ascagne's confidante, Frosine, the one character who shares her secret (because she is the daughter of Ascagne's wet nurse), hardly ever walks into the action together with any of the others, even though the five acts take place once again in a public thoroughfare; and when Frosine does appear at the same time as they do, she remains silent. For a second example, the two fathers meet at cross-purposes. Polidore means to apologize because he has discovered that his son married Albert's daughter—Lucile, as he thinks—without securing her father's consent. Albert fears that his ruse to keep the inheritance has at last come to light. The scene (III, 4) twinkles with evasions as the two old men, both reluctant to speak their minds and both terrified of committing a faux pas, fall to their knees and endeavor to outdo each other in repentance.

The overall pattern extends to a neatness in the matching of characters that is not quite symmetrical, like that of an oriental carpet that incorporates some wandering lines and clashing colors. The competition between Éraste and Valère for Lucile reverberates in a competition between the men's respective valets. Gros-René and Mascarille both desire Marinette, Lucile's *suivante* (a cross between a maid and a hired companion), in a contest Gros-René will win. Molière makes no attempt to complete the octagonal figure of four couples by pairing off Mascarille with Frosine, as in the resolution of a well-made play: a perfect balance in the plotting would have appeared mechanical and inhuman, if not lifeless.

Instead, he achieves a less obvious equilibrium by producing a second odd man out to match Mascarille and provide a role for an otherwise unused actor from his company. This is a variant of the pedant, a figure always good for laughs—not a philosopher but another type of word-chopper, a *littérateur* called Métaphraste whose name means translator from one sort of language to another, poetry to prose or vice versa; his scene (II, 6), written like the rest of the play in regular alexandrines, here and there cleverly rhymes Latin words with French. Albert tries to ask this tutor what is wrong with "my son," Ascagne, who "seems to be afraid of marriage." But going to a pedant for sensible advice is about as effectual as shaking an apple tree to bring down one piece of fruit. After Métaphraste refers his employer to Atticus, Virgil, and Quintilian, he grows impatient, like the Scholar in *The Jealous Husband*, and keeps urging Albert, every time the baffled father begins speaking, to come out with what he has to say, until Albert chases him offstage drowning out the metaphrastic chatter by ringing a bell in his ear.

The "spite" of the title expresses itself several times in the squabbles between the lovers. In dealing with love, Molière, the dry-eyed playwright, never stoops to the sentimentality deplored almost exactly a century after his death by Oliver Goldsmith. He appreciates the pains of love and their attendant jealousy all too well, but instead of wringing pathos out of them, he extracts laughter. In Corneille's drama, love is a handicap, a stumbling block in the way of honor or reputation and one's duty to others. In Racine, love is a disease; its aberrations of desire may turn into violence and wreak cruelty on the beloved. In Molière, love becomes a spur to activity; its anguish is real enough but it sets up in its victims frenzied efforts to talk around the subject.[16] When Éraste and Lucile meet, seconded by Gros-René and Marinette, who keep reminding them to hold their ground, not give an inch, they bandy words that are at odds with their feelings in a continuous play of unsuccessful concealment (IV, 3).[17] Éraste starts out by saying that he is not here to speak of his love for Lucile, "extreme" though it might have been, now that he has been made to see her indifference. They go on to agree that this represents their definitive break: "May I drop dead," says Éraste, "if I ever wish to speak to you again." They return each other's gifts and reread aloud the passionate covering messages. Meanwhile, they are still talking about the necessity for parting, but he wonders what might happen if he asked her pardon, and she suggests he not do so, for fear she may grant it, whereupon he does ask, and she gives him a brisk reply that repairs the break before it was made: "See me home."

Left to themselves, Marinette and Gros-René now repeat the same falling

---

16. The declarations of love in Molière thus contrast with today's sentimental comedy on Broadway, in television, films, and pop songs in which the speaker or vocalist shrieks, often through amplification systems, "I LOVE you! I NEED you! Can't you underSTAND!"—as though understanding were a key to requital.

17. The technique is not unlike that known as *marivaudage*, for which Marivaux gets the credit; but Marivaux practices it with less humor than Molière does.

and rising curve but on a less frosty level of gallantry (IV, 4). They swear never to weaken like Lucile and Éraste; they give back the gifts they have exchanged in the past, a ribbon, a knife, a package of needles, scissors, and a piece of cheese, and Gros-René regrets that he is unable to throw up the soup "you made me eat, because then I'd have nothing left from you." They will snap a straw, a homely gesture to signify that "an affair is over between honorable people." But they are looking at each other in peculiar ways and snapping the straw seems like a silly thing to do. Before they know what they are doing, they are laughing and making up, and Gros-René is forgiving her (not asking pardon, as Éraste did). She, forgiving him in return, allows that she is stupidly soft when she has to deal with "her" Gros-René.[18] Mascarille, who sees that Marinette favors his plump rival, declines to take part in a duel for her with Gros-René ("My blood is happy where it is—in my body") and withdraws from the contest.

> When I stop to consider how precious I feel
> To myself, and that two meager inches of steel
> Are enough to propel a live man to a grave,
> I marvel that anyone tries to be brave.

But he adds that "marriage doesn't close the door to flirting." Marinette promises to be faithful and Gros-René promises to be rough on Mascarille and other suitors, if any, but Mascarille says that after marriage men "often soften into permissive husbands." To which Marinette replies, "Shut up, you ace of spades *(as de pique),*" meaning fool but also, with its play on *pique*, implying a reference back to the "spite" of the title. Yet, Mascarille may enjoy a last grin to denote his satisfaction at sowing some premarital suspicion. And the happy ending, as is often the case with Molière, has a mixed flavor, for during the previous act, Gros-René, in a speech that haphazardly compares the tempestuous workings of nature with those of human nature (IV, 3), concludes that "women are worse than the devil."

Two Precious Maidens Ridiculed
(*Les Précieuses ridicules,* 1659)

In that part of the story that precedes the action, the *bon bourgeois* Gorgibus has brought his daughter, Magdelon, and his niece, Cathos, to Paris in

18. Molière would use the same "quadrille" effect of master and mistress, valet and maid separating and becoming reconciled in *The Bourgeois Gentleman*, but with a difference in the plotting: in the one scene (*BG* III, 10), he interweaves the remarks of all four characters rather than splitting the encounters into two scenes.

search of husbands and invited to his home a couple of wellborn bachelors, La Grange and Du Croisy, but the young women gave them a cold reception. As the action gets under way, La Grange suspects that Magdelon and Cathos would have behaved more warmly toward more affected suitors and says he will order his and Du Croisy's valets, Mascarille and Jodelet, to assume roles as a marquis and a vicomte and pay court to the women. La Grange was right: as the valets, who have foppish pretensions, put on airs, the women respond ecstatically, and the four of them literally have a ball, with musicians and dancing—until the masters burst in, denounce the valets as impostors, beat them, make them strip off their borrowed finery, and leave Cathos, Magdelon, and her father humiliated and enraged.

Summarized baldly in this fashion, the action sounds as though, for the first time (but not the last), Molière worked a partial reversal, making the servants dupes and the masters *fourbes*, or connivers, who play a mean trick on two naïve youngsters from the provinces. If, as Gorgibus hoped, the women had accepted the masters as marriage partners, it is questionable whether they would have been any better off than if they had chosen the alternative posed by their irascible father-guardian—becoming nuns. Similarly, if the servants had refused to oblige their masters, wouldn't they have taken a beating, anyway? Such a realistic view from inside the action reminds us of the plight of women in the seventeenth century, who for the most part "left the slavery of their fathers for the slavery of their husbands,"[19] as well as the plight of servants, who, like the wives, were animate property. Molière, however, gives us little opportunity to consider this one-act play as a sample of realism. His satirical treatment of the "precious," impressionable women and the snobbish valets occupies the bulk of the text, nine of the seventeen scenes. It overwhelms the social implications of the beginning and end. But it does not obliterate them. This slashing attack on *préciosité* has more ambiguity than it is usually credited with.

The adjective *précieux* carries the same two basic meanings as its English counterpart: having a high price or worth (and therefore being unusually valuable or dear) and unnecessarily finical or delicate. Early *préciosité* in which the Marquise de Rambouillet figured prominently began with literary salon gatherings that attempted, like the French Academy and its founder, Richelieu, to rid the French language of some of its dross—to purify it, to make it, in a similar word (which has a different root meaning), more *precise*. Over a period of twenty years or less, from the mid-1630s to the

19. Couton 1: 250.

mid-1650s, the cleansing process itself became corrupted by effusions that avoided triteness by substituting dainty, flowery, and sometimes tortured expressions. The extravagant, esoteric vocabulary took much of its inspiration from the romanesque novels of Mlle de Scudéry. While *préciosité* declined into something resembling the English euphuism of the century before, it had represented a striving on the part of women and some male admirers for artistic recognition and perhaps independence. Mlle de Scudéry felt it necessary to publish her novels under her brother's name; and as late as 1678 Mme de La Fayette had to borrow, for the publication of *La Princesse de Clèves*, the name of Jean Segrais, who also loaned his name as author to the books of his employer, the duchesse de Montpensier. Women, almost all of them from the educated, if not upper, classes, were putting forward claims to being arbiters of cultural taste as they tried to effect a quiet rebellion. Like noisier rebellions, *préciosité* was not a unified movement but different, contending groups with their own political, as well as literary, objectives. It threw to its flurried surface a number of extremists and exaggerated, irritating mannerisms.[20] And like any rebellion, it attracted adherents who were hangers-on and outsiders, nonaggrieved parties whose motives were sometimes less than altruistic. Men. Among the men were sensualists and mercenaries who played along in the hope of rewards, just as among the women were some leaders who, in escaping, as they thought, from the despotism of men, themselves became despots.[21] But the verbal and other excesses bespoke a desire on the part of women not to be taken for granted, not to be sold into marriage; hence, the coy and elaborate wooing procedures called for in Mlle de Scudéry's *The Great Cyrus* and *Clélie*, cited by Magdelon and Cathos (sc. 4), and responsible for the labeling by some critics of the *précieuses* as bluestockings. "I consider marriage quite shocking," declares Cathos. "How can one

20. The adverbs and adverbial phrases associated with *préciosité* were probably hardly more irritating than the ones endured today at academic conferences and in published "think pieces," with their repetitions of *importantly, significantly, paradoxically, ironically, interestingly, totally, completely, essentially, the fact that, in terms of, in the context of, in the sense of, in the framework of, the problem is that,* and other self-aggrandizing locutions.
21. There have been a number of accounts of the complex history of *préciosité*; it is detailed in the multivolume *La Préciosité, étude historique et linguistique* by R. Lathullère (Paris: 1966); but there will no doubt be histories published in the near future by feminists offering different emphases and interpretations.

support the thought of lying beside a man who is thoroughly naked?" (sc. 4).[22]

By not situating his farce in one of the acknowledged salons, Molière avoids direct criticism of the well-known Parisian *précieuses* of his time and concentrates his fire on provincial pretenders and servants dreaming of upward mobility; he also implies that there *are* inner, exclusive circles, and that those inside them want to keep interlopers out, while those outside either yearn to get in (Magdelon and Cathos) or claim to be already in (Mascarille and Jodelet). To the young women, *préciosité* appears to offer the most exhilarating route into fashionable society, their real purpose, as they see it, for coming to live in Paris. But the playwright contrives to have it both ways, to smite the provincials and at the same time to let Mascarille and the women enunciate some of the more prudish attitudes likely to be encountered in the salons of the late 1650s. The names of the heroines may roughly correspond to those of the actresses who played them, Madeleine (Béjart) and Catherine (de Brie),[23] but they also happened to suggest the names of Catherine de Vivonne, Marquise de Rambouillet, and of Magdeleine de Scudéry; and much as they were known to their followers as Arthénice and Sapho, so Magdelon and Cathos have adopted the names of Polyxène and Aminte.[24] Still, whether or not Molière meant to aim a few barbs in the direction of Rambouillet and Scudéry, he attended the salons of both, was evidently on friendly terms with the two women, and borrowed an episode from *Cyrus* for one of his comedy-ballets. Perhaps to avoid giving offense to them, he rewrote some of the scenes of *Maidens* after the first performance and before the second one.

The play's action supplies six principal routines. In the first, Magdelon and then Cathos disgust Gorgibus as they outline the spiritual nourishment of would-be *précieuses*, drawn from the fiction of *Clélie* and from its "Map of

22. A contemporary satirist Saint-Évremond wrote in *Le Cercle :* "If you wish to know what the *précieuses* would like considered their greatest merit, I will tell you that it is to love their lovers tenderly but without enjoyment, and to enjoy their husbands solidly but with aversion" (quoted in Couton 1: 250). Couton adds: "Thus physical needs are reconciled with the demands of platonic love."

23. Other members of the troupe, such as La Grange, Du Croisy, Marie du Croisy (Marotte the maid), and Jodelet used their own names for their characters; Jodelet's brother L'Espy played Gorgibus; Molière played Mascarille.

24. For the literary derivations of these names, and also possibly of Molière's own pseudonym, see Couton 1: 1217 nn. 2, 3.

the Lovescape" *(La Carte de Tendre).* A lover must woo by "the rules of chivalry and breeding," which include impassioned avowals, rejections, obstacles, misunderstandings, adventures, opposition from relatives (such as that of Gorgibus), and final acceptance of the emotionally drained swain by the placated maiden—who holds the upper hand in the insecure relationship. The second routine consists of the entry of "the Marquis de" Mascarille in a sedan carried by porters, the more polite one of whom he refuses to pay until the less polite one threateningly talks back to him, followed by the women's rapturous welcome. During this episode of arrival, deflation, and introduction, the first audiences could savor Molière's Mascarillian getup: ribbons, laces, and tassels, perilously high-heeled shoes, a wig that "swept the floor whenever he bowed," and a tiny hat—all in all, a multicolored feat by the costume supplier.

For the third routine, Mascarille drops names and connections; promises to bring his hostesses into the precious thick of things; recites and sings a four-line "impromptu" he has composed; then analyzes its self-evident meanings *("Stop thief, stop thief, stop thief, stop thief!* Wouldn't you say that's a man shouting and running after a thief to make him stop?"); praises his own outfit; and cries out that the women are taking unfair advantage of him. ("Both of you against my heart at the same time, attacking me from the right and left! It's against the rules of warfare.") The fourth routine brings on "the Vicomte de" Jodelet, and the two "former comrades in arms" vie for the attention of the women by boasting of their military prowess and wounds; at one point Mascarille starts to loosen his breeches to display a scar. To close this routine, all four characters dance to the strains of hastily summoned fiddlers.

La Grange and Du Croisy reenter for the fifth routine, the obligatory shaming and beating, which concludes with one of the actor Jodelet's special-ized turns, as he takes off an undergarment only to reveal another beneath, and beneath that, another, and so on, each article being of a different color from the one before. As the last routine, Gorgibus, instead of paying the violinists, chases them out of the house with his stick, then curses the women's papers and books as he hurls them in all directions.

Molière gave the first performance of this play some thirteen months after he had established himself at the Petit-Bourbon Theatre in Paris under the sponsorship of the king's brother. But did he perform it, or an earlier version, during his younger years on tour? If so, as Georges Couton notes, its meaning "would not be at all the same." It would then carry a clearer moral, aimed at country folk who might be lured to the glittering capital only to find themselves exposed to charlatans and other tempters; and it would form a sort of precursor of *Monsieur de Pourceaugnac* and *The Seductive Countess* rather than of *The Learned Ladies, The Bourgeois Gentleman,* and *The Misanthrope.* But if Molière had brought the play with him, Couton continues, "wouldn't he have put it on during the difficult period of his debuts" in Paris, when he badly needed material?[25] The question remains open. He might have delayed his presentation of the script, pending revisions and perhaps some updating, in the light of his year's stay in Paris. What we have now, in any case, is a text lifted in places from commedia scenarios featuring two Spanish capitano figures, two *innamorate,* and a Pantalone, spiced with jokes and business that go back well beyond the commedia to Plautus and the *fabulae atellanae.* These ingredients, combined with his observations and distillings of "precious" characteristics and with facts and satire gathered from a variety of seventeenth-century writings, fiction and nonfiction, add up to his first targeting of a specific corner of contemporary society and thus constitute his first link as a farceur with Aristophanes, so far as we know.

What are those "precious" characteristics? The women vamp prudishly. The men harp on their stylishness, which is all ornamental, superficial, imitative. They brag about their courage and wit, without exhibiting either, like effete political candidates on the stump who insistently try to persuade audiences that they are "tough." Both sexes are grotesquely insincere in their behavior and greetings. Both disguise themselves, the men in borrowed garb, the women with the aid of creams, pomades, whites of eggs, "virgin's milk" (for bleaching the complexion), and lard. This is a a play about snobbish aspirations (aping one's "betters") as much as it is about preciosity. Within the scenic subdivisions locked within their entrances and exits, *Maidens* is a farcical ceremony, an excuse for stand-up turns by two prevaudevillians backed by a pair of feminine partners who have moved into the dance ritual of seduction well before the violins arrive.

Sganarelle, or The Imaginary Cuckold
(*Sganarelle ou Le Cocu imaginaire,* 1660)

Along with intrigue, we find two other dramaturgical motors in Molière's earlier writings: coincidence and misunderstanding. They generally

---

25. Couton 1: 259. As Couton also points out, the troupe's unofficial record keeper, La Grange, calls *Maidens* in his *Register* Molière's "third new play" (after *The Botcher* and *Loving Spite),* and he again calls it "new" in his preface to the posthumous edition of 1682.

work in concert. The playwright takes them from older models and then rebuilds them. In the later plays, he uses them much more sparingly. Let the word *misunderstanding* stand, but I would like to look at coincidence from two separate angles. Jung supplemented the idea of coincidence with "synchronicity," which suggests that, in life, two events happening at the same time can often have a hidden connection; behind the apparently random operations of fluke or chance lies purpose, possibly a "higher purpose."[26] But synchronicity does not replace coincidence; it is its obverse. In life, we can reject all synchronicity; we do not have to believe in divinely ordained purposes. In the theatre and its sister arts, we cannot disbelieve in purposes, even when they come through to us warped and unclear because of ambiguities or incompetence or a clash of intentions or a faulty interpretation (by the director, actors, spectators) or, in the worst cases, all of these. When the playwright is not a surrealist, his plotting is by definition purposive. It may bring onstage (into the action) a character who sees or hears or overhears or deduces something that will lead to a conflict or will complicate a conflict already begun. It may keep offstage (out of the action, but still in the story) a character who has information or the sort of personality that could soften the conflict or negate the complication. And this presence or absence of consequential figures will always take place at the wrong moment, or for the dramatist's purposes, the right moment. Eric Bentley writes: "The playwright incorporates coincidences in a structure, which is to say that they will not be coincidences to his audience."[27] To the characters trapped within the confines of a farce-comedy like *The Imaginary Cuckold*, synchronicity looks like un-happy coincidence until the happy resolution, when they assume, not without a certain smugness, that all was for the best, and that providence has taken care of its own. But to us outsiders, from our superior vantage point, providence is the playwright and collaborators who, with their godlike prerogatives, have stretched synchronicity to (or if we are cynics, beyond) its acceptable limits.

Misunderstandings are to synchronicity what a thirst for vengeance is to an affront, an almost inevitable outcome.[28] Sganarelle's wife glances out of a

---

26. Some years ago the word "synchronicity" enjoyed a popular cachet due to two albums by the rock singer Sting.

27. *The Life of the Drama*, 245.

28. A misunderstanding can arise not only from synchronicity but also from a false or garbled report, defective hearing, and other causes, some of which Molière does use in his plays.

window of her house in Paris, just when her husband on the street below has a young woman in his embrace, his hand on her breast, and his lips only inches from hers. That settles it: he's having an affair. Lately he's behaved coldly toward his wife. She doesn't stop to think that if Sganarelle, who is anything but a reckless man, wanted to indulge in extramarital sex, he would hardly perform in broad daylight outside his own house. The audience, knowing what she doesn't know—that the young woman has collapsed and that Sganarelle is checking for a heartbeat and signs of breathing—basks in the dramatic irony and laughs.

This one-act in verse swamps its characters in as many coincidences, ten, as there are mini-intrigues in the five acts of *The Botcher*. From this last play, Molière extracts two characters with the same names but new roles, Lélie and Célie, and goes back to *The Flying Doctor* and *The Jealous Husband* to resuscitate Sganarelle, Villebrequin, Gorgibus, and Gros-René. Several of the remaining roles have no names, only titles, to identify them. For two of them, I shall borrow some names commonly found in Molière and other seventeenth- century writers and call one of them Martine, the other Lisette.[29]

In the story Célie's father, Gorgibus, has selected Lélie for her husband. The two young people have fallen in love, a rare circumstance for an arranged marriage. But as the action opens, Gorgibus heaves a wrench into his former plans: he now wants as his son-in-law Valère, who will come in for a fortune of "twenty thousand good ducats." Like many of Molière's later "masters of the house," Gorgibus will not stand for any quibbling from his daughter; and like his predecessor in *Two Precious Maidens Ridiculed,* he takes strong exception to the romances she reads, which win her over to the absurd notion that people should marry for love (I, 1). Célie, who has not heard from her fiancé for some time because he is traveling, is told by her *suivante,* Lisette, to accept the profitable new offer and reminded that Lélie may have changed his mind and abandoned her. Gazing at his portrait in a locket he gave her, she swoons at the suggestion (sc. 2).

Now there begins the synchronicity, a string of coincidences that will wrap

---

29. These are names supplied in my translation of the play in *One-Act Comedies of Molière.* By eliding the names Célie and Lélie, taken from the commedia's Celia and Lelio, we arrive at Clélie, the heroine of Mlle de Scudéry's novel (see previous section on *Two Precious Maidens Ridiculed*), which may well be one of the "romances" this Célie has read, to her father's disgust. Whether or not Molière was taking another jab, a padded one this time, at the *précieuses,* one critic, evidently confused by the similarity, has a chapter on the play in which every reference to Célie calls her Clélie.

themselves more and more tightly around the four principals and tie them together in a cocoon of jealousy:

1. As she passes out, Célie drops the locket.

2. Her neighbor, Sganarelle, happening by, holds her up while Lisette runs for help (sc. 3). His wife, Martine, sees him and assumes the worst (sc. 4).

3. By the time Martine reaches the street, the others are gone. She picks up the locket, opens it (sc. 5). As Sganarelle comes out of Célie's house—she has made a swift recovery—he finds his wife dreamily admiring the portrait of attractive, young Lélie and sniffing Célie's perfume. Is she kissing that picture? As Martine did, he assumes the worst. They accuse each other of infidelity and squabble over the locket. She runs off with it. He chases her (sc. 6).

4. Lélie chooses this moment to stagger home from his travels. He heard a rumor a week earlier that Célie was about to be married to someone else and since then has ridden practically nonstop to arrive home in time to forestall the wedding. He is tired out but will not admit that, and he lets his servant, Gros-René, who is even more famished than usual, go for food (sc. 7).

5. Sganarelle returns with the locket, which he snatched from Martine. He compares the portrait with the original and timidly asks Lélie to stay away from his wife. Lélie, seeing him with the locket that was given to Célie, and hearing the remark about the wife, also assumes the worst (sc. 9).

6. The exhaustion of his ride, combined with his disappointment at getting back too late and finding Célie, he thinks, already married to Sganarelle, causes Lélie to totter and almost faint, just as Martine reappears. Without recognizing him, she invites him into her house to rest (sc. 11).

7. Like Célie, Lélie gets his strength back miraculously fast. As he emerges from her house with Martine, Sganarelle sees them together, and assumes that the worst is now confirmed (sc. 14). And reconfirmed when Lélie tells him, apropos of Célie, "You're too lucky to have so beautiful a wife (sc. 15)."

8. Célie emerges from her house in time to see Lélie going away down the street. Sganarelle informs her the fop *(damoiseau)* is his wife's lover. Célie, brokenhearted, cries out threats and imprecations after Lélie. He does not hear them, but Sganarelle does and assumes the best: she is taking his part and railing at the stranger for having made a cuckold of him (sc. 16).

9. Lélie reenters to accuse Célie of having betrayed him. She throws the accusations back in his face and says he should be ashamed of himself for what he has done to Sganarelle. Sganarelle, by now covered in armor and

weapons, is trying to get up the courage to stab Lélie from behind for having seduced Martine. Martine joins in the fray, adding to the barrage of charges by attacking Célie. But Lisette, fortuitously present throughout this episode (scs. 19–22), appoints herself mediator and forces them to speak one at a time, until the misunderstandings are cleared up.

10. Gorgibus still, however, wants his daughter to marry Valère. Earlier, swayed by the misunderstandings and angry at Lélie for having, as she believes, deserted her, she agreed to accept Valère (sc. 18). Now that she is reconciled with Lélie, she goes back on that agreement. Gorgibus will not let her. But as the last coincidence, a benign one for a change, Valère's father walks onstage, not to complete the wedding plans, as Gorgibus hopes, only to confess that he has just found that his son has been secretly married for four months to another woman. To which Gorgibus, reversing himself in a flash, replies that he long ago promised his daughter to Lélie, and the young man's return now clinches the match (sc. 24). Sganarelle has the final word on coincidences and synchronicity: "When all the evidence as you receive it / Adds up to one conclusion: don't believe it."

By the time he wrote *The Imaginary Cuckold,* Molière had developed in his two previous plays a pliable, conversational verse; he would adapt it to a less frivolous content in the following year with *Don Garcie of Navarre* and go on to refine it further. For the moment, though, he had accomplished a play that appears to be in the commedia vein but is unusual in that the poetry conspires with the symmetry of couples and their square dance of jealousy to create a more formal pattern in the action. By taking its energy from one imposed coincidence after another, that action dispenses with intrigue. Nor does it rely on the revuelike, commedia format, despite some memorably comic set speeches.[30] Some critics have observed that the author has at last advanced beyond the imagining of types, and they have proceeded to study the characters as though they were living personalities—not a worthwhile expenditure of intelligence because the roles as written can each be adequately summed up in two or three adjectives, such as credulous, rash, quick-tempered. The principals all lack personalities of any depth or width; nor do they amount to the calcified attitudes that would stamp them as types. The springing of one coincidence on top of another turns them into sets of responses that are not

30. These set speeches are given to Gorgibus, Gros-René, Lisette, Martine, and, above all, Sganarelle, whose 68-line monologue about honor among cuckolds (sc. 17) is one of Molière's finest arias.

genuinely involuntary, into a ritual. Now, actors may certainly wish to furnish motives, real or unreal, in order to clarify those responses from one moment to the next, as well as the "through lines" of their performances. But acting, as almost any actor knows, goes well beyond role playing. A web of interacting movements and voices, *The Imaginary Cuckold* might be conducted as an accompaniment to music, actual or imagined, and its farce choreographed.

But what about the rhyming verse? English-speaking actors and directors, reared on the coachings of Sir Tyrone Guthrie, Peter Brook, John Barton, Terry Hands, and other pioneers of Shakespearean production, strive for a poetry spoken as naturally, as effortlessly as possible, for intelligibility and simplicity that will bring out the meanings of the lines and avoid the sonorous cadences of the nineteenth century or, come to that, the seventeenth-century snorting favored by Molière's rivals at the Hôtel de Bourgogne. But suppose that, like Monsieur Jourdain who suddenly becomes aware he is speaking prose, the characters became aware that they were speaking rhymes? And *played* with them, capitalizing on the line endings? Modern theatre has moved away from exploiting flourishes in dramatic language, as though ashamed of them, but here is one instance where they pulse outward from the heart of the play's theatricality.

Don Garcie of Navarre, or The Jealous Prince
(*Dom Garcie de Navarre ou Le Prince jaloux*, 1661)

The author or his first editors called *Don Garcie* a comedy, but it might more accurately be considered his first and most sustained spoof, since appreciating it calls for some familiarity with Spanish "golden age" theatre and its French and Italian derivatives of which he was indebted to at least two.[31] Yet, his contemporaries seem to have greeted it without pleasurable reactions, even though they must have known the originals that were being spoofed.[32] Onstage, the play had a short and dismal life of fewer than a dozen

31. *The Fortunate Jealousy of Prince Rodrigue* by Cignonini (1654) and P. Corneille's *Don Sanche of Aragon* (1649).

32. Although a spoof, the play is not a travesty, since it does not caricature its characters or make them seem ridiculous. Molière's contemporaries, for example, Donneau de Visé, and a number of critics since have wondered whether he meant the play as a tragicomedy, a genre that had already passed out of style, or a heroic comedy, as Corneille had called *Don Sanche*. For a further discussion of the genre, see Hubert, "A Burlesque Tragedy," 65–84, and his bibliographical references.

initial performances, a slumping box office, and no revivals. It has not been translated into English, so far as I can discover, since Ozell's brave prose rendering in "Volume the Fifth" of *The Works of Mr. de Molière* (1714),[33] possibly because of its long, intricately fashioned and sometimes pedestrianly rhymed speeches, or just as possibly because its singular reputation as this playwright's only out-and-out failure has triumphed over its many and considerable qualities.

The stage represents a hall or reception room in the mansion of the princess Elvire at Astorga, not unlike the impersonal interiors favored by Corneille and later Racine. As the rightful heiress of the kingdom of León in Spain, Elvire has been displaced by the usurper Mauregat who does not feature in the action (he presumably has ousted her from the palace in the capital city of León) and whose name suggests he is a Moor. The main plot consists of a one-sided contest for Elvire's hand between two princes: Don Garcie of Navarre, a kingdom well to the east of León, and Don Sylve,[34] thought to be from Castile in central Spain but actually the brother of Elvire; the fact of this blood tie is withheld from them until the fifth act. As in *The Botcher*, we have a man sexually (but unreciprocally) drawn to his sister, another incestuous attraction hinted at, although this dramatic device for creating a rival suitor and then disqualifying him has ancient sources and is mythical in its origins.

The contest here is one-sided because Elvire tells her confidante in the opening scene that although the two suitors are of equal merit and rank, she esteems Sylve but loves Garcie, to whose fighting prowess she owes her freedom. She would express her preference immediately, except that Garcie flies into rages of jealousy on the slimmest pretext: marriage with such a man could become a hell for both of them. The conflict in this main plot will therefore be not between Garcie and Sylve but between Garcie's jealousy and his self-control. The self-control will keep losing until he despairingly calls himself a thoroughly contradictory character, his own enemy: "Thanks to the fateful lengths to which I go, / Within myself I meet my greatest foe" (IV, 9).

Two secondary and, to some extent, overlapping conflicts fill out the requisite five acts and give rise to two more love triangles. Garcie's confidants,

---

33. 3 vols. (reprint; New York: Benjamin Blom, 1967), 3: 149–97.
34. In this chapter, as in the one on *Don Juan*, I have retained the French versions of the Spanish names but not the French versions of the Spanish titles, such as Dom for Don or Done for Donna. Ozell's translation anglicizes both titles and names.

Alvar and Lope, compete for the affections of Elvire's confidante, Élise. The loyal Alvar tries to smooth over Garcie's jealousy, explaining the outbursts as eruptions of his excessive love, whereas the subversive Lope provokes more of them for the sheer joy of starting mischief. The resolution of the Alvar-Élise-Lope triangle is implied but not explicitly dealt with in the action. At the same time, Don Sylve, in order to woo Elvire, has stopped paying attentions to a countess named Ignès and left her in León at the mercy of Mauregat the usurper. As the flattening-out of the second triangle, Sylve finds he is Elvire's brother and cannot very well marry her. The discovery makes him ashamed of his scurvy treatment of Ignès; but her love for him has not faltered, and he humbly asks her to be his partner. Since he now supersedes his sister as heir to the throne of León, Ignès will become its queen. Elvire, in marrying Garcie, will become queen of Navarre.

All well and tidy: the vacillations of the two principal men keep the final wrap-up at bay. But the substance of the action grows out of Garcie's jealous torments, for which the playwright offers ample provocation by means of his plotting. In the first act, Garcie invites the heavens to declare "eternal war" on him, to strike him down with blows, if he ever again succumbs to "the weakness of jealousy," following which imprecation Elvire opens a secret letter—and he goes into a transport of jealousy. He takes the letter to be a love missive and will not calm down until she forces him to read it and find that it comes from Ignès, whom the tyrant Mauregat still means to wed. From now on, Garcie swears, he will die rather than give in to false suspicions (I, 3).

But in the next act, he has found half of a torn letter addressed in Elvire's hand to a lover (II, 4), and again he foams at the mouth—until the missing part of the letter is restored and proves that the lover was himself. More abject self-recriminations and regrets follow—more oaths. But by the end of the act, the insidious Lope has given him fresh cause for alarm. In act III, this proves to be an unannounced visit from Don Sylve. Garcie again bad-mouths his beloved, accusing her of perfidy and of entertaining a secret passion for Sylve. By now Elvire has had enough of these accusations. In front of Garcie, she tells Sylve that she admires him (she stops short of saying she loves him); that he knows how to speak to a princess; and that she will need his assistance in ridding the kingdom of Mauregat. And she stamps out. Garcie then assures Sylve that "my rage will find the necessary force / That will prevent her from becoming yours" (III, 4), and that Sylve cannot feel sure of having won until he holds Garcie's dead head in his hands.

To continue the pattern, by now established, of one jealous spasm per act,

Garcie will next see his heart's desire in the arms of a knight (IV, 7). Elvire, after listening with mounting annoyance to his immediate reproaches, proffers a choice: either he must have faith in her, whatever he thinks he has seen, or failing that trust, she is willing to give him proof that she is innocent. But if he insists on that proof, she will sooner die than marry him. This choice unleashes a fresh outburst from Garcie: she is prevaricating; he will kill the traitor; and, yes, he will see her proof. To his acute chagrin, the knight turns out to be Donna Ignès in a soldier's garb (IV, 9). She assumed it to escape from Mauregat. What is left for Garcie? Only to die, he says, in Elvire's service, to recompense her for his mislaid suspicions. He is going straight off to kill Mauregat, and if he himself is killed in the attempt, perhaps she will understand, feel pity for him, and say to herself, "He outraged me by loving me too much" (IV, 9).

But the last act of the play deprives Garcie of the opportunity to make heroic amends. His rival, Sylve, has already defeated Mauregat, and Don Alphonse, the legitimate heir to the throne of León, has promised Sylve to his sister. By now Elvire, who still loves Garcie, says she has overcome her resentment toward him. To bring the lovers together will now require one of those thunderbolts of synchronicity—say, an act of renunciation on the part of Sylve (likely if the play were by Corneille) or his death. The death does happen, but symbolically. There is no Don Sylve; he is actually Don Alphonse the king, Elvire's brother, to everyone's surprise, including his own (V, 5). Further, Sylve-Alphonse admits that he did not overthrow the tyrant; that was done by the people themselves who rose against him, much as happens in *The Sheep Well (Fuente Ovejuna)* by Lope de Vega, and thus Garcie will not have to endure the disgrace of having been outbraved by his supposed rival. But the fifth act has left room, before the unraveling, for one more manifestation of Garcie's "monster" or "obstacle," for which he earlier blamed "the inhuman fates" (IV, 6). He finds the brother and sister smiling together, Sylve because the discovery of this woman as his sibling has magically restored his love for Ignès, Elvire because she has now steeled herself to cope in future with her lover's tantrums. But Garcie once again jumps to the wrong conclusion and pleads with her to have enough compassion for him not to look so openly and publicly gleeful at his defeat and anguish. The comedy ends with Garcie let into the latest developments, and his last word is "joy." As in *The Imaginary Cuckold,* the characters, if not the audience, might well deduce: Don't believe everything you see and hear—or at least, not until you've asked a few pointed but polite questions.

Is Molière capable of writing an undilutedly happy ending? It would appear

not. Amid the rejoicing at the union of three couples, a cynic will consider
that 1) Garcie is liable to turn jealous every time he sees Elvire glance at
another man; 2) Sylve-Alphonse returned to Ignès only when his sister
became unattainable; and 3) Élise faulted Alvar in an early scene for never
appearing jealous—for her, as opposed to her mistress, jealousy is the unmistakable sign of true love. But these flaws in the marriages to come belong to
the story's future; the closing action sweeps them aside.

Here again, we have a play that depends on synchronicity and misunderstandings, which in turn are due to withheld information. The manufactured
premises (a ruler who does not exist decrees that he shall give himself in
marriage and in a different guise to his own sister) and the *galanterie* of the
language might turn out to be even more difficult for a modern, realism-
soaked audience to appreciate than they were for those limited seventeenth-
century audiences. Elvire, despite her gratitude to Garcie for having fought
to rescue her from Mauregat, makes it clear from the start, in conversation
with her confidante, that she wishes to be wooed by having her slightest
gesture or response correctly interpreted: "A sigh, look, blush, a *pause* are
each enough / to signify a heart that speaks of love" (I, 1)—enough perhaps
for a suitor who listens attentively and fastens onto such clues, enough for
any suitor but Garcie, who searches for negative, rather than positive, signals.
For him, a reckless warrior unapt to the wiles and subtleties of courting,
sighs, looks, blushes, and pauses argue guilt, not innocent affection. In
addition, the severity of the dialogue (fortified by the length of the speeches)
goes unrelieved by those slivers of humor that might reveal more blatantly
that these characters dwell at the opposite end of the scale from the ones
who record similarly high-flown sentiments in the theatre of Spain and of
Corneille. Instead of proclaiming their unswerving will, like good Cornelians
or doughty Spaniards, the lovers either publicize their weaknesses or, when
they do express a firm intention, quickly go back on it. Garcie has sworn he
will sooner die than let himself be duped by false suspicions, and Elvire has
sworn she will sooner die than marry him. The very utterance of such vows
by such characters is a joke.

How might a play with so many strikes against it for today's theatre public
be reinstated? It would probably need to be presented in repertory with a
heroic tragedy, which it could play off with its subtle undercutting; or—
philistine as this might seem to purists—with the accompaniment of film or
television images, by means of which the close-ups of faces could catch the
rapid succession of contrasting emotions and the train of misapprehensions

by the listeners, together with medium-close shots to reveal the arms and hands, provided that the latter have something to say and are not wielded with the outward spraying movements so common on our stages. Filmed supplements would be not unlike the spoken asides placed with counterpointing skill by O'Neill in *Strange Interlude* and *Days Without End.* Close and medium-close shots have added force, color, and subtlety to the telecasts of opera, especially during the arias, and this play unwinds one "aria" after another. With monotonous vocal delivery, the harangues of Garcie might resemble the intolerably repetitive naggings of well-meaning mothers found in so much of today's theatre and cinema; but the meticulous grading of the speeches, reflected in a sensitive expressiveness on the part of the actors, would help to bridge the historical gap between our realism and Molière's affectionate parody of heroic grimaces.

The School for Husbands
(*L'École des maris*, 1661)

As soon as *The School for Husbands* announces itself as a conflict between a reasonable and an unreasonable man, it gives away its ending. But on the way to that ending, the conflict itself changes character and raises broader, unexpected issues, as well as doubts about whether this is the one didactic play by Molière that it is usually taken for. It certainly conveys a lesson of sorts: that a crabby, hidebound guardian like Sganarelle, who imposes severe discipline on his ward, Isabelle, must arouse her ire and fighting spirit; while a magnanimous guardian like his brother, Ariste, who lets his ward, Isabelle's sister, Léonor, grow up without parental constraints, wins her affection and even her hand in marriage. But the action never suggests that Sganarelle could, if he wanted to—he doesn't—evolve into a complaisant Ariste: the lesson is lost on him. You can't teach a middle-aged crab new tricks: Sganarelle is forty, but he behaves like the frowning parent of his brother who is sixty. What does unfold, though, is the typically Moliéresque tragedy-within-a-comedy of a man who is the amusing instrument of his own defeat.

The sisters' late father, that trusting and narrow-sighted soul, gave them into the care of the brothers, who are much older than the women, with instructions to marry them when the time came or find them suitable husbands. In the first scenes of the three acts, the two unconfirmed bachelors trade preachings. They stand on a street in Paris before their respective houses and that of a youthful neighbor, Valère—with possibly a fourth house nearby belonging to a *commissaire*, a police commissioner-cum-magistrate. There they bare their roles, if not their souls, sufficiently to tell us that Sganarelle will on no account dress as uncomfortably as a young blood to suit the fashion (with "tiny hats that let breezes blow into the brain," "short doublets that lose themselves below the armpits," and flapping "sleeves you see at table tasting the gravy"); nor will he permit Isabelle to run around wherever she pleases, as Léonor does; whereas we see that Ariste's conformity with the latest in clothing styles reflects his wish to melt into the crowd, not to seem conspicuous or be a subject of gossip—to live as an unremarkable citizen (I, 1). Ariste further lets it be known that if Léonor marries him he will continue to put no restrictions on her. He says this in front of her, Lisette, her *suivante*, and Isabelle, whom the other two have invited out for a walk. Sganarelle, however, will not allow Isabelle to go with them, whereupon Léonor and then Lisette whet their tongues on him, warning that domestic tyranny kills off love and that any man who oversees a woman too closely is taking a big risk. Says Lisette: "If any husband acted too severe / With me, I'd try to justify his fear" (I, 2). To no avail—secure in his cold folly, Sganarelle chuckles as he tells his brother, "I'd love to see her make a cuckold of you."

In the last two scenes of the act, Valère comes out of his house with his servant, Ergaste, and tries to strike up an acquaintance with Sganarelle. He greets him with courtesy, doles out flattery and neighborly sentiments, but receives only terse replies (I, 3). When Sganarelle takes his boorish self back indoors, Valère says that he has loved Isabelle "ardently" for four months, but that he has not managed to speak to her or find an intermediary to bribe, because Sganarelle, the "Argus," keeps no servants. To cheer up his present master, Ergaste remarks that he has served twenty different "hunters" in the past and that their "greatest joy" was to run across a sour watchdog like this one, because the woman at stake was always eager for release. They reenter Valère's house to dream up a plan (I, 4).

But they will not need one. A plan will be thrust upon them. The second act abandons the contented partnership between Léonor and Ariste in order to explore the rivalry between Sganarelle and Valère for Isabelle. In enlarging upon the three sides (or corners) of the triangle, Molière works several innovations into what had looked like standardized roles. First, Isabelle, a normally reticent heroine who spoke only thirty-one words in the opening act, turns out of desperation into an initiator of several intrigues. Pretending she has had written overtures from Valère, she asks Sganarelle to carry the unopened messages back to Valère: these "unopened messages" are enve-

lopes containing her sealed instructions. Second, Valère and his valet, in
complying with the instructions, will play almost passive agents in the action,
unusual roles for a hero and his servant. Third, the villain of the piece,
Sganarelle, will not only act as a willing go-between in the plan to cheat him
but will also come to feel sympathy for his rival, Valère, who, he thinks,
doesn't stand a chance with Isabelle. By filtering into these "types" certain
characteristics that are atypical, if not the direct opposites of the norm, the
playwright approaches more nearly than before the creation of what we
call "rounded" characters, although they remain roles-in-action—what they
"are" fulfills exactly what they "do," and he supplies no more of what they
"are" than is necessary.

French critics who claim that Molière has at last begun with this play to
apply himself to Comedy of Character, as an advance over mere Comedy of
Intrigue and Comedy of Coincidence, believe they are praising him for
achieving a drama that is more difficult or artistically rich.[35] But a reader or
spectator will not find *The School for Husbands* particularly revealing for
its characterizations; its rewards proceed more from its eventful intrigues,
especially in the second act, and from the clashes of ideas. Another topic
touched on by critics has to do with the author's standing up for women's
rights here to compensate for his caustic treatment two years earlier of Cathos
and Magdelon. He may have felt disappointed that some people had taken
him to task for apparently lashing out at women in that play; yet *Maidens* is
as much a mockery of pretentious male fraud as of two young women's easy
susceptibility to impostors; and *The School for Husbands* would make theatrical
sense if it took place in a matriarchal society and the sex of the five principal
characters were reversed.[36] It is difficult to see this play as an apology or an
attempt to curry favor with outraged women; instead, in its discrediting of
parental oppression, it joins forces with many of the later plays. It is the
unjust exercise of power that Molière baits with laughter.

Isabelle's stratagems work triumphantly for a time, and then backfire.
When Sganarelle brings Valère to meet her and hear the rejection from her
own lips, she recites a series of double-entendres. One of the two men, she

---

35. As has become obvious from much contemporary theatre, a comedy or other kind
of play that consists of character studies is not inherently superior to other drama,
any more than a play called a tragedy is inherently superior to one called a melodrama
or farce.

36. In one of Molière's sources, Terence's *Adelphi (The Brothers)*, the youngsters
subjected to contrasting skills of upbringing are male, not female.

declares, is the honorable choice for her because he has all her esteem and love; the other fills her with anger and aversion—she would rather die than marry him. Moist-eyed with gratitude and misunderstanding, Sganarelle gives her a hug as she holds out her hand behind his back for Valère to kiss (I, 9). But Sganarelle, in high excitement, now decides she wants him so much that he will marry her on the following day (I, 10).

Isabelle must escape fast. She improvises a lie: that her sister has loved Valère for a long time, is now hiding in her room, and intends to marry him secretly (III, 2). Sganarelle cannot help gloating over his brother's mistake and misfortune. He summons a notary and the *commissaire* to perform the marriage between Valère and Léonor without further delay (III, 4) and calls Ariste to witness the consequences of his leniency (III, 5). Sganarelle doesn't know, however, that Isabelle will impersonate her sister in order to get out of his house and into Valère's, under cover of the inky darkness of a Molière night. He joyously signs the consent papers and gets Ariste to sign (III, 7).

To round out the lesson, the real Léonor returns from a dance, where "all the young idiots" bored her with their blond wigs and forced wit. She is now ready to accept Ariste as her husband, the sooner the better (III, 8). Isabelle apologizes to her sister and then tells Sganarelle with delicate irony that she "does not deserve" a heart like his. Small consolation for him. Four of the other assembled characters—Ariste, Lisette, Léonor, and Ergaste—then take turns to sprinkle salt on his wounds by saying that circumstances have worked out for the best and proved him wrong.

The plotting, which had circled Sganarelle, now focuses on him again. His last ten-line speech is all resentment and defiance. He cannot believe that "Satan in person could be as wicked as a slut like her." Rising momentarily from satanic to biblical cadences, he exclaims, "Woe unto him who trusts a woman after this!"—but he ends by renouncing "this deceitful sex forever and consigning it to hell with all my heart." In one startling line, Molière flicks his infernal references back at him: "For her I'd have put my hand into fire." The affirmation, which I would say has to be uttered with sincerity (if not heat!), has a pathetic ring that will sound again in the next play, a course of variations on the same theme, the art of rearing a child-wife, when Arnolphe realizes that he is in love with the ward he intends to marry (V, 4).

Sganarelle, a generation younger than his brother, behaves like a rebellious son, but a literal reactionary against Ariste's liberalism and liberality.[37] He has left the prospect of marriage until late in life and seems to want an obedient daughter for a wife; but Ariste, marrying at a much later age, doesn't mind setting up house with a granddaughter who will soon become his nursemaid. Do such realistic considerations matter? In production, hardly. The age differential illustrates not that older men make the best husbands, but that marriage is not for the mean, rigidified man of whatever years, only for him who is prepared to give more than he takes. Even so, the positive lesson—which, if it bothered some men, delighted many women spectators, who made the play a commercial success—counts for less than the edifying manipulation of Sganarelle. In him, Molière has stretched the negative hero well beyond the dimensions of his two Mascarilles, two Gorgibuses, and Don Garcie, and colored him antisocial and malevolent, a prefiguring of Harpagon. Like the Miser, he assumes that to be fashionable is to acquiesce, surrender, play false to oneself; and like him, he has a weakness for flattery. If he does love Isabelle, he loves what he sees of himself in her, the attitudes she adopts precisely to deceive him; and if he cannot help liking and feeling sorry for Valère, it is because he perceives some sort of resemblance between them, which makes his rival a shadow of himself, as when he speaks a strange line to Valère, *"Tenez, embrassez-moi: c'est un autre elle-même,"* or, "Come, let me hug you: you're two of a kind," or "you're just like her," or literally "you're her other," or figuratively "you're *my* other" (II, 9). To be wholly himself means to Sganarelle not to be anybody else's mark or prey; but his approval only of others who reflect him back to himself is a condition of astigmatism, brought on by a desire to see the world populated in his own image.

37. In Slawomir Mrozek's play *Tango* (1965), the hero, Arthur, stages a filial rebellion at home, an embracing of the conservative principles and practices long since spurned by his avant-garde parents.

PART TWO

Diversions

Why did the man who would become the author of *The School for Wives*, *The Misanthrope*, *Don Juan*, *Tartuffe*, *The Miser*, *The Learned Ladies*, and other plays that rank with the lasting works of literature, expend so much of himself on a series of *divertissements* that had to be assembled in a rush, and drained him, and may have aggravated his ill health during the last twelve years of his life? Seldom are these spectacles revived, and never with the grandiosity that seventeenth-century France could accord and afford. The potential in their very size and splendor may have been a principal reason why Molière attempted them: to see whether he could bring them off; to discover and broach fresh theatrical forms.

But there were other reasons. Although commissioned for the elect, the shows drew tremendous crowds, thousands of people other than courtiers. The director in Molière could call on the finest designers in Europe and spread his dramatic wares over huge outdoor spaces wrapped in greenery. The budgets were virtually unlimited, and the generous salaries fed into and subsidized his troupe during leaner seasons. He used the productions to make himself necessary to the monarch and the court; in his time he became celebrated more for these shows than for his "legitimate" drama. They provided him with the opportunity, as of 1663 and *The Forced Marriage*, to work with Lully who, although younger than he, had already become the royal "superintendent of music"; with Lully he went a long way toward inventing a new medium, comic opera and, in the case of *Psyche*, toward a tragicomic opera. He seized on opportunities to sing, to prance, to dance. Finally, there is no evidence to suppose that he thought these diversions inferior to his other writings as literature; he even appears to marvel retrospectively at how much he contrived to do at precipitant notice.[1]

Here I am treating the comedy-ballets principally as drama, although much more could be said about the music, the dancing, scenic conjuring, costumes, and the other theatrical infusions and flourishes.

The Nuisances
(*Les Fâcheux*, 1661)

With *The Nuisances*, Molière made his debut as a showman. His audiences and monarch had seen him before as playwright, artistic direc-

1. Molière's justifications, actual and probable, for taking on the comedy-ballets are dealt with in Pellisson (17 ff.), who believes that Molière had something like a seventeenth-century equivalent for productions by Aristophanes in mind for this medium, as opposed to his other drama influenced formally by Plautus and Terence.

tor, and actor. Now, on the grounds of Foucquet's chateau at Vaux, he masterminded the first thoroughgoing comedy-ballet. It had landscape architecture by Le Notre, scenic painting by Le Brun, music by Beauchamp (with one air by Lully), and machinery designed by Torelli. The spectacle consisted of an address by the author, pretending to be bewildered by the presence of the king and other spectators; a prologue[2] recited by a naiad in the form of Madeleine Béjart, who emerged from a rock that "undetectably turned into a shell," according to one witness, La Fontaine; dryads, fauns, and satyrs, summoned by the naiad to materialize from behind or within trees and statuary; then a three-act play in verse, the acts culminating in balletic movement by croquet players and inquisitive lookers-on (after act I), bowls players, a gang of urchins, "cobblers, male and female, and their fathers and others," plus a solo dance by a gardener (after act II), and (after act III) masked actors, Swiss halberdiers, four shepherds and a lone shepherdess "who," says the last stage direction, "in the opinion of all who saw them, brought the *divertissement* to a graceful enough close." The sheer magnitude of this enterprise and its successors makes Molière the most expansive impresario after Leone di Somi, who was active as producer-writer-director-designer about a century earlier. In his preface to the published play,[3] Molière tells us that he believed it was "quite a novelty" for the show to have been "conceived, put together, learned, and performed in two weeks." Some critics conjecture that he had already written or partially written or thought about certain of the scenes in the play well beforehand, even during his years of touring the provinces. As another novelty, invariably pointed out by commentators, this is the first endeavor to write in verse realistic scenes and dialogue about contemporary life.

If we except Mlle Béjart, we do not know how many of the regular members of Molière's troupe and the *gagistes* (extras hired for the occasion) took part in the ballets. But the strictly dramatic segments of *The Nuisances* add up to

2. The prologue, a tribute to the king, was written by Paul Pellisson, a friend of Foucquet, a platonic suitor of Madeleine de Scudéry, and (who knows?) possibly an ancestor of the Pellisson mentioned in the previous footnote.

3. In this same preface Molière says drily he is not sure "whether it could all have been better, and whether those who were entertained laughed according to the rules"; he also promises that the time will come when he publishes "my comments on the plays I've done, and I am not unhopeful that it will be seen that, in the role of great author, I can quote Aristotle and Horace." The promise may not have been serious, but only a dig at the theoretical prefaces of Corneille; if it was serious, he did not live to fulfill it.

his most daring instance of providing roles tailored to his actors, including two or perhaps three for himself—while the action envelops them in a simple but suspenseful dramatic structure. A young marquis and man-about-court named Éraste, initially played by La Grange, waits for his lady friend, Orphise. But he is standing in a public place, where the nuisances of the title, others who move or hope to move in court circles, go by and spot him: today we would probably call each nuisance a pain in the neck or elsewhere. One after the other, they buttonhole him, so that every time Orphise does show up, he looks as if he is preoccupied with them, although he is inwardly cursing them, fidgeting, muttering asides and trying to tear himself away. The ballet interludes, also plotted to serve as nuisances, fit thematically into the action; they edge him temporarily offstage after the first and second acts.

While the revue format has the advantage of elasticity, it also spells danger. The nuisances who plague Éraste might in theory grow tiresome to spectators. But in practice, the playwright skirts the danger by introducing types he has sufficiently individualized to give his actors and himself plenty of room for exploration with a variety of personalities, grievances, and (within the confines of the alexandrine) sentence structures. During the episodes in which they discomfit Éraste for our amusement, the portraits accumulate as a living tableau of French court manners and mortifications in the 1660s, many of them painfully resurrected in our own uncourtly days. For instance, the first of them, not seen in the action but described by the hero, talked noisily during a show about the episodes to come, changed seats, shifted around to obscure the views of others, loudly greeted friends who had come in late, and tried to accompany Éraste to his appointment with Orphise.

The next nuisance is his valet, La Montagne, who insists on fussing about Éraste's appearance, straightening and dusting his master's clothes, combing his wig, taking off his hat to brush it and letting it fall to the ground. Meanwhile, Orphise passes by in the company of another man and turns her head away when Éraste nods or waves. He, struck to the heart by this snub, instructs La Montagne to go after them and spy on them:

LA MONTAGNE What, all the way?

ÉRASTE   Yes.

LA MONTAGNE   Do I hide en route?
               Or look as if I'm frankly in pursuit?

ÉRASTE   (Sarcastically) No, let them know you're following
               them, and
               You're doing so at my express command. (I, 2)

The next nuisance, a fop named Lysandre, has just composed a ditty set to his own music, which he sings five or six times, kicks a few dance steps to fit the melody, and asks whether Éraste isn't eager to learn it. But luckily, intoxicated with his own gifts, he scampers off to perform before another friend (I, 3). Orphise returns alone and remarks on Éraste's sad appearance. The man he saw her with was a nuisance she shook off by asking him to escort her to her coach. Éraste doesn't know whether to take her word but affirms that he is prepared to suffer all her deceptions, and after nine lines of complaint, that he will sooner die than complain (I, 5). Her reply is curtailed by the arrival of Alcandre, who whispers that he wants Éraste to carry a challenge to a rival who uttered an insult and must pay for it with a duel. Éraste declines, but by this time Orphise, offended by the whispering, has left (I, 6). The first act ends with him on his own again, waiting again, but almost instantly the first ballet displaces him.

In the second act the procession of nuisances does not let up. A certain Alcipe lost a hand of piquet the day before and reenacts the game, card by card, for twenty-eight lines, before leaving to impart the sad news to the rest of the world (II, 1). Two ladies next want Éraste to resolve a dispute already laid out at play-length in *Don Garcie:*

> ORANTE   You'll end this great debate if you can tell us
>   Whether a lover should—or not—be jealous.
> CLYMÈNE Or, to explain my view, and yours, precisely:
>   Do jealous folk, or others, love more nicely?

To placate them both, Éraste says that the jealous person loves more, while the nonjealous one loves better (II, 4). But by this time, Orphise, who had been detained by her own set of nuisances, returns to find him in conversation about love with the two women (II, 5). She stalks off, leaving him prey to Dorante, the longest-winded nuisance in the play, who must narrate in excruciating detail how, the day before, he, his horse, and his hounds lost a stag he had almost caught to a bumpkin who shot the poor beast in the head with a pistol—a gross breach of hunting etiquette. In disgust, says Dorante, "I clapped my spurs to my horse" and rode off without saying a word to "the ignorant fool." Éraste congratulates him with sad self-consciousness: "Well done. It's rare and sensible to find / A way to leave such nuisances behind" (II, 6).[4] After which envious sentiment, he is bustled offstage by the end of the act and four consecutive dances.

Act III opens with Éraste's announcement that Orphise's uncle-guardian has forbidden her to see him, but that she has defied the order and set a new time for their meeting that evening. Before he can hurry away, Caritidès accosts him. This pedant professes to be appalled by errors and lapses in taste committed by the people who make up street signs, tavern signs, and other public inscriptions and wishes Éraste, evidently a man with some clout, to present the king with a petition in which he asks to be appointed national superintendent of signs. To shake him off as briskly as possible, Éraste agrees (III, 2) but is almost instantly beset by Ormin, who is even more ambitious than Caritidès and dreams of "a string of ports along our coast, for off it / His Majesty would reap tremendous profit." Meanwhile, Ormin would like to borrow a couple of *pistoles* until the rewards for his idea roll in. Éraste is glad to get rid of him so easily; but alas, the next pest hovers nearby. Filinte claims to have heard that Éraste needs a second to support him in a duel with a man he has quarreled with. This is the obverse of the encounter with Alcandre (I, 6). Éraste protests that he has had no quarrel with anybody, but Filinte persists and is driven away only by the threat of being made the opponent, not a second, in the duel.

Finally, as Éraste leaves for his appointment with Orphise, he faces the supreme nuisance, her uncle, who has hired some mercenaries to ambush and murder him. But Éraste's servants, hiding close by, hear of the plot and indignantly attack the uncle. Éraste arrives with drawn sword just in time to intervene. Thus, in spite of all the vexations caused by his nuisances, they delayed him until the right moment, with Molière's cooperation; and the uncle gratefully hands over his niece to the man who saved him.

It is hardly surprising that Louis enjoyed the show, besieged as he must have been every day by importunings like those endured by Éraste. Molière had hit on a theme that could hardly have appealed more to a ruler, a man with a crammed schedule, a dispenser of power and wealth. But we cannot

---

4. In his published dedication to Louis, Molière expresses warm thanks for a suggestion that came from the king, who knew in advance of the subject of this piece, to "add a character to the nuisances . . . which everyone has [since] found to be the finest part of the work." Did he thank the king so strenuously in order to distance himself from the sponsor of *The Nuisances*, Foucquet, who fell (indeed, plummeted) from royal grace after the production at Vaux?

help noticing that most of the nuisances are people of leisure, whose obsessions fix on their recreation: writing lyrics, dancing, singing, cards, hunting, sporting with love and duels.[5] Two of them are seeking money or influence, a scholar and a sort of inventor, but their schemes are hare-brained. Like some of the other obsessed nuisances, they predate in psychologically milder forms the warped personalities at the center of the later plays.

The Forced Marriage
(*Le Mariage forcé*, 1664)

This playlet, which has reached us in one act, originally had three acts bulked out by eight "entries" danced by the king, the composer, Lully, and a number of male courtiers, some of whom performed the women's roles in drag. Once again the theme is that dread of deception, articulated a century earlier by Rabelais' character Panurge and experienced by one or more characters in most of Molière's comedies: the prospect of a man's being cuckolded by a wife or wife-to-be or a woman's being let down by a male lover. The ten scenes divide neatly into two segments. In the first, the rich, middle-aged Sganarelle seeks advice. A bachelor, he has found a pretty, teenaged coquette, secured her father's permission, and will marry her that evening. But he has doubts, which deepen as the advice he receives becomes more and more ambiguous. In the second segment, having found out that his bride loves somebody else and looks forward to making merry with his money, Sganarelle does what he can to avoid entanglement in a marriage that will make his fears come true.

The conventional setting, a street, has entrances to three houses belonging to Sganarelle, his old friend Géronimo, and his future father-in-law, Alcan-

---

5. Dueling had long been banned in France, but the rulings against it had not been vigorously enforced. After an edict of 1651, ten years earlier, which imposed penalties of confiscated property, capital punishment for those surviving, and no burial monuments for those killed, there were nevertheless hundreds of duels and deaths. In 1661, when *The Nuisances* was played, Louis had begun to enforce the legal prohibitions "inflexibly" (see Couton 1:1,259 n. 5). This is probably the reason why Alcandre tells Éraste about his impending duel in a whisper.

tor.[6] After asking Géronimo to "swear in good faith" to give him an absolutely frank answer, Sganarelle wants to know whether he should get married. The reply is an unequivocal no: he will make a fool of himself and should not dream of marrying at his age, which, by backtracking through Sganarelle's years of domicile in France, Holland, England, and Italy, Géronimo estimates at fifty-two. But Sganarelle disowns the frankness he had invited and received, declaring that he has better health and more vigor than a man of thirty, will not "let the tribe of Sganarelles vanish from the earth," and means to wed Alcantor's young daughter, Dorimène, this very evening. Géronimo immediately capitulates and goes off chuckling (sc. 1). Sganarelle tells himself he is now the happiest of men because he brings laughter to every person to whom he mentions the marriage.

Enter the bride. Sganarelle exults at her youthful face and body, of which he will soon be the "sole master." But when she tells him how much she looks forward to breaking free of her family, going out, having a good time ("every kind of pleasure" because she grows "desperate" when alone at home), putting no constraints on him and expecting none in return, she notices that he has turned pale; she then reassures him that their marriage will dissipate the "vapors" he feels rising in his head. She leaves "to buy all the things I need" and send him the bills (sc. 2).

When Géronimo returns with news of "the most perfect diamond wedding ring" available from a neighborhood vendor, Sganarelle is in no hurry. He has been brooding about a dream he had the night before, of being in a boat on a choppy ocean, and—but his friend cuts him short; he doesn't know anything about dreams[7] and gets himself off the hook by suggesting a consultation with two local philosophers (sc. 3). The first of these, Pancrace, keeps shouting offstage at someone with whom he has just been squabbling or

6. Engravings by Brissart, which serve as frontispieces for the 1682 edition of Molière's plays, represent royal command performances in nontheatrical settings. Thus, the Brissart illustration for *The Forced Marriage* sets the scene in a narrow room papered with a design of an open countryside. This room may be part of the queen mother's apartment in the Louvre, where the play in its one-act form had its premiere, for on the rear wall, which serves as a scenic backdrop, hangs a portrait of a portly lady.

7. Géronimo, the cheerful, life-loving old neighbor or friend, resembles some of the stock figures in the plays of Plautus, such as Periplectomenus in the *Miles Gloriosus* or Callipho in *Pseudolus*. Versions of him have already appeared as Ariste in *The School for Husbands* and Chrysalde in *The School for Wives;* in Molière's later plays he will evolve into the sensible confidant-mediator-interlocutors Cléante in *Tartuffe*, Anselme in *The Miser*, Béralde in *The Imaginary Invalid*, and others.

changes the subject or interrupts Sganarelle in mid-sentence or speaks over his words, until the latter has to bundle him into his house and hold the door closed. In some productions, the audience catches glimpses of Pancrace at one window after another, still audibly orating (sc. 4). The second philosopher, Marphurius,[8] a Pyrrhonian, or skeptic, drives Sganarelle into another rage as he refuses to admit that he knows or understands anything at all: there are no certainties in life. Sganarelle has to chase him around the stage, hitting him with a stick and answering the cries of pain and threats of a lawsuit by quoting Marphurius back to himself: he is not sure that he is hitting him; the philosopher may have wounds on his body, but "nothing is beyond belief," and so on (sc. 5).

Two gypsy women (one played at the first performance by the king and the other by a male courtier) dance their way onstage as they sing and accompany themselves by thumping tambourines. When the troubled fiancé questions them, they ironically predict a marriage to "a woman who will be loved and cherished by everybody" and bring him many friends and "a great reputation."[9] But to his stark question, repeated four times with increasing urgency, "Will I be a cuckold?" the gypsies sing and dance their tantalizing no-answer: "La, la, la, la" (sc. 6).

Sganarelle finds himself sliding off the plateau of uncertainty and onto the downward slope of despair. He hears Dorimène saying to a young admirer, "I'm not marrying this man for love; I accepted him only because he's rich . . . and he'll be dead and flat on his belly within six months" (sc. 7). He swiftly approaches her father with his misgivings. Alcantor, in the midst of making preparations for the wedding, "would sooner die than go back on my word," but when Sganarelle pleads, "I want to be like my father and his forefathers before him; none of them wanted to get married," he will "see what can be done" (sc. 8).

Sganarelle is congratulating himself on having escaped just in time when Alcantor's son appears, fully armed. With the utmost civility, he challenges the defaulting bridegroom to a duel. As alternatives, he can choose a beating "or marry my sister." Sganarelle would rather make no choice at all. He then suffers a beating with a stick, accompanied by the son's fulsome apologies, until he gives in: "I'll marry her, I'll marry her!" (sc. 9). (The exquisite

8. Marphurius is, like Pancrace, the stock name of a pedant from Italian comedy.

9. Marrying an attractive woman who will bring many friends with her (as she turns her husband into a cuckold) is another of the ideas Molière borrowed from Rabelais' *Gargantua and Pantagruel* (bk. 3, chap. 28).

politesse shown by the son as a mask for his cruelty will be revived in the characterization of Monsieur Loyal in the last act of *Tartuffe.*) The closing scene of seven or eight lines has Alcantor, his son, and Sganarelle present, but the latter speaks not one word as his in-laws rejoice at the happy outcome of having at last unloaded the family's giddy, free-spending flirt.

A *livret*, or program, for the original *Forced Marriage*, describing the work as a "ballet," lists the entries by number and identifies the participants. One entry consists of the dance and singing of the two gypsies; another of an episode in which a magician brings on four demons who terrify Sganarelle. There are several songs too. The contents of the remaining entries are described hardly at all; they seem to supply elaborate transitions between the scenes of what would later be published as the "comedy" in one act. In the initial performance, Molière introduced, as the last of the "entries," four young *galants*, who "cajole Sganarelle's wife." Modern productions generally go on to stage the marriage celebrations—a slapstick, rather than shotgun, wedding—and show Dorimène contemptuously leaving her husband standing in isolation as she mingles with the young male guests.

Some directors like to add actors who will play an onstage audience peeping at Sganarelle and enjoying his distress. In the text, though, the author has plotted the scenes with economy of casting throughout. Seven of the ten scenes have only two characters present at a time; in an eighth, Sganarelle's encounter with the pair of gypsies, those two transvestite fortune-tellers function conceptually as one. The effect is, once again, of a series of cameos or turns as Sganarelle wanders, or is pushed, from one vaudeville partner to the next.

The Princess of Elis
(*La Princesse d'Élide*, 1664)

In Western Europe, the month of May generally offers the most reliable weather of the year, warm but not hot, an agreeable postlude to the showers and freshness of April. In 1664, therefore, May 8 saw the start of a weeklong festivity, a seventeenth-century spring fertility rite, on the newly and vastly enlarged and refurbished grounds of Versailles. *The Pleasures of the Enchanted Isle* was designed to honor the queen, the queen mother, and as many courtiers believed, the twenty-five-year-old king's most recent fancy, eighteen-year-old Louise de La Vallière, who had already borne him a child. The sumptuous proceedings, under the supervision of the Duc de Saint-Aignan and Molière, began with "ring coursing" *(la course de bague)* or jousting in which court figures, the monarch included, played roles chosen by Saint-Aignan from Ariosto's early sixteenth-century epic of chivalry *Orlando Furioso.* The alfresco events continued with mythical and allegorical pageantry that featured Molière's troupe,[10] a performance of *The Princess of Elis,* parades, ballets, fireworks, feasting, and the introduction of the first version of *Tartuffe,* shortly to be suppressed.[11]

Some writers have speculated that Molière undertook to rush together his *Princess* and to manage the complex array of "pleasures" in order to ensure a showing for *Tartuffe* before the king, who had read the script and found nothing objectionable in it. The playwright may have guessed or heard that the fierce Compagnie du Saint-Sacrement, which had somehow learned of the existence of *Tartuffe* after the king's brother read it, would prove less tolerant, as would the archbishop of Paris, Hardouin de Péréfixe, who was to attend the Versailles extravaganza. Yet, so far as one can tell, Molière, whatever his feelings about *Tartuffe,* relished the chance to do another grand show and his position as combined Philostrate and most-favored author; took pains and pride in mounting the dazzling entertainment; and wrote himself a leading part. The fate of *Tartuffe* had almost certainly been on his mind before the festival, but he and his company had only six days in Versailles to prepare for the seven crowded days to follow—which must have driven that mind into more pressing considerations. Diversions like these sapped his strength and, by the next year, would endanger his health; but they earned high wages and royal gratitude. They also solidified the king's patronage. *The Pleasures of the Enchanted Isle* amounted to one of the most lavish series of spectacles ever staged. Molière, a skilled organizer, guided a team of artists that included his actors, the designer Carlo Vigarani (who had managed to

---

10. Molière as Pan, his wife as the Age of Gold, Mlle de Brie as the Age of Bronze, André Hubert as the Age of Silver, Du Croisy as the Age of Iron, La Grange as Apollo, Mlle du Parc as Spring (on a horse), René Berthelot (Du Parc) as Summer (on an elephant), La Thorillière as Fall (on a camel), Louis Béjart as Winter (on a bear), and Madeleine Béjart as Diana (on a traveling mountain). For a colorful account of the *Pleasures,* see Palmer, 296–303.

11. This first *Tartuffe* in three acts is assumed by many critics, following Michaut, to resemble the first three acts of the version in five acts that has come down to us (see Michaut, *Les Luttes de Molière,* 56 ff.). Other critics, including Guicharnaud, believe that most of the action and story in the five-act version would have been incorporated in the original, so as not to leave the ending ragged and unresolved.

oust and replace Torelli), Lully, the poet Benserade, and a certain Périguy, these last two assuming responsibility for the incidental and introductory verses.

We can get some sense of the scope of the *Pleasures* from the engravings by I. Silvestre. In two of them, an extensive sward, the acting area, enclosed by trees, shows dozens of horses and riders in a virtually military formation; between the trees are lofty portals and other scenic elements. In another engraving, three actresses—Du Parc, De Brie, and Armande Molière—sit astride sea monsters floating in a circular lake *(le grand bassin)* with wind baffles on either side. Behind the lake a larger, connecting lake accommodates "the enchanted isle," an artificial mound on which stands the palace of the magician Alcine. On the third day, this palace, as we see from another engraving, bursts into flame and fireworks. A throng of spectators are densely packed into semicircular rows for each event. For the performance of *Princess,* an ornate proscenium frame, which looks to be about fifty feet high, has a pit in front for the musicians and is lit by five immense chandeliers. Behind it stretches a long perspective, the playing area, defined by rows of trees and shrubbery—or convincing imitations.[12] The stage managers and sceneshifters, aided by Vigarani's machinery, must have had their work cut out.

Molière took the action of *The Princess of Elis* from a then-recent Spanish play,[13] interleaving its five short acts between bouts of pastoral playfulness. Thanks to a *relation* or narrative published as a guide for the participants and guests, we have a reliable text for the spoken portions. An Aurora figure urges "young beauties" to yield to their admirers and not withhold their charms. A hunting party and musicians then sing and wind their horns to arouse several of their sluggish colleagues, including one named Lyciscas, played by Molière, who curses early-morning activities.

The play proper begins with a colloquy between Euryale of Ithaca and his old tutor. Euryale is one of the princes invited from all over Greece to join in the games of Elis and to compete for the favor of that state's unnamed princess. We learn from him that the Princess, a beauty at whom Aurora's song might have been aimed, has a haughty manner that should repel suitors but has the effect of enhancing her desirability. She reserves her passion for hunting and other horsey sports. (The original actress, Armande Molière,

12. The engravings are reproduced in Chevalley, illustrations 440, 442, 446, 447, 449.

13. *Disdain Conquers Disdain (El Desdén con el Desdén)* by Augustín Moreto, 1654. The title means, in effect, "fight fire with fire."

apparently looked very fetching on horseback.) Euryale has grown badly smitten and has bought the support of her court fool, Moron, another role for Molière, who does not reappear until the second scene, after hurriedly changing out of his Lysiscas costume and into cap and bells. In subsequent scenes, Moron proves to be a coward who ran away from a wild boar, sacrificing the glory that might have accrued from a bold victory or a valorous defeat ("I'd rather have two days on earth than a thousand years in history"). The boar then attacked the Princess. The Prince of Pylos slew it and rescued her. Far from being grateful, she bridled at his interference, which stopped her from killing the boar and saving herself. She further announces that she considers marriage no better than death, an attitude taken up and exaggerated about a century later by Gozzi's Turandot.

Euryale, seeing how useless are declarations of love and other accepted methods of ingratiating oneself, makes up his mind to affect an indifference toward the Princess even chillier than hers toward her swains. He tells her bluntly that, in distinction to the other visiting princes, he has no aspiration to winning her, only to winning the racing events. She grows piqued and resolves to make him love her (II, 5). The conflict has turned into a contest between an Artemis and an Hippolytus. (In the dialogue, the Princess is compared several times to Diana, the name given the character in the original Spanish play.) The question remains: which of them can hold out the longer? Euryale confides to Moron that he keeps being tempted to "forget my resolution, throw myself at her feet, and own up to my desire for her" (III, 2). The Princess also confides in Moron; she doesn't confess that she loves Euryale, only that she yearns to "punish his disdain and practice on him all the cruelties I can imagine" (III, 5).

Molière fends off the unavoidable smoothing-out of the love discrepancies for two more acts, not permitting Euryale to win the Princess until he has won the races. Few psychological or dramatic subtleties arise. But the depicting of love as mutual umbrage and the comic treatment of it provide a basic model on which the author will work variations in future plays. As an additional postponing of the dénouement, he turns the interludes into a thinly connected subplot in which Moron also takes the leading part. From alternating between court buffoon and shrewd adviser to both lovers in the main plot, he switches in the subplot to the role of scorned lover. He is devoted to one of the Princess' *suivantes* with the traditional sheepherding name of Philis. Philis prefers his rival.

Before getting down to the business of wooing Philis, however, he performs an antiheroic deed (interlude II). He clambers up a tree to escape from a bear. This bear is a character in the action, unlike the boar who bristles and dies only in the story. Luckily for Moron, some hunters arrive on the scene and kill the bear. Moron then delivers "a thousand blows" on the poor animal's corpse, much like Falstaff claiming Hotspur's body as a trophy after Prince Hal has fatally wounded him. Philis, played by Madeleine Béjart, says she will listen to Moron's entreaties only when he learns to sing as well as his rival (interlude III, sc. 1). He picks up a tune from a passing satyr, then falls out with him, and departs hastily to avoid a fight, while more satyrs dance and sing in chorus (interlude III, sc. 2). In the next interlude, Moron comes upon his rival, Tircis, sweetly singing to Philis. He offers some competition

> Your extreme rigor
> Tears my heart apart.
> Ah, Philis, I die.
> Deign to help me!
> Will you be fatter
> For having made me die? (P. 805)

and then applauds himself. Philis warms to the thought that a man will die for her sake. She and Tircis encourage the clown to do away with himself. When he pretends to put a dagger into his heart, though, she turns away and asks Tircis to sing for her again (interlude IV). In interlude V, Philis and a woman companion sing a dialogue praising the joys and lamenting the pains of love. To conclude the performance, interlude VI abandons the subtale of Moron and Philis, leaving its untold ending easily guessed at, in favor of music and dancing by four pairs of shepherds and shepherdesses.

Since Theocritus and Virgil, the durable and romantic appeal of pastoral literature, its idyllic ideals, reborn Arcadias, fictitious ages, and climes of innocence and (sometimes) social equality does not altogether account for their popular incidence among the French nobility of the 1600s. Molière may well have been nudged in the direction of the pastoral by Lully, who was born in Italy where the pastoral had enjoyed its revival and flowering during the Renaissance. An element of mockery seems to have crept into the language and performances, especially in Molière's contributions, but never so obtrusively as to shatter the charm of a clean, tanned humanity dwelling in harmony with its domesticated animals; all those sheep must have been raised for their wool and peaceable, woolly personalities, not for mutton. The playwright's jarring notes merge cleverly (because comically) into the tradition. The boar, and then the bear, terrify Moron. These are wildlife; they must be mercilessly despatched. Fearsome scourges have no place in this sunwashed Mediterranea, this latter-day paradise. Hence, the hunting parties, which smash into the last hour of sleep, its most sweet, refreshing, and hard-to-part-from climax. And hunting, that prepastoral means of survival, has become a source of frolic, a royal pastime at that, organized on a grand scale and lacking the heroic affirmations implicit in the deeds of a monster-conqueror like Heracles or his cousin, Theseus.

But there is a further element of mockery. William Empson writes: "One strong help for the pastoral convention was the tradition, coming down from the origin of our [British] romantic love-poetry in the troubadours, that its proper tone is one of humility, that the proper moments to dramatise in a love-affair are those when the lover is in despair."[14] Molière includes in his assortment of interludes for the various comedy-ballets plenty of heartbroken shepherds, counterparts of his other unloved male characters and forebears of the tearstained Harlequins who appeared in the following century. But Moron's sighing and singing for Philis has none of the crooning pathos that belongs to the tradition; it is an unsatisfactory form of self-comfort. He can successfully pander on behalf of Euryale but cannot win love for himself.

Doctor Love
(L'Amour médecin, 1665)

Doctor Love has maintained a firm hold in the Molière repertory not because of its infrequently revived ballets, though they do tie in thematically with its main plot, nor because of the main plot itself, which resembles several different plays by this author and countless others not by him, but because of its second subplot, his most unflinching affront to medical practices and practitioners. One might almost say that the rest of the play exists to subtend that second subplot. In the main plot, which occupies the first of the three acts and the latter part of the third, we have a quartet of players: the Parisian bourgeois, Sganarelle, his daughter, Lucinde, her companion,

14. *Some Versions of Pastoral* (New York and London: New Directions, n.d.), 13. According to Harold E. Toliver, however, unrequited love belongs to an "antipastoral nature"—*Pastoral Forms and Attitudes* (Berkeley: University of California Press, 1971) Or perhaps it represents a non-pastoral intrusion into the pastoral world.

Lisette, and Lucinde's lover, Clitandre. Sganarelle is worried; he keeps asking himself and others why Lucinde is sorrowful and apathetic; he refuses to heed the repeated replies of Lisette and Lucinde that she wants to get married.

The first subplot, introduced and disposed of in the play's opening scene, brings on another quartet, Sganarelle's neighbors. He may have summoned them for advice or they may be visiting him to commiserate over the recent death of his wife. When he explains Lucinde's condition, their recommendations are not disinterested: the jeweler suggests cheering her up with some costly jewelry; the tapestry merchant thinks new tapestry in her bedroom would do the trick; a woman whose lover has been paying attentions to Lucinde believes it would do her good to pack her off in marriage to some other man; and cousin Lucrèce feels Lucinde is too delicate for marriage and childbearing; she should be settled in a convent—as a result of which Lucrèce would become her uncle's sole heir.

After this prelude, the main plot pushes forward. Lisette scares Sganarelle when she says his daughter has considered killing herself and, as though by an exertion of will power, now lies prostrate and may not last out the day. He summons four doctors—a third quartet—and after their diagnoses and prescriptions prove conflicting and in large part unintelligible to him, he admits another young doctor who cures not with "emetics, bleedings, medicines, and clysters" but "with words, sounds, letters, talismans, and astrological rings," as well as seventeenth-century psychiatry: "In my practice I swiftly come to the mind before I get to the body." This doctor concludes what Sganarelle knew all along, that Lucinde yearns to marry. He tells the father he will therefore make her well by pretending to marry her; his assistant can pretend to be the notary. The young doctor is, naturally, the man Lucinde wanted to marry in the first place; the assistant is a genuine notary; and the mock ceremony is real. Doctor Love wins out. Main plot disposed of.

But before that happens, the second subplot has taken over most of the middle act and part of the third. As the act opens, Lisette, before announcing the doctors' arrival, asks Sganarelle:

LISETTE How come you need four doctors? Does it take more than one to kill somebody?

SGANARELLE Quiet! Four opinions are better than one.

LISETTE Couldn't your daughter die on her own without the help of these gentlemen?

SGANARELLE You mean that doctors make people die?

LISETTE Certainly. I knew a man who proved logically that you mustn't say, "So and so died of a fever or lung inflammation," but that "he died of four doctors and two druggists." (II, 1)

The four doctors have Greek-derived names—Tomès, Des Fonandrès, Macroton, and Bahys[15]—and are caricatures of actual contemporary physicians with a clientele that included many nobles and royal connections. Molière most likely had them in masks that unmistakably identified the target figures. They have already examined the patient and, after some joshing from Lisette, are prepared to deliberate together. Sganarelle now proves himself a fool by paying them in advance.

When he goes out, they "sit and cough" and force some irrelevant conversation, disputing mildly over whether it is easier to get about Paris on the traditional doctor's mule or on a speedier horse. The discussion turns to a dispute that "divides our profession" and has erupted between two other doctors, one of whom killed a patient, but he did stick to the rules, while the other, who might have saved him, was wrong for not agreeing to observe the formalities. Dr. Tomès then tells a story of how he kept insisting on pro forma procedures during a debate with unnamed doctors, in the course of which the patient "bravely died" (II, 3).

Sganarelle returns for their verdict. There is some uncertainty (and hostility) over who will speak first.[16] Tomès then orders the patient to be bled. Des Fonandrès contends that she must take an emetic, instead; bleeding will finish her off within fifteen minutes. The pair of them become abusive, reminding one another of patients recently deceased under their respective treatments (II, 4). So much for second opinions, insisted on today by our medical insurance companies. The third and fourth opinions are still to come.

Of the two remaining doctors, Macroton speaks haltingly and draws out his words, while Bahys gabbles; in answering them, Sganarelle (originally Molière's part) unconsciously mimics them. The burden of their discourse is that one must be cautious—and therefore apply not as few but as many

15. The names were said to have been devized by Boileau, and each is meaningful (see Couton 2: 1320–21 n. 2).

16. Apparently, it was protocol for the youngest doctor to commit himself to an opinion first, and then the others in ascending order of age (see Couton 2: 1324–25 n.1). This inverse order of seniority (juniority?) is observed in *Monsieur de Pourceaugnac* (I, 8).

remedies as are necessary. The young woman may not survive them, but "it makes more sense," snaps Bahys, "to die according to the rules" (II, 5).

After their departure, Sganarelle, in confusion and despair, hails a passing medical con artist, known at that time as an "operator," who is hawking a product named Orviétan (so called because it was supposed to have come from Orvieto in Italy), whose hyperactive ingredients were guaranteed to cure a bold assortment of maladies, from scabies and bad temper to smallpox, measles, and an organic prolapse (II, 7).[17] But we never learn whether the Orviétan is later administered or its results and side effects, if any.

The third act finds the medical quartet reassembled for a tongue-lashing by a senior colleague, Dr. Filerin, who pours out the longest speech in the play. Its earnest and cynically confidential tone, together with its apparent candor (the revelation of professional secrets), makes it one of the most explosive pieces of writing in Molière's thirty-three plays. The subject of the action has now changed from malpractice to deception and covering-up, as Couton notes.[18] The doctors have committed the cardinal sin of differing in their opinions, going so far as to quarrel in front of members of the public. Filerin contends: "Since heaven has been kind enough over the centuries to grant us men's infatuated confidence, let's not disabuse them with our wild and open disagreements, but take advantage of their stupidity as tactfully as we can." He goes on to compare the "art" of doctors in deceiving and in amassing riches with the skills of alchemists and horoscope readers, in order to "profit from the vanity and ambition of gullible minds," for "people's greatest weakness is their love for life." The browbeaten Tomès and Des Fonandrès shake hands. The latter says that if the former will agree on an emetic for this patient, he can go unchallenged with whatever he wishes to prescribe for the next patient (III, 1). The bargaining here sounds like that of legislators each of whom tries to load down a bill with clauses that truckle to his or her constituents.

Lisette cannot let them leave without a parting shot: she has just heard of

---

17. Orviétan was one of the more notorious "universal remedies" or panaceas of seventeenth-century France. Another was "drinkable gold" (l'or potable), mentioned in *The Doctor in Spite of Himself.*

18. "*Doctor Love* takes part in the most bitter cycle of Molière's comedy: the cycle of hypocrisy. *Tartuffe* is [at that time] under a ban, *Don Juan* has been withdrawn from the repertory; Molière is denouncing the great social taint, hypocrisy, which persists with official sanction, comfortably, honorably, as it exploits people's inexhaustible credulity" (Couton 2: 93).

a man who had the effrontery to invade their turf: he killed another man with a sword and without a medical prescription. Tomès replies darkly: "You can joke now, but some day you'll fall into our hands" (III, 2).

The doctors' roles are not so much characterized as sketched in swiftly and broadly. The playwright provides enough material for the actors to differentiate themselves in their several scenes. But the roles of Lisette and Sganarelle have more pliability. Lisette belongs with the cheeky women servants, those surrogate mothers who take the children's parts against the fathers and whose down-to-earth reasonableness is made more palatable by a biting sense of humor. Sganarelle is a master of the house, less assertive at first than such others as Arnolphe, Orgon, and Harpagon in that he is still grieving over his wife's death. While he "cannot think about her without weeping," he admits with disarming frankness that "I wasn't ever quite satisfied with her behavior, and we often got into arguments. . . . If she were still alive, we'd still be arguing" (I, 1). But he is as dogmatic as the other masters in opposing marriage for his daughter. Lucinde is the only one left of "all the children heaven granted me," and it seems clear that he doesn't want to be left at home on his own (I, 1). Subsequently, though, he aligns himself with Harpagon when he speaks of the hard work required for amassing some wealth and "raising a daughter with care and tenderness," only to be "stripped of both by a man I don't even know" (I, 5). That he loves her is unquestionable; but the love may be consuming and onerously tinged with selfishness. Lucinde, after all, pines to marry a man she has never formally met, only seen from a distance (she has, however, observed the adoration in his eyes); as a teenager, she may be traditionally made helpless by calf love, but she also will use this stranger as an excuse to move out and away from her father.

The relative realism of the scenes in the main plot contrasts vividly not only with those featuring the four doctors but also with the balletic elements. The prologue consists of a brief song and dance by three figures who represent Comedy, Music, and Ballet, and sing, "Let us all three unite to bring / More pleasure to the greatest king," a sentiment that is integral in that it previews the reconciliation between the four doctors.[19] The first interlude takes Sganarelle's servant, named Champagne, in a dance to the houses of the four doctors and brings them back, all dancing, to Sganarelle's

19. Arthur R. Harned suggests that this plea for unity may be directed at Molière's collaborator, Lully (see "Molière and Lully," in Johnson, Trail, and Neumann, 31–48).

home. The dance that makes up the second interlude follows Sganarelle's purchase of Orviétan from the "operator" and is performed by the latter's helpers, here played by two groups of commedia figures, Trivelins and Scaramouches, probably hired for the original production from the Italian comedians who shared their playhouse with Molière's company. After act III, the epilogue reintroduces Comedy, Ballet, and Music, who sing a ditty with the following refrain:

> Sickness would be rife
> Without our compositions.
> For a healthy life
> We're the best physicians.

Doctor Love may have healed Lucinde, but the efficacy of the procedure was due not so much to love as to an impersonation, a performance. And perhaps the giving of a performance is a subspecies of love.

Mélicerte,
1666

Some eighteen months after *The Pleasures of the Enchanted Isle* ended at Versailles, the new festival that came into being at the Saint-Germain-en-Laye chateau lasted for almost seven weeks, from early December until late February—a winter rite dedicated to the arts and thick with nauseating tributes to their sun-blessed French patron, the king. *Ballet of the Muses* comprised no fewer than fourteen "entries," three of them, including the fourteenth, *The Sicilian,* provided by Molière's troupe. There is some question about the chronological order of the first two, *Mélicerte,* a "pastoral, heroic comedy," and *Comic Pastoral,* but at least one reason for believing that *Comic Pastoral* came later and substituted during January and February for *Mélicerte.* The leading male role in *Mélicerte,* that of Myrtil, was written for, and played by, the very young actor Baron. At some point, he had a falling-out with Armande Molière and asked the king's permission to retire from the play. Molière had no actor who could suitably fill in at short notice, and therefore slammed *Comic Pastoral* onto paper and into production before the festival ended.[20]

At the *Enchanted Isle* festivities, the time pressure on Molière as purveyor

20. Couton 2: 1352–53 n. 3.

of royal entertainments had begun to show: he did the first act of *The Princess of Elis* in verse, but the remainder in prose. In *Mélicerte*, he completed the first two acts, twelve scenes in all, mostly in regular alexandrines, but then stopped writing. "Having satisfied His Majesty for the festival in which [the play] was presented, le sieur Molière did not finish it," testifies a note in the 1682 posthumous edition of the complete works in which the text appeared in print for the first time. Nor did he revive the two-act play in Paris. Armande's son by her second husband later added material and expanded the title, but his addenda have not survived. He does, however, mention that the author had taken the story from an episode in one of Mlle de Scudéry's novels, *The Great Cyrus*, a derivation that may account for its maintaining a "heroic" and occasionally pretentious tone, even in the speeches between shepherds and shepherdesses.[21]

Molière laid the action in the Vale of Tempe in Thessaly during a conveniently vague classical era, which allowed allusions to Pan, Ceres, and other deities—with their Latin, not Greek, names—and created an atmosphere of the overlapping hinterlands of myth and fantasy. Two shepherds cannot understand why the two shepherdesses they love respectively repel them (I, 1). When the shepherdesses have shaken off their unwanted lovers, we and they discover that they are both smitten by the adolescent Myrtil (I, 2). He, however, has set his heart on his playmate, Mélicerte, a "nymph or shepherdess" of slightly inferior social rank to the others, and she returns his love (I, 5; II, 1, 2, 3). His father, Lycarsis, opposes the match at first, but when Myrtil argues fiercely with him—

> I tell you, you rejoice in vain:
> Your plans will bring you naught but pain
> And all your efforts to deter
> Will not make me relinquish her (II, 5)

and then pleads heartrendingly, Lycarsis (something of a clown's role, played by Molière) relents. But a new complication supervenes. The king of Thessaly is paying a visit to Tempe in search of Mélicerte, whom he intends to marry to a "great lord" (II, 7).

Here the action ends, with Myrtil frantic. The love between the two young people, if Molière had persisted with the play, might have had a cheerful resolution. Lycarsis is the "supposed" father of Myrtil in the list of characters, while another shepherd, Mopse, is the "supposed" uncle of Mélicerte. The

21. See Couton's *notice* for the play, 2: 285–86.

revelation of the young people's identities might have established them as nobility, an outcome hinted at by Lycarsis when he tells Mopse and another shepherd that he has some "news," which the plotting does not give him the chance to reveal: no doubt that Myrtil is the true son of parents on a loftier social rung.

The *livret*, a program booklet handed out free to participants and selected spectators (others had to pay for it), introduces the framing *Ballet of the Muses* with a synopsis the tone of which typifies Benserade's toadying for the occasion ("The Muses, charmed by the glorious reputation of our monarch and the care His Majesty takes to promote the flourishing of the arts through-out his empire, leave Parnassus to visit his court"). Twenty-three gentlemen of the court dance their roles as the "nine sisters," the "seven arts," the "seven planets." Melpomene, the muse of tragedy, receives a bouquet in the form of a performance of a version of *Pyramus and Thisbe;* and the muse of comedy, Thalia, gets another, the *Comic Pastoral* mounted by "the king's actors and composed by him who, of all our poets in this form of writing, may most justly be compared with the ancients."

Comic Pastoral
(*Pastorale comique,* 1667)

Molière neither kept nor published a copy of this play. In most editions, extracts have been taken from the official *livret;* but they consist of only scene notations and a few passages of rhyming dialogue, most of which take place between two rich sheep farmers, Lycas (Molière) and Filène, in love with the beautiful young shepherdess, Iris (Catherine de Brie), who repulses them. For the rest, the action is not summarized, only the plotting, the characters who appear in each of the fifteen scenes. No act division is intimated. Presumably, Iris eventually goes off with Coridon, a young shep-herd (La Grange) listed as a confidant of Lycas.

The passages of dialogue reproduced were, in all likelihood, the most amusing ones. Lycas and Filène think of committing double suicide, once they discover that Iris wants neither of them, but their resolution breaks down when they cannot agree on which of them should die first. A "young, playful shepherd" comes in and exclaims, "Ah, what folly / To give up life / For a beauty / Who turns you down!" In the final scene a gypsy lass is "followed by a dozen men who seek nothing but joy, dance with her to songs she sings agreeably," the songs ending on an upbeat note of making the most of love while one is still young enough to taste its delights. And the skeletal account of the play gives way to a listing of ten more entries devoted to dance, music, and the other arts, bringing on scores of courtiers, as well as the king and Lully, as shepherds, Latin orators and Greek philosophers, Indians, satyrs, fauns, nymphs, Jupiter, Alexander the Great, and other cavorters. To an especially melodious setting by Lully, Molière also introduces a lyric with an unusual line of nine syllables : "But, alas! when age ices us o'er, / Our lovely days will return no more."

The Sicilian, or Love the Painter
(Le Sicilien ou l'Amour peintre, 1667)

Afourteenth entry, added late to the *Ballet of the Muses* to serve as prefatory material for *The Sicilian,* found a justification in offering some music and dance by performers disguised as Turks and Moors, two nationalities not represented in the thirteen previous entries. Written in prose, which in places can be seen to scan as free verse, the twenty scenes of this brief comedy play in front of the houses of a Sicilian citizen (doubtless of Spanish extraction) named Don Pèdre, a "French gentleman" named Adraste, and a senator or magistrate.[22] The action, an intrigue, comes from Roman comedy: Don Pèdre keeps a beautiful Greek slave called Isidore as his mistress; Adraste has for some time loved her from a distance and now, with the aid of his valet, a male slave named Hali, resolves to snatch her from her owner. First, he hires musicians to charm her with several serenades (scs. 1, 2, 3). Next, he wants an assurance that she returns his love. He therefore takes the place of a painter hired to do a portrait of Isidore and, while wielding his brush, contrives to converse secretly with her (scs. 10, 11, 12). Then he enlists another female slave, wearing a veil, to present an excuse for getting into Don Pèdre's house, lending the veil to Isidore, and so letting her escape (scs. 14–18).

22. John Wood's excellent translation, and the only modern version of the play in English, reproduces the three acts as three scenes, the first and last played outdoors and the middle one indoors. For such an interpretation, the front of Don Pèdre's house might be a gauze lighted from the outside and, in the indoor scene, backlighted and then furled. But there seems to me no reason not to play the entire action as though out of doors.

Although the play derives from no known single source, it was a common enough dramatic ploy for a suitor to insinuate himself into a home, often in the guise of a music teacher, rather than a portrait painter, in order to free a young woman from the watchdog behavior of a father, guardian, or master.[23] Here, the device makes possible several acts of impersonation. Adraste, a bland figure as himself, the heartsick swain, becomes more sprightly as the painter. Hali, a far more colorful character, who opens the first scene with a monologue cursing his fate as a slave ("Never living for my own benefit. . . . No rest, night and day"), plays a Spaniard who comes into the house during the portrait session to distract Don Pèdre while his master makes an assignation with Isidore (sc. 12). And the second slave woman pretends to be Adraste's put-upon wife, a role taken over by Isidore after she has borrowed the veil and is able to leave with Adraste as his purported wife and actual wife-to-be. The most striking piece of theatricality, however, is the creation of the extravagant Don Pèdre, played by Molière in the elaborate costume of a Sicilian, that is, a Spanish grandee resembling the commedia's capitano. In the last dialogue scene (14), finding himself tricked out of his ward and swearing vengeance, he accosts his neighbor, the senator. There ensues a cross-conversation like the ones in *The Jealous Husband* and *The Forced Marriage* in which a man with a grievance cannot get a straight answer. The senator takes no notice of Don Pèdre's complaint. He bubbles over with a description of a masquerade he has arranged, and the play ends (sc. 20) with a dance by several Moors (the masquerade itself), which Don Pèdre will probably get swept into.

But why Sicily, that seething island in which the author had already ambiguously set his *Don Juan?* As a Mediterranean crossroads, it had a mixed population of French, Italians, North African and Mideastern Muslims, Spaniards, and others—merchants, servants, and holdovers from the countless conquests by various nations to which it had been subjected in the long turmoil of its recorded history. At the time when the play was written, it was under Spanish rule, together with the kingdom of Naples—a locale mentioned in *The Miser* and later to be the setting for *Scapin.* Sicily was a hot spot

---

23. In Molière's work alone, the suitor as intruder-cum-woman-stealer had already appeared in *The School for Husbands, The School for Wives, Doctor Love,* and most recently in *The Doctor in Spite of Himself* (in which he pretends to be an apothecary), and he would turn up again in *The Imaginary Invalid* and numerous plays by other authors, the best-known being *The Barber of Seville.*

politically, as well as climatically.[24] The Spanish, who had won and lost it a number of times and had long been rivals of the French for influence there, become targets of satire in the form of Don Pèdre and the capitano figure played by Hali, and must have given Louis some pleasure. But although the early history of the theatre is anything but established, Sicily also appears to be one of the places where comedy originated. Did Molière know this?

Monsieur de Pourceaugnac, 1669

The name and title add *pourceau* (pig, swine, or beast) to an ending that denotes a province or region, and so the whole name means something like "gentleman from Pig Province." Restoration and post-Restoration translators and adapters drew on English words like "looby" or "lubber" that had to do with lumpishness, with being a boob or rube or hayseed; they called the character Squire Trelooby or Squire Lubberly.[25] But Molière's character is not so much dense as naïve, a victim, fresh from ruralia, of merciless city intriguers.

Poor Pourceaugnac walks into a Paris setting and trouble. The scenic design for the premiere at the Chambord chateau, as for the reprise several weeks later at the Palais-Royal, probably showed a recognizable square with two houses and either an inverted *V* perspective or a crossroads to allow for a chase. The arrangement needed to be spacious enough to accommodate the "overture" (a serenade rendered by musicians and singers), two interludes, and a finale. For these visual and musical ornaments, there could have been shallower sets dropped into the principal one to mask it temporarily and elicit gasps from the audience, but they were not strictly necessary, for Molière and Lully also integrated a number of songs and dances into the action of the play proper, which is very like a modern comic opera with spoken dialogue in place of recitative.

One of the houses belongs to Oronte who has arranged to marry his daughter, Julie, on the recommendation of his brother, to the stranger,

24. Spain, which had won and lost Sicily a number of times, was not quite successful in quelling an anti-Spanish uprising in 1670. It had to surrender the island, under the provisions of the Treaty of Utrecht, in 1713, and recovered it—but not for long—after 1738.

25. Cf. the name in *George Dandin* of Clitandre's rural messenger, Lubin, a French equivalent for "looby."

Pourceaugnac. The latter, a man of means, has offered a generous marital settlement and traveled by slow (and inexpensive) coach from Limoges, about three hundred miles to the south, a wearisome journey at that time. But Julie, without her father's approval, already has a lover and intended mate named Éraste. In the opening scenes, Éraste and two hired assistants, a "woman of intrigue" named Nérine and a "man of intrigue" who is named Sbrigani and hails from Naples, assure Julie that they have prepared for Pourceaugnac a reception that should send him scurrying back to Limoges without a bride.

When Pourceaugnac appears, turning to remonstrate with some people (off-stage) who are laughing at his outlandish outfit, Sbrigani instantly befriends him (I, 3) by upbraiding the mockers and telling Pourceaugnac that anyone who laughs at him "will have to take it up with me." Next, Éraste greets Pourceaugnac warmly and tells him he had the honor of seeing him almost every day during a stay in Limoges five or six years before and of meeting every single Pourceaugnac, big and small. Pourceaugnac, who has never seen the man before and is astonished by this outbreak of chumminess, is now persuaded by sly questioning that he really is meeting a former acquaintance:

ÉRASTE What's the name of that fellow again who used to entertain so generously?
POURCEAUGNAC Petit-Jean?
ÉRASTE That's the one. We used to go to his house all the time and enjoy ourselves. What do you call that place where everyone walks?
POURCEAUGNAC The cemetery?
ÉRASTE Exactly. . . . Tell me something about your family. How's that gentleman, you know, your . . . ah, that very decent man who . . .
POURCEAUGNAC My brother the consul?
ÉRASTE Yes.
POURCEAUGNAC Couldn't be better.
ÉRASTE Delighted to hear it. . . . And your uncle, the, ah . . .
POURCEAUGNAC I have no uncle.
ÉRASTE You had one at that time.
POURCEAUGNAC No. Only an aunt.
ÉRASTE That's what I meant. Your aunt, that great lady. How is she?[26]

And so on. After eliciting more personal details, making the stranger feel at ease by reminding him of his hometown and relatives, and allowing us to see

26. This manner of wheedling out information comes from the commedia dell'arte. Molière had used it before, notably in his previous work *The Miser*, when Maître Jacques fishes for facts to describe Harpagon's cashbox, which he hasn't seen (V,3).

Pourceaugnac as an innocent out of his element in the capital city, Éraste insists that the visitor must stay in his house (I, 4). But not yet. He has some business elsewhere and will put Pourceaugnac in the hands of someone who will take very good care of him (I, 7). This "someone" is a doctor, the occupant of the second house onstage, whom Éraste has already paid to treat Pourceaugnac as a mental patient.

After his lulling introduction to Paris, the man from the country will now be subjected to a train of humiliations: treated like a maniac by the doctor and his colleague, by an apothecary, and by two musicians dressed as "grotesque doctors" as they sing in Italian,[27] plus eight *matassins* or "armed dancers" who carry fearsome syringes (I, 8–11). They urge Pourceaugnac to face his medication cheerfully, because "folly / Is nothing but melancholy." He runs for it. When he reappears, panting, they descend on him again with the apothecary wielding clyster pipes for administering enemas and repeating his lines like an incantation ("It won't do you any harm. It won't do you any harm. It's a little clyster, a little clyster. Benign, benign. It's to deterge you, deterge you, deterge you"). The act ends with this musical fantasy, a dance, the flight of Pourceaugnac, and a pursuit offstage.

Sbrigani now moves more actively into the picture, telling the doctor that Pourceaugnac intends to become Oronte's son-in-law and reminding him that he will lose "fifty hard-earned pistoles" if the patient is not found (II, 1). The doctor hurries next door and warns Oronte that the patient has been placed in his care and is therefore his property; that he is suffering from a malady that he, the doctor, is not at liberty to reveal (hinting at venereal disease); and that unless he recovers Pourceaugnac, "I'll claim you and cure you, instead." Oronte cries, "I'm in perfect health!" The doctor replies, "That doesn't matter. I must have a patient. I'll take anyone I can get" (II, 2).

Sbrigani blotches Pourceaugnac's reputation even further by impersonating a Flemish merchant and saying he represents ten or twelve others to whom the Limousin owes money; he tells this to Oronte, pretending he doesn't know whom he is speaking to (II, 3). Pourceaugnac reappears, smelling, as he says, of clysters, and looking for Oronte's house, where he can take refuge from the apparently insane doctors and their henchmen and oversized syringes. Sbrigani then drops the Flemish accent and plays Iago, hinting that the fiancée Julie is man-crazy and that Oronte has planned to dump her on an out-of-towner who does not know about her behavior (II, 4). When

----

27. The Italian verses were probably composed by Lully to go with his music.

Pourceaugnac calls on Oronte to protest this deceitful match, he finds that Julie, to his and her father's embarrassment, keeps flinging herself at him; this act of hers is another deliberate step in the attempt to drive him away.

There are more humiliations to come. A woman named Lucette alleges that Pourceaugnac has been her husband for the past seven years in Gascony; while Nérine, the "woman of intrigue," puts on a Picardy accent and also claims to be his wife, releasing three children who surround him and pluck at his clothes, calling him, "Daddy, daddy, daddy!" Pourceaugnac escapes and, running across Sbrigani again, wails, "In this country it rains enemas and women" (II, 10). He pleads with Sbrigani to find him a lawyer, and the Neapolitan shyster conjures up two musicians dressed as lawyers, two other attorneys, and two police sergeants. One of the fake lawyers has a slow drawl, the other a rapid, clipped delivery, like the doctors Macroton and Bahys in *Doctor Love*. But instead of speaking, they sing at him, several verses with a refrain: "Polygamy in every sense / Is a capital offense" (II, 11).

In act III, Sbrigani, capitalizing on his sadistic success so far, has told Pourceaugnac that in cases of bigamy the inevitable sentence, hanging, means that he will never get out of town alive (III, 1). Pourceaugnac has now put on women's clothes and calls in the manner of a peremptory "lady of quality" for his coach and pages (III, 2). But two rough Swiss men enter, and at the sight of this demoiselle, each declares that he wants to sleep with "her," either without noticing "her" beard or without caring about it (III, 4).[28] Pourceaugnac is saved from rape by an officer, who gets rid of the two importunate Swiss but then recognizes and arrests the bearded lady (III, 4). The officer and, possibly, the pair of Swiss are doubtless in the pay of Sbrigani, for the latter appears almost immediately and, still playing Pourceaugnac's friend, advises him to bribe the officer—twice—if he wants to go free. Grateful for any relief, Pourceaugnac pays up and hastens out of the city and the play, telling Sbrigani he is the one honest man he has found in Paris (III, 5). It remains only for Sbrigani to warn Oronte that Pourceaugnac has run off with Julie (III, 6) and for Éraste to pretend to have rescued her and to be willing to take her still, despite her coquettishness (III, 7). To compensate for this newly acquired flaw in his daughter, Oronte adds ten thousand crowns to the marriage portion. The show ends with a masquerade in which gypsies and a chorus sing in praise of seeking pleasure, although a

28. The two Swiss, like the performances of Lucette as a *Gasconne* and of Nérine as a *Picarde*, provide excuses for comic accents, as in *The Botcher, Don Juan, The Doctor in Spite of Himself*, and *Scapin*.

short solo adds a cutting edge: "When we gather for the sake of laughter, / The wisest people, it seems to me, / Are those who are most mad (III, 8)."

Pourceaugnac used to be accounted Molière's most cruel piece of writing, because the central figure, although moderately conceited and simple, did nothing to deserve his punishment. Recent critics have pointed out that the play is, after all, a farce. A musical, dancing farce, one might add. Like most farces, it is a continuous nightmare, a classic of the species, an actualizing of a character's worst fears: falling into the clutches of ruthless, fanatical medicos; being accused of insanity and of debts one knows nothing about; undergoing one public embarrassment after another; having to keep on the run and then take refuge as a transvestite *and* be detected; finding oneself engaged to a shameless stranger and alone in a remote, hostile environment.

Only from the inside of the central role is this a cruel show. From the point of view of the performers, it is a generous gift. We have no full listing of the cast at Chambord or in Paris, but both Sbrigani and Éraste are uncommonly rewarding parts, an oily swindler and a malicious hero. The first doctor, who takes every response from his "patient" as incontestable proof of illness and insanity, has a two-page speech, an elaboration of his "diagnosis, prognosis, and remedy," that compares in its ferocity with that of the medical quartet and Filerin in *Doctor Love*, the remedy, as always, calling for copious bleeding and clystering. His senior colleague's refinements include a literal oddity, "giving the bleedings and purgings in odd numbers," because, he adds in Latin, "God likes odd numbers," thereby completing the portraits of these healers as superstitious gargoyles. As the original Pourceaugnac, Molière—the only identified piece of casting—offered himself a sampling of opportunities, which may have included dances and acrobatics, as well as one heartfelt authorial remark during his consultation scene: "If you two are doctors, I'll have nothing to do with you. I laugh at medicine."

The Magnificent Lovers
(Les Amants magnifiques, 1670)

Sostrate loves Ériphile. He is a young warrior of proved valor and integrity. She is surpassingly fair. What stands between them? Rank and rivals— or so Sostrate believes. The belief is not unfounded. Ériphile's mother, Princess Aristione, rules the Vale of Tempe in Thessaly—the same geography as in *Mélicerte* —and is playing host to suitable suitors from all over, of whom the two most eligible are a couple of princes, the magnificent lovers of the title, magnificent because of their dress and manner and the cost-be-damned entertainments they provide to impress the princess and her daughter.

Sostrate's love looks hopeless. In the opening act, he has stayed away from the first of the entertainments and is wandering gloomily in a forest and asking himself how he can bear to go on living. The court clown Clitidas accosts him, guesses his secret, suggests that the lovely Ériphile must have guessed it too, and implies that she may not frown upon a respectful approach. What? From this soldier of humble birth? Clitidas persists: Is Sostrate not a general who has defeated the Gauls and helped rid Greece of "that deluge of barbarians" (I, 1)?

But Sostrate will not allow himself to be convinced. His anxieties mount when the princess deputes him to ask her daughter to make up her mind which of the two *magnifiques* she prefers (I, 2). To fortify their chances, each of the princes promises a reward to Clitidas if he can sway Ériphile's choice, though neither offers anything as tangibly welcome as an advance bribe. Ériphile, however, keeps to herself, not confiding even in her confidante (1, 5).

Act II begins with Clitidas seeking out Ériphile, as he did Sostrate at the start of act I, and questioning her. He tells her Sostrate is in love. She puts on an indignant front—how dare he, a commoner, think of her as a marriage partner! But no, says Clitidas swiftly; the man is in love with one of her maids. Seeing her dismay, he tells her the truth, promises to keep quiet about it, and goes (II, 1). Sostrate arrives on his unwanted mission and puts the question: Which prince will she will pick over the other? Instead of answering, she asks his advice, as an inducement to him to confess his love. But he does not see what she is getting at. Advice? He hardly knows how to reply and avoids an answer (II, 3). He is saved from the embarrassment of having to nominate one of the princes by interruptions (II, 4, 5), those historical standbys of suspense.

As the third act proceeds, Ériphile continues to back away from a decision and again proposes that Sostrate be the arbiter, this time in front of her mother and the two princes. He declines to commit himself, but the court astrologer, Anaxarque, is less hesitant and declares that the stars will inform them which prince to choose. Sostrate cannot let this pass, and delivers the longest speech in the play, an attack on astrology and, by implication, other forms of superstition: "What bearing, what commerce, what correspondence can there be between us and the globes that lie at such a terrifying distance from us? And how does man come by this fine knowledge? What god revealed it to him? What experience enabled him to make deductions from that great number of heavenly bodies that are never seen twice in the same relationship to each other?" (III, 1)[29]

The baffled princess then asks her daughter in private whether she is not keeping some secret from her and receives unsatisfactory replies (IV,1). Without warning, Venus descends in a flying machine, surrounded by four Cupids, and instructs the princess in rhyming verse "to give your daughter as a wife / To the man who saves your life" (IV, 2). This apparition of the goddess, it turns out in the following scene, was a trick arranged by the venal astrologer, who is going to set up a dangerous situation for the princess and a rescue by one of the princes who has bought him off (IV, 3). Sostrate and Ériphile again meet, only this time they reveal their mutual love but feel anything but optimistic over its outcome (IV, 4, 5). [30]

Clitidas still works diligently as a go-between, but as often happens with Molière's servants, his efforts are thwarted by fate or modified synchronicity—but so are those of Anaxarque. For the princess does find herself in danger, in the story rather than the action (between acts IV and V), although not the danger set up by the astrologer. As Clitidas later relates, she was walking through a forest when she came upon a boar, shot an arrow at it, but merely wounded and enraged it. Sostrate came on the scene just in time and dispatched the animal. Having saved her life, Sostrate can now marry her daughter, as "Venus" decreed (V, 1). The two princes, understandably frustrated, offer threats of war, but the princess brushes them aside, and even disarms the royal gentlemen by forgiving them for having the bad taste to mention war at a time of celebration (V, 3, 4).

The scenes of *The Magnificent Lovers* are in prose, except for Venus' prediction, but the six interludes are in free verse. For this production, Molière was entrusted with the "writing" of the ballets, a disappointment to their usual fabricator, Benserade. Two of the interludes consist of the entertainments provided by the princes: a seascape featuring river gods, tritons, Cupids on the backs of dolphins, fishermen, Neptune, Aeolus, sea gods, and other novelties; and the third interlude offers a sylvan scene with the usual nymphs, shepherds, satyrs, fauns, dryads, and other pastoral

29. Sostrate's assault on astrology is also, it goes without saying, an assault on astrologers, but in particular, some contemporaries say, on an influential charlatan named Morin. For more information and further sources, see Couton 2: 643.

30. Molière almost certainly took the idea of a princess who rejects her royal suitors in favor of a gallant general from Corneille's heroic comedy *Don Sanche of Aragon*, first performed twenty-one years earlier.

population and accouterments—this interlude forming a self-contained play within the play with its own prologue and five scenes. Three of the remaining interludes are straightforward ballets. The final one (number VI) is a danced imitation of the Pythian Games, another excuse for a parade of figures from all nations interpreted by courtiers.

We have no record of the members of Molière's troupe who took part in *The Magnificent Lovers*, save for his own performance as the mischievous Clitidas. The action moves forward steadily with ease and grace, as do the written-out interludes; there is no sign of the rushed conditions under which he must have worked. Inside the loose confines of the comedy-ballet's conventions, the language is inventive and affords the creator opportunities to let off a few arrows at superstitions like astrology (which carried weight among the credulous in many seventeenth-century courts, as in our own White House from time to time), at expensive entertainments as a means of winning love, and even one jab at French ancestry in the reference back to Sostrate's heroic defeat of the second Brennus, that "scourge" who led a Gallic invasion of Greece in the third century B.C.E.

Psyche
(*Psyché*, 1671)

Molière's one "tragicomedy-ballet," *Psyche* belongs with the comedy-ballets insofar as its text became subordinated to its spectacle (not necessarily the case with *The Bourgeois Gentleman* and *The Imaginary Invalid*), although the text itself consists of a prologue, five interludes, a five-act play, and synopses of entries galore. The playwright-impresario planned the outline and wrote the prologue and two of the scenes in verse. He commissioned Quinault to compose the interludes, and Pierre Corneille (whose *Titus and Berenice* he had in simultaneous rehearsal) to write the remaining verse dialogue—the overwhelming bulk of it—in two weeks.[31] Corneille's contributions are of consistently high quality, better, one is tempted to say, than was deserved by a project designed primarily, it seems, to take advantage of the ultrasophicated "hall of machines" in the Tuileries palace. The house, lighted

---

31. *Psyche* is included in editions of the complete works of both Corneille and Molière. The synopses of the entries come from the official *livret* program, which included "arguments" or abstracts of each scene; these are skillfully written and probably also attributable to Molière.

by thirty chandeliers, had a capacity of seven thousand spectators. The show ran for five hours. Seventy to one hundred dancers trooped onstage for the finale, but they had already been outnumbered in an earlier sequence when Vigarani's machines lofted three hundred performers into the air at the same time, some aboard clouds, others apparently free-floating.

As a mythical fancy, the play itself has no *comic* scenes in the older sense of the word (no significant characters below royal rank) and only a few in our conventional sense (humorous or witty). The *comedy* component of the *tragicomedy* denotes tragedy averted, a happy resolution, imposed by Jupiter.

The prologue, appropriately Greek in inspiration, tells us that Venus feels unworshiped and outclassed because young lovers from all over the world are flocking to the feet of Princess Psyche. Hovering in her flying machine, Venus feels especially disturbed that Juno and Pallas Athene will be able to crow because she has lost her votaries to a "mere mortal." She instructs her son, Love (Cupid), to make Psyche fall in love with "the most hideous mortal creature"—she is thinking of something more horrific than an ass-headed Bottom—and suffer the pangs of loving without being loved.

The first act opens in a long perspective of cypress trees culminating in an arch of triumph, where Psyche's two jealous older sisters form a momentary mutual admiration society; they each find the other distinctly more attractive than Psyche is. They cannot understand why two visiting princes bent on marrying Psyche are immune to their superior looks (I, 2). Psyche, when she appears, shows herself to be modest, loving, considerate—virtuous through and through (I, 3). But a captain of the guards brings her a summons from the king, her father, and then reveals to her sisters that an oracle has decreed that she must be delivered to a poisonous dragon (I, 4). Like Cinderella's stepsisters or Goneril and Regan, they could not be happier with Psyche's disastrous fate (I, 5).

For the first interlude, the scene changes to a desert with a dismal cave in the background. Here some "afflicted persons" sing and dance dirgefully out of sympathy for Psyche. And here, as the second act begins, the king arrives, accompanied by his two older daughters, to tell Psyche how miserable he is to have been compelled to relegate her to this sterile spot. Her generous heart goes out to him in his distress (II, 1) and then to the two devoted princes, who have come to rescue her or die in the attempt (II, 3). But under orders from the airborne Cupid, Zephyr, the god of winds, has her whisked away by two of his minions (II, 4), while Vulcan, we learn, is toiling at designing a new palace for her. Instead of punishing Psyche, Cupid has fallen in love and made up his mind to have an all-out affair with her (II, 5).

For the second interlude, the palace is rapidly put together by a contingent of Cyclopes and fairies. In the third act, in place of the poisonous dragon ordered by the oracle Cupid appears, having put on the age, voice, and mien of an astonishingly handsome youth, despite a reminder by Zephyr that "your mother Venus is like all beauties, / Who don't want to admit they have grown-up children" (III, 1). The confused but greatly relieved Psyche is captivated by this mysterious lover, and there follows a blissful exchange of vows. Cupid will shower her with everything she wants, even require Zephyr to bring her sisters, whom she unaccountably misses. But he will not tell her who he is, and she must not ask (III, 3).

The third interlude, a song and dance by four minor Zephyrs and four secondary Cupids, gives way to the fourth act, set in a different gorgeous palace with a view of a garden and orchards. The sisters land after their flight, not too tired to feel awe at the sight of the palace and surroundings, which sharpen their jealousy (IV, 1). They tell Psyche that her lover's refusal to divulge his identity is suspicious; then, having sown discontent, they depart for home on a Zephyr-powered cloud (IV, 2). Psyche asks Cupid to share his secret. He warns her that if she insists on knowing his name, she will wreck their happiness. She insists. He disappears; so do the palace and grounds (IV, 3). Psyche is now on a vast plain intersected by a river. She would drown herself, but a river god dissuades her (IV, 4). Then, Venus returns to the stage in her machine and condemns Psyche for pride and insolence, for being competitive, and for corrupting her son, who has been lax in his duties, neglecting the suppliants who have come asking for supplies of love (IV, 5). Sad Psyche is despatched to hell.[32]

In and around the palace of Pluto, encircled by a sea of fire and burning ruins, eight furies dance the fourth interlude. Psyche glides across the burning expanse in Charon's boat, reciting a lengthy lament (V, 1). She meets the two lovestruck princes who died because they could not go on living without her (V, 2). With characteristic solicitude, she feels sorry for them (V, 3). She recklessly opens a box given her by Proserpine. The vapors that come forth

---

32. It may be that *Psyche* was devized as a means of dusting off the hell set left over from an earlier production. The king had enjoyed it and thriftily wanted it reused. Couton relates that a story, possibly untrue, had the king inviting three of his leading poets to submit ideas for incorporating hell in a new work. Racine suggested an *Orpheus* and Quinault a *Rape of Proserpine*. But Molière won the bidding with *Psyche* in which he placed his hell scene strategically after the desert, sumptuous palaces, and plain, making its impact more dramatic by contrast (see Couton 2: 792 n.1).

make her swoon, and Cupid, finding her dead, goes into a tantrum of rebellion against his parent (V, 4). Venus, condescending to be seen in hell, tells him that she could restore Psyche to life, but will not. He threatens and pleads (V, 5). Luckily, Jupiter flies in on his eagle, calms both parties, and promises to do away with the difference in their rank by making Psyche an immortal (an appropriate reward for her superhuman virtue), so long as Venus restores her to life (V, 6). The play proper is over but not the production. It continues for some time with the nuptials for Psyche and Cupid: speeches by Apollo, the muses, Bacchus, Momus, the god of mockery, and concluding ballets and choruses in praise of love and loving, doubtless meant as a sop to Venus.[33]

In many of his plays, but especially in the comedy-ballets, Molière likes to introduce characters in pairs. The two malicious sisters and the two admirable prince-suitors in *Psyche* recall those two *magnifiques*, the prince-suitors in *The Magnificent Lovers*, the two sheep farmers in *Comic Pastoral*, the pairs of shepherdesses and shepherds in *Mélicerte*, the two peasant girls in *Don Juan*, and the two pairs of lovers in *The Bourgeois Gentleman*, among other couples. This type of plotting gives a rhetorical edge to both comic and serious scenes because of the repetitions and variations played on particular sentiments, which sometimes create an echolalic effect and provide for coordinated—either matching or contrasting—choreographed movement.

With this production Molière touched the limits of baroque staging: total theatre with minimal characterization. Bits of personality glint in the lines of the two sisters and Zephyr, but most of the speeches (and more broadly, the roles) represent attitudes. To say this is certainly neither to fault the script nor to criticize the artists who made it but rather to mention that Molière and Corneille could, at the height of their powers, achieve an operatic theatre that is in line with the quality, as conception and as writing, of their most memorable drama, while making it distinctive. Corneille brought to his hurried task a pliable poetry of varying line-length that accommodates conversational lines of dialogue as comfortably as it does the exclamatory, heroic and majestic solo arias. *Psyche* is an Olympian work of art.

33. The role of Apollo, intended for the king, was not ultimately played by him. Of the leading roles in *Psyche*, Cupid went to Baron and Psyche to Armande Molière. Molière himself took on the modest role of Zephyr; his and Armande's six-year-old daughter, Esprit-Madeleine, had a tiny walk-on.

PART THREE

Fulfillments

1. MASTERS OF THE HOUSE

2. MISTRESSES OF THE HOUSE

3. LONERS

1. Masters of the House

The School for Wives
(*L'École des femmes*, 1662)

The School for Wives plays further variations on that favored, even obsessive, theme of the French and other Latin-derived drama, cuckoldry—the fear of it, precautions taken to fend it off, and the antagonism aroused between the sexes and the generations as a result of those precautions. But as this ambiguous comedy also deals with a second theme, an artist's failure to accomplish the work of art he set out to create, its author reinvents an ancient myth.

The play's pattern, versification, and characters derive from *The School for Husbands*, with some sharp differences. The three-act structure has been expanded into five acts, a neoclassical format that promises a more serious work and a deeper plumbing of the dramatic material. Intrigue is as rife as in the earlier comedy, only now it grows out of the defects in the central figure and in the young lovers, who are not as clever as their predecessors. The Isabelle and Valère of *Husbands* scheme; she invents off-the-cuff deceits and double-entendres; together, they see through the weaknesses of their opponent, Sganarelle, and trade on them. In *Wives* the young lovers, Agnès and Horace, are an innocent and an unstoppable bumbler. Their intrigues do not exactly succeed; rather, the countermeasures adopted by their opponent, Arnolphe, fail. We could impute the failure to the triumph of true love over possessiveness or to fate—Arnolphe, like Don Garcie, speaks of the "star" that persists in robbing him of hope (IV, 7)—or to built-in flaws in the countermeasures, in Arnolphe's personality, and in his master plan.

He hatched the plan long before the action opens, fourteen years earlier, when Agnès was a little girl of four. He purchased her for adoption from an old peasant woman, on the understanding that with him she would enjoy a richer life. But after having her raised in a convent,[1] he intended to train her,

---

1. Convent life and education in seventeenth-century France are discussed by M. E. Lowndes in some detail in *The Nuns of Port Royal* (London: Oxford University Press, 1909) and more lightly by W. H. Lewis in two chapters of his fascinating *The Splendid Century* (1953; reprint, New York: Doubleday Anchor, 1957), "The Church" and "Female Education," 80–124 and 239–59.

virtually to brainwash her, into becoming an Arnolphe-centered wife by never letting her out of his house, denying her the society of others, especially other women, and keeping her ignorant of everything but the chores of a housewife. He would thereby score over the many husbands he knew (and jeered at) whose wives deceived them.

Molière reduces the principals in the action from the five in *Husbands* to three in *Wives;* there is no contrasting couple corresponding to Ariste and Léonor, only the triangle of Arnolphe, his ward, Agnès, and her swain, Horace; the remaining characters, although adequately motivated, serve as adjuncts to the main plot. All five acts take place outdoors in the square adjacent to Arnolphe's house in an unspecified town, so that accidental meetings between the various characters occur in an impersonal setting, which is out of Arnolphe's control. In four of those acts (I, III, IV, and V), Horace encounters his father's old friend and boasts of how he means to free Agnès from her cage in order to marry her. He has no idea that he is addressing her keeper nor that Arnolphe has adopted a new name, Monsieur de la Souche, in line with his pretensions to settling down as a tranquil, wife-managing city squire. At these encounters, forewarned is disarmed: once Arnolphe has got over his shock at the risk of being cuckolded before he has even married the woman, he serenely cooks up counterplans to keep the trustful marauder at bay.

The conflict between a young lover and a guardian or father or older suitor, familiar long before Molière fastened onto it repeatedly, and a dramatic staple down to our own day, becomes distinctive in *The School for Wives* for several reasons: because of the plotting, the deployment of the characters on and off the stage; because the playwright invokes piercing irony by having one rival obliviously tell the other how he intends to outmaneuver him; because Horace lacks the aid of a smart servant, such as Mascarille or Scapin or Beaumarchais' Figaro, usually the agent when a young woman has to be rescued from an oppressor; and finally because the lovers do not meet and conspire in the action (on the stage), only in the story; we do not see them together until almost the end of the play. As a result of these dramaturgical ploys, Arnolphe has drawn the top four cards in the conflict: he functions as a biased intermediary with the audience; as Horace's competitor; as the surrogate parent of Agnès, not merely her intended husband; and *in loco parentis* for Horace, who insists on confiding in him as in a sympathetic father—the true father, Oronte, does not appear until the seventh scene of the last act. While Arnolphe holds those four aces, how can he possibly lose? In *Husbands*, the joke is on Sganarelle, who turns into the messenger of his own defeat; in *Wives*, the joke ought to be at the expense of Horace, but it gets deflected because Arnolphe's aces prove worthless in a game of jokers wild. The tautness of this plotting compares with that of Racine's *Bérénice*, written eight years later.

The play's narrowed focus, in comparison with that of *Husbands*, marks another turning point in Molière's theatre. It brings him to the first of his searching examinations of an imperious male temperament haunted by a passion to rule others wholly. The despotic motif is used in his preliminary works, but not so unrelentingly. Beginning with Arnolphe, a line of central characters will parade past us, doing their utmost to establish themselves as masters of the house—George Dandin, Harpagon, Orgon, Monsieur Jourdain, and Argan. They will each be foiled by opponents and/or circumstances from imposing their will, to which, like monarchs, they accord the force of law in their own domain. Is the thwarting in every case a foregone conclusion? Yes. But the playwright staves off that conclusion so artfully that the expected comes as a surprise and compels us to view the defeated man in a new light.

The opening scene of *The School for Wives* in which Arnolphe announces the consummation of his master plan, his marriage to Agnès, now that he regards her as trained to his wishes and worthy of his hand, also projects doubts about the plan. His friend, Chrysalde, says directly in the play's sixth line: "Your plan makes me tremble with fear for you," and adds that it would be rash for Arnolphe to marry at all. Chrysalde will reappear at intervals as a remonstrative figure. He was interpreted by some earlier critics as a *raisonneur,* the author's unabashed stand-in, who mouths good sense and moderation; but he performs more as a warning signal, like a buoy floating in and out of the text with an attached revolving light that shows up dangerous rocks ahead. If Arnolphe represents the first of Molière's psychologically complex masters of the house, Chrysalde represents the first of a line of friends and kin who argue forcefully, do not convince the central character, but refuse to stop trying.[2] As an apostle of sweet reason, Chrysalde (like Cléante in *Tartuffe,* Philinte in *The Misanthrope,* and Béralde in *The Imaginary Invalid)* talks sound, pragmatic logic but makes no headway with a listener impervious to this particular logic. If anything, Chrysalde achieves the opposite of what he, the character, intends; he merely hardens Arnolphe's resolve by disagreeing with him. He does, however, fulfill what the *playwright* intends; he tightens

---

2. The difference between Chrysalde and the Ariste in *The School for Husbands* consists in Ariste's disputing with his brother out of self-justification—he is less of a disinterested bystander than Chrysalde is.

the suspense and he draws Arnolphe out. This last function, making Arnolphe reveal himself to the reader and spectator, suggests that it might be helpful to think of Chrysalde and comparable figures as interlocutors rather than *raisonneurs*. All roles draw others out. They may simply engage them in amiable conversation or may go so far as to provoke them into a dispute. What differentiates the interlocutor in this respect from the general run of roles is that he is a self-appointed chastener who purveys unwanted advice, a conventionally sensible, uncontroversial point of view, not unlike that of a Greek chorus or of a confidant in the tragedies of Molière's contemporaries.

(A number of Molière's comedies also incorporate a woman, usually a servant, who argues with the master of the house and may even ridicule him. Such dissonant voices sound more brassily [and bravely] than those of the male interlocutors because the women play more active roles. Not content to plead, they intrigue, opposing their masters openly and secretly, and by means of the ridicule, setting out to arouse the masters' wrath.)[3]

Much as the Sganarelle role has been transposed into the more gentlemanly Arnolphe, Valère into the more headstrong Horace, Isabelle into the naïve Agnès, and Ariste by a splitting process into Chrysalde and Oronte, so the two astute servants of *Husbands*, Lisette and Ergaste, are replaced in *Wives* by Georgette and Alain, whom Arnolphe has deliberately chosen as wardens for his ward because they are simpletons. The witticisms (intended funniness) of Lisette and Ergaste give way to the humor (unintended funniness) of Georgette and Alain. Through contact with them, Arnolphe hopes, even assures himself, that Agnès will never catch a glimpse of the sophisticated world, the one outside the house, which runs amok, according to his nervous fancy, with sybaritic, duplicitous women dedicated to the most effective ways of ensnaring and ruining men. His pair of maladroit guardians, terrified of their *patron*, compete not to open the gate when he knocks, then compete to open it when he yells at them, and Alain almost decks him with a blow aimed at Georgette (I, 2). They try to run away when he tells them to approach (II, 2). Georgette even cries, "Don't eat me, Monsieur"; and when he demands to know whether Agnès missed him while he was away for several days, Georgette tells him that "she thought she saw you coming back every moment, and there wasn't one horse, ass, or mule we heard passing the house that she

---

3. These antagonistic female roles include Lisette in *Doctor Love*, Claudine in *George Dandin*, Dorine in *Tartuffe*, Nicole (and Mme Jourdain) in *The Bourgeois Gentleman*, Toinette in *The Imaginary Invalid*, and Martine who, in *The Learned Ladies*, sides with her master against her mistress.

didn't take for you (I, 2)." Oh, the penalties of being an employer! In trying
to convert his house into a barricaded fortress, Arnolphe is too clever to hire
clever helpers because they may accept bribes; instead, he hires helpers who
are dumb but at least as open to bribery as anyone else.

As the action progresses, Horace hardly changes; there is no need for him
to become other than what we see at first, a fervidly optimistic swain attempting one intrigue after another to circumvent his unseen rival and get to Agnès.
But signal changes take place in the personalities of Agnès and Arnolphe.

Agnès starts out as a female Caspar Hauser sheltered almost beyond belief
by convent walls, studies, precepts, and preparations for docile housewifery,
a teenager marooned in a second-floor room where she sews together head-
gear and nightshirts for Arnolphe and is bitten by fleas that keep her awake
all night. Her first appearance is restricted to an exchange with her guardian
of thirteen lines of which he allows her to speak only three and a half. He
then sends her back upstairs and gloats for five lines over his ownership of
"this nice and modest ignorance" and its superiority to the showy love letters,
poems, and novels written by "the heroines of our time, *Mesdames les savantes*
(I, 3)." Further along in the play, not yet suspecting that he has reserved her
for himself, she blithely describes how she has welcomed his rival's attentions
and been charmed by them. After being told by an old lady that the young
man was stricken by her glances, she replied that "he can come and see me
here as often as he likes," and he did and was cured. He took her hands and
arms and kissed them. As she revels in the delights of this first love, Arnolphe
demands, in a colloquy that became notorious, whether Horace took anything
else from her. Yes. But what? He'll get mad if she tells him. He won't. Will
he promise? Her ignorance, which he had earlier joyed in, now drives him
frantic. But all that Horace took, it appears, was a ribbon given her by
Arnolphe, who now turns over an ace and slaps it down violently. She must
have no further truck with Horace. If he calls to her from the street, she must
throw a stone at him. Arnolphe cuts off her protests with "Enough!" and a
stern line borrowed from Corneille's *Sertorius*, which had had its premiere
not long before: "I am the master; when I speak: go, obey (II, 5)."

He later continues in this high-handed vein by requesting her to recite a
document written in rhyme and entitled, "The Maxims of Marriage, or The
Duties of a Married Woman, and How She Must Practice Them Every Day."
There are twelve maxims, one to each verse, of which he has her read ten
aloud, his marital commandments, enjoining her to stay out of other men's
beds; not to dress up or use cosmetics or leave the house without a veil over

her face or admit anyone to the premises or accept gifts or write anything at
all or attend social functions of any kind or gamble or go out for walks or
picnics (III, 2).

By such compulsions he incidentally compels Agnès to grow up suddenly,
if only out of self-protection. The stone she throws at Horace has a message
tied to it. She invites him into her room; when Arnolphe comes up and rages,
Horace takes cover in a closet, subsequently recounting to Arnolphe with
satisfaction and pity the enraged language and behavior (thumping a table,
smashing vases, kicking a dog) of that "dear old cuckold," Monsieur de la
Souche. Later yet, when marriage to Arnolphe looms, she will plan to elope
with Horace and would succeed, save for the latter's attempt to keep her out
of sight of Monsieur de la Souche by entrusting her for a few hours to his
friend, Arnolphe.

During her second conversation with Arnolphe, when he asked her, "Any
news?" she replied, "The kitten died." The line has become famous in France
(*"Le petit chat est mort"*) as an expression of inconsequential happenings, and
Arnolphe uses it as a springboard for a remark about the inevitability of death,
but it echoes soundlessly thereafter as a token of her initiation from wardship
into womanhood—the death of one Agnès leading to the birth of a quite
different one. The domestic pet has turned into an independent human
being. To put it another way, our image of the Agnès of the first two acts is
of a figure removed and inaccessible—one story off the ground, looking out
at the square, the great beyond, with wide eyes from behind a shuttered
window or standing on a balcony. In the last two acts, she has come, or been
brought, down to ground level.

Arnolphe's parallel transformation can be seen in the contrast between his
first appearance and his disappearance. He opens act I with his cheerful
confirmation to Chrysalde that he will marry Agnès the next day and goes on
to laugh at cuckolds who meekly wear their horns and think themselves bright
for having chosen wives bright enough to fool them. He congratulates himself
on the realization of his master plan after fourteen patient years. Everything
has fallen into place, the place he decreed for it. He overpowers Chrysalde
with his certitude, his exuberance, his stream of oratory. As king of his
minicastle and three subjects, one of them the queen-to-be, he will organize
his world to his own design.[4]

---

4. J. D. Hubert (chap. 8, 66–85) says that Arnolphe will be God. The play does
indirectly sustain the notion of him as a deity when, for example, he has Agnès read
his ten commandments aloud. Later, he characterizes his rival several times as the

Act V, however, sees the return of two parents: Oronte, the father of Horace, and his brother-in-law named Enrique. The latter sailed off to America fourteen years earlier to seek his fortune, which he found. (The European belief that every European who braved the Atlantic made his fortune on the other side predated this play by centuries as one version of the Eldorado myth.) Enrique left his small daughter, Agnès, in the care of a peasant woman. It was from her that Arnolphe purchased the child, without knowing who her father was or that he was alive. By an additional stroke of synchronicity that is less of a mental strain to accept than to question, Oronte and Enrique have already arranged a match between their children; and to stretch the synchronicity almost to breaking point, they arrive in the square in time to avert the forced marriage of Agnès to Arnolphe. After these well-laid coincidences thunder down on him, Arnolphe departs with a mere exhalation: "Oh!," as a stage direction informs us that he is "transported and unable to speak," an abject contrast to his earlier self.

Arnolphe starts out resembling not only a king but also a theatre critic who has made up his mind to outwrite all the dramatists he has savaged in the past. He will work the same sort of material, but with more literate results— no grammatical errors, no halts in story development, no sidetracking, or inconsequential conclusions. But fate has thrust upon him a co-writer who keeps altering the projected narrative. Arnolphe tries to absorb the new events, caused by Horace's intrusions, into his original plan, growing more intent, more rabid, more cruel. A notary who calls to write the contract for Arnolphe's marriage finds him engaged in a dialogue with himself, so that his distraught mutterings about his troubles are at cross-purposes with the notary's businesslike replies.

ARNOLPHE *(Not seeing the Notary)*
          I'm scared, because if I don't play this down
          They'll talk of nothing else all over town.
NOTARY   The contract? Easy! We'll avoid a fuss
          And keep it secret, just the three of us. (IV, 2)

When Horace announces that he intends to climb a ladder into Agnès' room, Arnolphe prepares a welcome by instructing Georgette and Alain to lean out of the window and wallop the young man with sticks (IV, 9). But in the offstage story, as Horace later relates it, he ducked the swipes and fell off

---

devil and tells Agnès she will be roasted in hell. At the end when he sees his godlike powers over her dissolved, he says that the very heavens conspire against him.

the ladder onto soft ground beneath, leaving Arnolphe with the impression for a time that he was responsible for a murder.

The final mishap, the clincher, is inflicted by Arnolphe on himself, and comes, slightly adapted, from *The School for Husbands.* Just as Sganarelle in that play thought he was marrying off his rival, Valère, to Léonor, not to Isabelle, so, on learning about the arranged pairing-off of the daughter of Enrique and the son of Oronte, Arnolphe argues in its favor to get his rival married off to someone else, only to discover that Enrique's daughter is Agnès, and he has convinced the others to take her away from him. In both plays, this apparent prankishness on the playwright's part has a symbolic coloring: neither Sganarelle nor Arnolphe "knows" the young woman he wanted to possess. The character flaw lay not in Agnès' ignorance but in the ignorance of Arnolphe.

The truth is that Arnolphe never tried to *win* Agnes, only to take her. She tells him this at one point, but her remarks roll off him. He didn't believe he needed to win her. He believes she owed herself to him; he forgets that she did not sign the unwritten contract. He tells Chrysalde, "I already think of her as a wife." Chrysalde may sound futile when he talks reason to Arnolphe and tries to restrain him from marrying; but Arnolphe sounds just as futile when he talks reason to Agnès or thinks aloud about her. He says that Horace has corrupted her mind, when Horace has tampered with her feelings; and he asks himself despairingly how, when he made his choice after "so much philosophizing," he can have fallen in love with her—for the pains of opposition are now being overtaken by the pangs of jealousy (III, 5). He imagines, because he worked out his plan rationally, that it was a rational plan to begin with.

If, like most plays, this one deals with irrational behavior, we can ask two questions about Arnolphe. Is he mad? And does he really love Agnès? In the introduction to his splendid translation, Richard Wilbur restates an idea earlier suggested by J. D. Hubert, among others, namely, that Arnolphe is "a madman, and his alienation is of a harmful and unlovable kind. What ails him is a deep general insecurity, which has somehow been focused into a specific terror of being cuckolded" (p. ix). The second sentence in this judgment is unexceptionable. But the first? A madman? If madness means anything, it implies the psychotic maladjustment between a person and his surroundings. Arnolphe's madness, if it existed, would have to extend to all his relationships. It doesn't. His comeuppance has to do with his conviction that he is utterly reasonable in his expectations; that the master plan will work because it has been so conscientiously thought out. If Arnolphe were indeed mad, Chrysalde would not waste time talking to him; while Horace, blinkered though he is, would see through him. In his dealings with his servants, Arnolphe does adopt here and there a tone of almost-mad ferocity, and his attitude toward Agnès has an unswerving resolution; but these are lapses from his normally balanced behavior, which is supported by flashes of foreboding, as when he pleads with heaven, if it ordains that he shall have his brow decorated with horns, to give him the fortitude displayed by "certain men" (III, 5), the cuckolds he laughed at in the opening scene. Arnolphe is not a madman but a fanatic when it comes to cuckoldry, especially in persuading himself that he has concocted *this* method of avoiding it: a loveless union with a gauche prisoner. In performance, a crazed Arnolphe throughout would rob the play of its subtleties and falsify its ambivalent ending—when we feel that he has earned his deserts and, at the same time, feel sorry for him for having precipitated what he strove so vigorously to evade.

And does he love Agnès? He is forty-two; she is eighteen. She is too youthful and inexperienced to resist his will. She will be manageable, pliable. She will not make demands or lay down conditions, as other wives do, because she knows nothing of demands or conditions. Like Humbert Humbert in *Lolita* and Solness with Hilde in *The Master Builder*, by "capturing" her youthfulness, he fools himself into believing he has recaptured his own. In the opening scene, he tells Chrysalde that he did not seek beauty or wisdom in his marriage partner. No, he looked for a negative quality, that she not deceive him or make him into a laughingstock—he assumes a person of her age and social greenness would not know how to. But he happened to acquire a beauty, although he did not appreciate her looks until Horace wanted her and praised them. He now desires her because she is coveted by someone else. A number of critics have remarked that Arnolphe's mistake was to fall in love with Agnès. The play seems, rather, to suggest that he *thinks* he loves her and is infatuated less with her as she is than with the notion of keeping her as she was. Some of the avarice that showed itself in the personality of Sganarelle in *Husbands* itches in him too. He is afraid of losing a possession, but his possessiveness takes a disguised form. Arnolphe is intelligent, sophisticated, imaginative, a sculptor who took this child as a four-year-old piece of clay and made out of it a woman he might cope with. She is a Galatea to his Pygmalion or Eliza Doolittle to his Henry Higgins, and Horace is the young puppy of a Freddy Eynsford-Hill who has done nothing to deserve her.[5] A

5. I would suggest that Shaw deliberately drew on the *School for Wives* triangle—in *Candida* as well as in *Pygmalion*. In the fifth part of *Back to Methuselah*, Shaw introduces

staging concept that would take account of this Pygmalion-Galatea theme, and of the play's structural artificiality, might begin with the concept of Agnès as a doll who comes to life, stiff and statuelike at first but growing more animated through the action as she finds herself more and more compelled to defend her feelings. Conversely, Arnolphe, who starts out bouncy and apparently unbeatable, grows older, tired, stiff. On his last exit, he moves like an automaton, and matches his adopted name, Monsieur de la Souche, *une souche* being a block or stump of wood.

From the middle of the play onward, Arnolphe's confidence in his own powers wanes as he labors under the festering suspicion that he is the butt of cosmic injustice; that he had a right to own what he considers this live statue because he made her over into an image he required; and that he is thus losing a part of himself. He is wrong on all three counts. We might be tempted to laugh at him during the final scene, as we have done throughout the play, and relish the happy, imposed, satirically convenient wrap-up; but this comedy abruptly takes on tragic overtones *because of* the forced ending. Arnolphe was not a villain outwitted by the hero (a comic format) or outdu-elled by the hero (a melodramatic format). His fanatical adherence to a flawed plan makes him close to being tragic in his disappointment. He is absent from the stage for the play's last eight couplets. The closing one, delivered by Chrysalde, who also spoke the opening line, carries an ironic weight as it invites the other characters to pay tribute to Arnolphe for the pains he took in bringing up Agnès, and to heaven, "which does everything for the best." This couplet implicitly alerts us that Arnolphe's real foe was not Horace but either himself or heaven, the ultimate and all-purpose culprit, which made him what he inescapably is.

another Pygmalion, a scientist who creates two living puppets, one of whom bites and kills him.

The name Galatea has mixed mythical origins. It belongs to a goddess, the daughter of Nereus (who reappears in John Gay's libretto for Handel's opera *Acis and Galatea*); refers to a statue by Apollodorus; and was applied by W.S. Gilbert to the heroine of his *Pygmalion and Galatea*. In Ovid, the principal source for the modern usage (*The Metamorphoses*, bk. 10), the statue that comes to life has no name.

The Criticism of The School for Wives
(*La Critique de L'École des femmes*, 1663)

J ust over five months after *The School for Wives* had its premiere, Molière
staged a discussion of the kind most playwrights would like to conduct, a
postperformance evaluation in which he plays his own critic and takes a few
whacks at his detractors, without deviating from what one of the participants
calls "the grand rule of rules . . . to please" the public. The salon comedy in
one act has a generally good-natured tone, which verges in places on the
jocular and sometimes the farcical. But it registers a number of percipient
comments on playwriting and play judging. Its title affirms that the subject
is the criticism of *The School for Wives*, not a defense of it, which would have
sounded more self-serving, but the comic content does contrive a defense of
The School for Wives in particular and, in general, of Molière's ideals and
techniques as a dramatist.

The informal debate takes place in the home of a young society woman
named Uranie who liked the play.[1] Uranie and the two guests she has invited
over, her cousin, Élise, and a young man named Dorante, constitute the
defense team. The prosecution is leveled by three uninvited visitors, for
people in the *haut monde* of Paris seem, if Molière's theatre accurately
represents it, to have strolled at any time and without warning into one
another's drawing rooms. The visitors consist of an older society woman
who is something of a *précieuse* named Climène, a giggling marquis, and a
playwright called Lysidas whose writings are not wildly popular. The lineup
of three guests against three visitors is not at first as balanced as it might
appear, for Lysidas, who makes the more telling accusations, does not show
up until after halfway through the action. As a result, the criticism in the first
half consists mostly of unsubstantiated opinion-mongering by Climène and
the marquis; they call *The School for Wives* detestable, filthy, witless, and
insulting to women; they deplore its appeal to the lowbrows standing in the
pit; they object to some colorful and mildly erotic phrases, as when Alain

---

1. As several French editors have mentioned, Uranie was the name of the muse of
astronomy, and since the character liked *The School for Wives*, the author has given
her a name that suggests she is a "lady of quality."

tells Georgette that a man guarding his woman is like a man preventing others from eating his soup (II, 3), or when Arnolphe says that the reply he would like the artless Agnès to give to the question, "What shall we put in my basket?" in the game of *corbillon* is "cream tart" *(tarte à la crème).* [2]

With the arrival of Lysidas, however, the disagreements begin to strike deeper and build to a more serious consideration of the principles of seventeenth-century play making. For a time, Lysidas declines to be drawn into condemning the work of a fellow writer; he calls *Wives* "one of the finest" plays, although he concedes that it has not won the approval of people of good taste.[3] But before long, he cannot hold back his true feelings, a mix of envy, resentment of the reception of comedies compared to that of tragedies (such as his), and annoyance at Molière's flouting of the "rules" that have come down from Aristotle, Horace, and other names sacred to Renaissance and early baroque critics. He goes on to complain that the play lacks action— it consists of reports (i.e., offstage story) rather than events; that certain of the funny lines are cheap, such as Agnès' asking Arnolphe whether children are born through the ear (I, 1);[4] that an early scene between the servants is too lengthy—this scene (I, 2) happens to abound in knockabout business, hardly the sort of fare to appeal to a writer of tragedies; that Arnolphe is either ridiculous, in which case he would not give money to Horace like a gentleman, or intelligent, in which case he would not make a ridiculous figure of himself when he declares his love for Agnès (V, 4). Most of these charges resemble the ones tossed at today's (and yesterday's) playwrights by produc-

---

2. In the game of *corbillon* the players, usually children, have to find a rhyme for the sound *on.* Arnolphe's remark tells his interlocutor, Chrysalde, that he doesn't care if Agnès is so ignorant that she doesn't understand that a rhyme is called for; she simply answers with the first item, a cream tart, that a child might desire. Over the question of whether *tarte à la crème* is suitable language for a play written in verse there was, to start with, a storm in a teacup, which turned fairly serious and may have led to verbal and even physical assaults on Molière. Couton provides some details on the "cream tart" controversy in 1:1289–91.

3. According to the abbé d'Aubignac, Lysidas is modeled on Pierre Corneille, but the abbé was an enemy of Corneille, and another witness, Donneau de Visé, says that the abbé was himself the model for Lysidas. Couton (1: 1287–88) deduces that Corneille's younger brother, Thomas, corresponds to Lysidas in a number of particulars—if it matters.

4. The story of the birth of a child through its mother's ear comes from *Gargantua and Pantagruel* by Rabelais, published more than one hundred years before *The School for Wives.* Did Molière know this? Almost certainly, but the play offers no clue.

ers, directors, literary advisers, playwriting teachers, and critics. The last charge seems to question the "consistency" of Arnolphe's character—as though any striking character is ever "consistent" in motivation or behavior—but it actually muffles the real criticism, namely that Arnolphe is neither likable nor admirable.[5]

Molière resists the temptation to answer these criticisms in his own voice. He allots the principal defense and counterattacks to the character Dorante, supposedly a friend of the author and performed in the original production by Brécourt, the actor-playwright who had played the valet, Alain, in *Wives*, while he gives himself the role of the simpering marquis.[6] Dorante applies energy and loquacity to the task of reviewing the playwright's objectives and results. He contends that comedy is more difficult to write than tragedy and high drama. For the elevated marvels of the last two, their wondrous unreality, the author must substitute truth to life, convincing portraits of characters whose flaws invite recognition and arouse laughter. If the plays people enjoy are fashioned by time-honored rules, and the plays that are popular ignore the rules, the rules must need revision.[7] At the same time, he insists that *Wives* does adhere to the current rules, so that this criticism is twice invalid. Some of the lines and phrases singled out as being unfunny or witless are not necessarily the author's own comments about life and art but revelations of the character who speaks them, an observation that applies to plays written in every age.

Uranie supports his arguments and so, indirectly, does her cousin, who relies heavily on sarcasm and irony as she pretends to agree with the other side by means of double-entendres. The debate ends inconclusively. Dorante

---

5. Since long before Molière, writers—not only dramatists—have had to confront the difficulty that a protagonist who is not wholly sympathetic will arouse the antipathy, rather than the healthy curiosity, of many spectators and critics. Typical of a modern review is the statement: "I just couldn't care less what happened to this unsavory hero." The topic of the unsympathetic hero will be discussed further in reference to Harpagon, Orgon, Alceste, and Don Juan.

6. These choices of casting are not absolute facts but reasonable, almost-reliable inferences (see Herzel, pp. 46–50).

7. There is more than a hint in Dorante's arguments that in criticism, descriptions and analyses of what playwrights do write, rather than prescriptions of what they should write, have more value than rules do. Today commentators on Aristotle believe for the most part that the *Poetics*, the fount of all subsequent theatre "rules," was meant to be largely descriptive, not prescriptive. It is clear, nonetheless, that Aristotle preferred some plays he mentioned to others he mentioned.

continues with his assiduous justification of Molière's artistry until the marquis begins to interrupt him after every few words and then, as the arguments strike home, refuses to listen any more: he drowns out Dorante's voice by singing. At which point, Uranie suggests that a play might be made out of the debate; the others agree (for the first time); and *The Criticism* turns into self-conscious theatricalism with an open end, except that dinner is now served.

The blending of satirical fact with satirical fiction in the roles has been much imitated since. Lysidas is probably based on a real playwright or more than one, the marquis on a real marquis or more than one, and Climène on a pseudointellectual or more than one. Dorante is an invention who is said in the dialogue to be a friend of Molière, and Uranie and Élise are probably outright fictions. Dorante's arguments have more substance and eloquence than those of Lysidas, but Lysidas and his two allies are far more entertaining *as characters* than their opponents—the author knew what he was doing when he took on the role of the marquis. As a result, our enjoyment of the opposition rectifies the imbalance in the polemics.

The gist of the play may lie in a remark of Dorante's to the effect that what some people disliked the most in *Wives* was what others liked the most. But the summary of the action one comes away with is Molière's unspoken but unmistakable implication: Let my critics outwit me by writing better plays than mine—if they can.

The Rehearsal at Versailles
(L'Impromptu de Versailles, 1663)

It is no exaggeration to pronounce *The Rehearsal at Versailles* the most prodigious one-act play in the history of the theatre, the first utterly realistic drama (ahead of Hebbel by some 200 years) and at the same time an anticipation by 270 years of Pirandello's *representation* of improvised dialogue and his deliberately uncompleted plays-within-plays. It also reviews a number of the playwright's writing and acting principles and reveals how they are at odds with those of his contemporaries.

Molière displays his troupe at work on a new, untitled, unrehearsed script called for only a week earlier by the king, who is expected to arrive within a couple of hours for the first performance. The script, aired now in October 1663, ten months after the production of *The School for Wives* and four months after *The Criticism of The School for Wives*, answers many of the countercriticisms provoked by those plays. It is aimed in particular at a satire due to open at the Hôtel de Bourgogne the following evening, *The Painter Painted (Le Portrait du peintre)*, written by Edmé Boursault but, according to Molière's play, instigated and sponsored by a flock of *antimoliéristes*.

Despite the pressing deadline for his production, the king's appearance, Molière allows himself to be distracted when his actresses encourage him to show off some of his routines in a pastiche of five of the actors who belong to the Bourgogne company.[1] Not long after the rehearsal of the script gets under way, the king and his retinue show up early. The author-director desperately pleads for more time, since his performers have not yet learned their parts and are terrified. The king sensibly grants a postponement of the new play and will be satisfied with one he has seen before.

The Rehearsal at Versailles has been called a polemic and a dialectic rather than a play; Voltaire and many subsequent critics have accused the author of

---

1. The published text names these actors (Montfleury, Mlle Beauchâteau and her husband, Hauteroche, De Villiers) in the stage directions, but the dialogue does not. The audience, we can assume, would recognize their stage personae as readily as the actors in Molière's troupe do.

being spiteful in his spoofing of his rivals.[2] He did enjoy the protection and favor of the king and might have deigned to overlook the gossip and charges against him by actors who were accomplished and popular, and whose traditional style, so different from his, may yet have had artistic validity. But it can be argued that, within the compass of this short comedy, with its series of apparently false starts, interruptions and discontinuities, Molière fashioned a work of dramatic art that meets its own structural requirements with exceptional boldness and efficiency; and that the impersonations are surprisingly temperate.[3] They also give the leading actor some histrionic opportunities. Because of its ending, the play can also team up with, and lead into a production of, one of the earlier plays.[4]

The realism is self-evident. *L'Impromptu* finds the actors in costume on the stage at Versailles, where it was first shown (or later on the stage of the Palais-Royal when it came to Paris), but they play themselves and are unwilling to start rehearsing for a variety of reasons: They have not yet mastered their lines and will need prompting; the lines are prose, which is harder to learn than poetry—though, as Molière replies, prose is easier than poetry to improvise, in case they go "dry"; this script (the play-within-the-play) is too indirect as a retort to his detractors—he should have written a frontal assault, for example; and they voice other gripes that sound like natural, if not inevitable, extracts from an actual rehearsal. The actors and Molière speak conversationally; even their longer speeches sound unrhetorical, not at all elevated, the only exceptions being some quotations from Corneille, with which the playwright-director illustrates the Bourgogne manner of declaiming heroic drama. As though to heighten the realism and the tension of preparing a new play, a marquis (performed by La Thorillière, a newcomer to the company) crashes the rehearsal, almost driving the director frantic with his unwanted presence and niggling questions. The most notable realis-

---

2. See, e.g., Gross, 75 n.

3. W. D. Howarth points out that if Montfleury really did accuse Molière of having "married the daughter [Armande] after he had slept with her mother [Madeleine]," as Racine is reported to have written to the king, and if this accusation was typical of "the weapons his jealous rivals were prepared to use against him, one can only admire Molière's moderation as a polemicist" (Howarth, 174).

4. Occasionally, a company will follow it with a later play, as the Association of Producing Artists did in the 1960s when *The Rehearsal at Versailles* prefaced *Scapin;* such an arrangement is historically illogical, but surely only a hidebound historicizer will object if the plays are well done.

tic touch consists of the basic premise that the king has commanded a new play at maddeningly short notice, a condition the author would have to cope with, on and off, for his remaining ten years as head of the *Troupe du Roi*.

At the same time, the impression of improvisation and the enactment of the play-within-the-play make this comedy a choice example of theatricalism, not the first by any means in seventeenth-century France, but one in which the inner and outer plays support each other. The plotting works ingeniously. As a preface and supplement to the inner play, the character Molière yields to the blandishments of Mlles Béjart and de Brie to entertain them with some of his impersonations; he thereby heads off an incipient revolt by the actors. He has discarded an earlier idea: "I was thinking about a comedy in which a playwright—I'd have taken that part myself—offers a script to an acting troupe that has just come into town." He goes on to imitate two actors and an actress from the troupe, in addition to the playwright, who scorns their portrayals and demonstrates how the recitation of certain lines, all taken from Corneille, should accord with the acting techniques at the Hôtel de Bourgogne—emphatically accented, teamed up with extravagant gestures, and "smiling . . . through the greatest afflictions."[5] Having denied his intention to mock the Bourgogne actors, he has now done exactly that; he has also used his company as an onstage audience. Next, he gives out acting instructions to the cast, as if seeing them standing there spontaneously reminds him of how they should each tackle their roles.

La Thorillière's irruption as the marquis sets him back some precious minutes, but he then manages to launch the inner play, which takes place in the king's antechamber, where courtiers and other suppliants meet to advance their careers, feverishly plead for lower taxes, and casually exchange rumors, slanders, and insincere compliments. The playlet brings together two marquis, who resent Molière's plays for their mockery of the generalized marquis figure ("The marquis is your clown in modern comedies . . . today you must have a foppish marquis to get the laughs," Molière has just told his wife), with an unsuccessful playwright who has the same name as the one in *The Criticism*, a clutch of noblewomen, and a *chevalier* who will defend the author and his writings. But Molière reintroduces the semblances of improvisation several times when he breaks off the run-through of lines in order to give advice to the actors—one does not sound like a marquis; the

5. Molière must have had a special talent for quick switches in voice and personality. He had done this several years earlier in his roles as Sganarelle in *The Flying Doctor* and Mascarille in *The Botcher* and would do it again in the sack scene in *Scapin*.

other sounds exactly like a marquis, but is not supposed to be playing a marquis—an occurrence familiar to anybody who has attended a rehearsal and noticed that one actor picks up another's vocal mannerisms, to the director's chagrin. He cuts in again when Brécourt, the actor playing the Chevalier, is not performing "strongly enough," and he takes over to give a line reading of a lengthy speech. This is the sort of demonstration that would be anathema to actors of our day, and may well have been in Molière's day, for at the end of it Brécourt curtly remarks, "That's enough." But Molière either could not resist the temptation to speak his own argument or, more likely, did not want to appear to avoid the responsibility for that argument by foisting it off onto Brécourt. (In the rest of the inner playlet he takes the role of the more foppish marquis.)

The final improvisational turn chops off the inner playlet apparently before it is over, when Mlle Béjart tells Molière to come up with a more "vigorous reply" to his critics, and he refuses to single out Boursault for a target as he explains why he will not take offense at most of the critical jibes: "I willingly offer up my plays, my face, my gestures, my words, my tone of voice. I sacrifice my tricks of the trade for them to use as they will. I have no objections to whatever they take, if only the audience likes it. But in yielding all this to them, I reserve the rest as my own property. They must be fair and not accuse me of moral and religious delinquency, as they have done in the past" (sc. 5). The statement sounds eminently reasonable, and is. But there is a sly dig in the first four sentences quoted here. He implies there that if his rivals succeed in caricaturing him accurately they are stealing a free ride on his popularity. He understands, as Chaplin much later did, that the price of popularity is to be plagiarized. (The accusation of plagiarism has already been planted in one of Brécourt's speeches. He says he has seen the script of *The Painter Painted* and "since the most amusing lines in it are lifted from Molière's own work, he won't object if the audience likes them" [sc. 5]).

By the time Molière, as himself, makes this announcement, the inner playlet has broken off with no ending; the king will shortly arrive; and the theatricalism has given way to the realism of an unfinished rehearsal—for, like a work of art, a rehearsal is never finished, only abandoned.

Molière's review of his writing and acting principles crops up piecemeal. Some of it occurs during his advice to the players, which resembles Hamlet's in its repudiation of overacting, and the rest in remarks scattered through the texts of the outer and inner plays. It is worth noticing that he does not aim for neutral acting throughout, only for economy of means. He tells La Grange, who plays a marquis, to take his voice into a higher register, because "most of these fellows affect a special way of talking" (sc. 3). He caricatures the greetings and sycophantic compliments exchanged by courtiers (sc. 4), which we can imagine punctuated by little shrieks and mannered exclamations of pleasure, the sort of affectation that will revolt Alceste in *The Misanthrope*, produced less than three years later. Mlles du Parc and Molière are advised, "Wiggle your hips correctly and exaggerate your behavior" (sc. 4). Even so, he is recommending acting that belongs aptly to the characters in question, and by means of which, exaggeration actually makes for authenticity. He draws a distinction between the requirements of tragedy and those of comedy when he has Madeleine Béjart say:

> Your portrait of them would be a much more accurate picture than theirs of you. They tried to spoof your comic acting, but they weren't imitating you at all, only the role you were playing, your makeup, and the mannerisms you adopted in trying to draw a comic character from life. But if you mock an actor in a *serious* part you'll come very close to mocking him as a man, because serious acting doesn't allow him to cover up his personal faults with ridiculous tricks and comic gestures. (Sc. 1)

Molière the character concedes that she is right. Yet, in *The Criticism of the School for the Wives* Molière's defender, Dorante, seems to say the opposite, namely, that it is far easier "to soar aloft on great sentiments, to defy one's fortune in verse, to accuse the fates, and speak ill of the gods, than to venture, as one should, into ridiculing men and making everybody's flaws amusing in the theatre. When you portray heroes, you follow your own fancy . . . But when you portray [ordinary] men [in comedy], you must draw them according to nature" (sc. 6).

In the first quotation, Béjart says in effect that tragic characters are more natural, or at least, have a closer resemblance to the actors playing them, than comic characters do. In the second quotation, Dorante suggests that it is comic characters who are more lifelike. I see no way to resolve this contradiction other than to attribute the first quotation to Madeleine Béjart herself, since it does not square with what Molière proposes elsewhere, and to assume that he, playing himself, agrees swiftly and allows it to pass so as not to delay or complicate his subsequent arguments. This is admittedly a weak attempt on my part to reconcile the two statements written only a few months apart. And after all, there is no reason to hold him to an inhuman standard of consistency. But if Madeleine really said the lines she is given to speak in the play, it may be that other lines assigned to various actors are also direct or indirect quotations, in which case *The Rehearsal at Versailles* becomes not only a pathbreaking play but also a partial *record* of his actors' attitudes toward their parts, their obligations to him and to the king, and the actual conditions in which they sometimes rehearsed.

Did he believe that tragic characters had to be more "true to life" than comic ones? If so, why does Madeleine remember to add that the comic ones, for all the actors' additions and elaborations, are drawn from life? Dorante, Molière's defense counsel in *The Criticism*, gives the impression that tragic speech derives primarily from its author's invention, comic speech primarily from observation. But the comic arises from observation *of classes of people*, from types, rather than from individual models. Brécourt, Molière's defender in *Versailles*, insists that Molière's characters have traits "that could fit a hundred people" (sc. 4). Here, the author openly dismisses the charge that he pilloried specific people in *The Criticism of the School for Wives*. Whether he did so or not, his claim to have created recognizable types has been upheld over time, for we do recognize certain of those types, especially the gushier ones, when this or other Molière plays are mounted today, and while we may not exactly "recognize" certain other types, we can still appreciate their entertaining failings.

Many of his contemporaries—and not only his avowed enemies but also some friends such as Boileau—believed that Molière was not suited for tragic roles, in part because he lacked the heroic stature and voice, and in part because of certain unavoidable *manies*, or tics, his cough, for instance, which he could plausibly impose on a character like Harpagon, but not on a tragic hero. The conclusion among many twentieth-century critics is that, realizing his shortcomings as a tragedian, he wrote for himself roles that were comic while endeavoring to raise comedy as a genre to a parity in critical esteem with tragedy.[6] The conclusion is a tempting one. But we cannot assume that his contemporaries were correct in their assessment of his ability as a trage-dian. It may be that they were so habituated to the "heroics and flourishes" he deplored that they could not imagine tragedies performed in the lower-keyed style that Molière favored. Whether we ascribe this style to his convic-tions or to his limitations or to both is immaterial. It sounds, in truth, not far removed from the style Shaw thought appropriate for playing Ibsen when he praised Janet Achurch and Eleanora Duse; and something like this style has become ingrained in acting in this century. Even that bastion of heroic acting, the Comédie-Française, has undergone a drastic revision in its performing

---

6. This conclusion seems to have been put forward first by W. G. Moore, then by Renè Bray, and later by other writers.

since the 1950s that may well have brought the House of Molière closer to Molière.

In the opening scene of *The Rehearsal at Versailles*, Madeleine Béjart mentions that the king had not merely asked for *a* play but for a play in which the dramatist would answer his critics. In his text Molière satisfies his royal patron on both counts. He makes the king appear considerate for not insisting on a new work, while, at the same time, he produces such a work for the king's edification. In addition, he artfully jabs at his critics by saying that they have attacked a play the king liked, implying that their distaste is impertinent, if not disloyal. Best of all, from his point of view, he makes fun of Boursault's play and rushes his own play into production one day ahead in order to forestall the criticisms he expected and neutralize them ahead of time. People who see the Boursault play first will now feel compelled to see Molière's for its responses; whereas some people who see Molière's play first will believe they do not need to see Boursault's because Molière has already answered it.

Yet, the play's last minuscule scene of eleven lines has an ambiguous flavor. The playwright fervently thanks the king's messenger for the reprieve he brings—"Monsieur, you restore me to life!"—and pronounces his gratitude to Louis for his "extreme kindness." At that moment we understand that Molière who, throughout *The Rehearsal at Versailles*, has played the master of the playhouse is not much more than an indulged servant at the mercy of the real master of the house.

In the mid-1960s, the late Fred Stewart produced a staged reading of *The Rehearsal at Versailles* at the Directors' Unit of the Actors Studio in New York. The engaging performance in which Roscoe Lee Browne took the role of Molière lasted for about thirty-five minutes, after which the audience, consisting mostly of other directors, tore Stewart's "concept" to shreds and offered all sorts of alternative interpretations as they each asserted their notions of how the play *could be* done. Then, the late Lee Strasberg, who ran the Studio, sat in his director's chair with his name on it, a tape-recorder was switched on, and Strasberg proceeded to talk with eloquence, erudition, and understanding of Molière's art and of seventeenth-century theatre for ninety recorded minutes, almost three times as long as the duration of the play. He compared the rivalry between Molière and the Bourgogne company to the recent rift between himself and Elia Kazan, who had left the Actor's Studio and "betrayed" it by becoming one of the artistic directors of the theatre program at the newly inaugurated Lincoln Center, for Kazan had neglected to invite the Studio personnel to participate in the Lincoln Center enterprise. Strasberg neither defended nor attacked Stewart's interpretation, but he did obliquely criticize one aspect of it when he noted that there would originally have been one or two rows of privileged spectators, courtiers most likely, seated on the two sides of the stage and that the king would also have sat onstage, down center, facing the actors. Thus, his director's chair should have occupied the same position as the king's throne did. This observation led Strasberg from the analogy between Molière and himself into an extended analogy between the king and himself, between Louis and Lee, as he put it, as rulers of their respective domains. Once again, this potent little play had called forth a contrast between a real and an apparent master of the house.

George Dandin, or The Confounded Husband
(*George Dandin ou le mari confondu*, 1668)

George Dandin is a friendless figure who talks out his anguish in six soliloquies, dozens of asides, and the formal second person plural. But he does himself no good. This born loser, who lacks a good French *s* on the end of his first name, is Molière's nearest approach to an authentically tragic character, yet he lives in the farcical environment of one of the playwright's two most pessimistic works, the other being *Don Juan*. Dandin, whose name sounds like a reduction of "Don Juan," elicits a grudging pity similar to that which we feel for Arnolphe, Orgon, and Alceste; but whereas they finally undergo a liberation of sorts, a limited release, which may not have been at all what they wished for, Dandin remains trapped and, if anything, worse off than before. His plight is of his own making; he is cursed with a tragic flaw. Three times, once in each act, he has the chance to free himself from that plight, and three times, because of his flaw, he fails. Although he is all too aware of mistakes he has made in the past, he never comes to see the true reason for his failures; as a result, he stays wedded to a false wife and a false remedy, a belief that he must expose his wife's infidelities if he is to separate from her. In the last lines he gives way to despair: "Once you've married an evil wife like mine, the only way out is to throw yourself headfirst into deep water" (III, 8).

The monologue that opens *George Dandin* creates overwhelming first impressions of the central character and his torments. Dandin, middle-class and of yeoman or peasant stock, had pretensions to moving up the social scale when he married Angélique, the young daughter of a rural aristocrat. He doesn't understand his wife, while she shows no respect for him as a husband or for his money; nor has she provided a real home for him. Dandin is not a schemer but a whiner, who cannot seem to help himself out of his troubles. He now takes barren comfort in reviewing his grievances and citing his own example to warn others who might feel tempted to marry above their station, to teach them a lesson now that it's too late for him to teach anything to himself. Those others consist of the spectators, people outside the play. He is talking to thin air, creating figments of an hypothesis—to an audience in his head.

But he has not yet touched in this first speech on the circumstance that will vex him through the rest of the play: that Angélique is deceiving him. The news of this deception caps his misery after he stops talking, and it reaches him by way of a thick-witted peasant. This man, Lubin, a go-between hired by Angélique's admirer (in an imperfect reprise of Horace in *The School for Wives*), does not know Dandin to be the master of the house as he speaks of that master's churlishness, swears Dandin to secrecy, and reveals details of the lovers' affair and their plans for a rendezvous (I, 2).

The play's punning subtitle, *le Mari confondu*, tells us ahead of time that Dandin, even though alerted to the plans, will be both confused and confounded, perplexed and defeated, and it reinforces that first impression of him as a beleaguered husband. The action will do likewise as his parents-in-law, the Baron and Baroness de Sotenville, repeatedly bully him; as Angélique and her maidservant, Claudine, abuse him; and as Angélique's lover, Clitandre, threatens to put a sword into his belly. When he watches Lubin come out of his front door after delivering a love note to Angélique, we can appreciate that the opening sequence has characterized Dandin further by keeping him out of his own house, an image (this figure on that landscape) that the play will revert to a number of times and on which it will conclude.

The image comes from the earliest play attributed to Molière, *The Jealous Husband*, which supplied the dramatic situation for the third act of *George Dandin* and was in turn based on older French and Italian farces and other literary texts.[1] Dandin himself, like Harpagon and Arnolphe and Orgon, traces his lineage from Pantalone. The scenes are riddled with a variety of other comic and farcical elements: a relentlessly satirical tone; a beating; collisions and fumblings in the dark during the third act; the presence of four secondary buffoons (Lubin, the De Sotenvilles, and Dandin's manservant, Colin); dramatic irony, which is most telling in the meetings between Dandin and Lubin and between Angélique and her parents; and some of

---

1. Sources for the play are suggested in Joan Crow's "Reflections on *George Dandin*" in Howarth and Thomas, 3–12; the sources she mentions may include the epic *Roman de la Rose* and *L'Avare duppé ou l'homme de paille* (*The Duped Miser*, or *The Man of Straw*), written by Molière's contemporary Chappuzeau in 1663, five years before *George Dandin*. The play is also indebted to the *Decameron* (VIII, 4; VII, 8). Thomas Betterton's adaptation of the Molière, published thirty-eight years after *George Dandin*, was called *The Amorous Widow, or the Wanton Wife*.

the names.[2] In the original outdoor production, the play formed part of *Le grand Divertissement royal de Versailles* in which there were interludes of pastoral opera and ballet with music by Lully. Two shepherds who, after misunderstandings, win the shepherdesses they love, wait for Dandin at the end of the play and induce him to go out and celebrate with them. But the work came to the Palais-Royal theatre in Paris shorn of the opera and ballet. It has been played variously since as a straight drama, a comedy, a farce, and a tragifarce.

However it is interpreted, its comedy and farcical antics shade off into an experience that seems at times to be scarcely funny at all. We watch a coward being baited from all sides. Instead of fighting back, he asserts himself feebly or chooses to withdraw into mutterings of self-reproof, such as, "You wanted it, you wanted it, George Dandin, you wanted it. You asked for it and you got what you asked for." His father-in-law later drags out of him, phrase by phrase, a formal apology to Clitandre, ending with the words, "And I beg you to believe that I am your servant." Clitandre is himself embarrassed by the apology as Dandin lets out an unavailing cry from the heart: "You want to make me the servant of a man who wants to make me a cuckold?" (I, 6). After the painful apology has been delivered and Clitandre has left, De Sotenville carelessly twists the knife in his son-in-law's wounds as he assures him that he belongs to a family that will always back him up and protect him from affronts.

In only one scene does Dandin enjoy any respite from the humiliation, when he hopes to outwit his wife for once after she has had an outdoor tryst with Clitandre. It is night. He has bolted the door on Angélique and Claudine, sent Colin to fetch her parents as witnesses, and now taunts her from an upstairs window. But she is too clever for him. She threatens to commit suicide and let her parents know he is responsible. He hurries downstairs to check up on her, bothered less by her possible death than by the possible consequences for himself: "Could she be wicked enough to kill herself so as to get me hanged?" (III, 6). As he unbolts the door and steps outside, she and Claudine slip into the house and bolt the door on him. Her parents duly arrive and she claims that he has been out on one of his nightly benders (III, 7). Foiled again.

2. The name-play includes Sotenville ("fool in town"), Mme de Sotenville's maiden name of Prudoterie ("prudishness"), Angélique ("angelic"), Lubin (a "looby" or simpleton), and Dandin (an assonance for *dindon*, meaning "turkey" or "dupe"), a name borrowed from Rabelais and used later that same year by Racine in *The Litigants (Les Plaideurs)*.

The play, then, can and should be disquieting *and* amusing to sit through, and all the more riveting for that. But those first impressions are misleading. If husbands in the audience pay attention to his message and expect to draw a nugget of practical instruction out of this drama, it will not be what the first impressions convey, namely, that Dandin has been sorely put upon; that he has unwillingly become a catspaw of his wife and in-laws; that he is paying for having married snobbishly; or that one can accept at face value what he says has happened to him and to his marriage.

J. D. Hubert proposes that Dandin is "harmless" and that his downfall comes about as a result of his "lucidity"—his awareness of his fate and his determination to share his realization (Hubert, 190–98). But Dandin is not lucid *enough;* he goes off on the wrong tack and talks to himself in vain. The true cause continues to elude him. Lionel Gossman discerns a mixed motive in Dandin: he yearns to mount the social ladder and put himself on a par with his in-laws; but if he succeeded he would no longer be able to look up to them, as he wishes to do (Gossman, 147–63). But Dandin's main impulse in the action seems to be not so much to elevate himself as to shake free of Angélique, her parents, and their monetary dependence on him. He does let them intimidate him; he does obey their orders; but in the play's first sentence he regrets his marriage into a higher caste. The action thenceforward does not initiate his downfall, which began with his marriage; it merely continues and reaffirms it. Gossman says further that Dandin married Angélique "precisely in order that she should mediate between him and his gods," the De Sotenvilles. The play, however, never shows us Dandin seeking the company of his in-laws so that he can fraternize with them or exploit their impoverished nobility to enhance his standing in the community. Rather, he unwisely or unfortunately contracted the marriage with them, not with their daughter. To break out of the contract he believes he must make *them* see that it is unsatisfactory. But toward them he can act only as a representative of a socially inferior class, not as a contractual equal. He lacks the nerve to affirm his rights, while his in-laws behave as though the marriage were a stroke of condescension on their part: "There's a chasm between you and us," says his mother-in-law. "Remember who you are" (I, 4). They have compelled him to change his name officially to Monsieur de la Dandinière, the owner of an estate. They may familiarly call him "son-in-law," but he must address them as "Monsieur" and "Madame," and he must also refer to his wife as "Madame." "In the house of Prudoterie, thank heaven," cries Mme de Sotenville, "there hasn't been one woman for over three hundred years about whom anything can be said" (I, 4). Her mate's strongest claim to respect is that his father, "Monsieur Jean-Gilles de Sotenville, personally took part in the glorious siege of Montauban" (I, 5). In the final scene, to the incidental music of his meek protests, the parents insist that Dandin kneel to beg his wife's forgiveness. He does. He has again deferred to these ridiculous figures of fun infatuated with a sense of their importance, although he does burst out once that "without me, your affairs were, if I may say so, in pitiful shape. My money plugged up plenty of sizable holes" (I, 5).

In the production brought to the Unites States in the late 1960s by Roger Planchon's Théâtre de la Cité de Villeurbanne, the play became an illustration of a class struggle, which it almost is. Planchon's company, viewing Molière as a "realistic visionary," showed the yeoman class being debilitated by marrying indolent, provincial minor nobility (not unlike the families in Chekhov's drama), who are in turn fascinated by the *haut monde* of the court and the capital. This mildly Marxist interpretation, supported by the play, gave the Villeurbanne company, magnificent exponents of Molière that they were, excuses to compose lovingly detailed, Watteau-like stage pictures of seventeenth-century French rurality. However, the class differences support the personal differences in this play; they do not altogether govern them. Dandin is not a "worker," but a country cousin of Monsieur Jourdain, the Parisian bourgeois. He has the money to buy himself a wife who will know her manners, do him credit, and serve, he hopes, as a compliant housekeeper and ornament.

A company wishing to stage *George Dandin* and able to afford sufficient actors might want to have a chorus of rustics, an onstage audience, present throughout, particularly to listen and react to Dandin's soliloquies and asides. The listeners might become by turns sympathetic, mocking, attentive, skeptical, conspiratorial, and so on. This device could add some theatrical, even spectacular, suggestiveness to the play, which, like all of Molière's work, is full of references to performing and role playing, and would serve as a substitute for the *grand divertissement.* The idea struck me while I was reading reviews of the Planchon company's interpretation, which I did not see, and also some reviews of the production staged in 1912 by Max Reinhardt at the Deutsches Theater in Berlin in which Viktor Arnold played Dandin and during which the director interpolated pastoral scenes resembling those of Molière's production at Versailles. The reviews were less than explicit, as reviews sometimes are, in recording what actually happened onstage. It could be that either Planchon's troupe (Planchon himself did not direct the play, though he may well have had a hand in it) or Reinhardt's, or both of them, did feature an onstage audience, in which case the idea is secondhand or thirdhand, but still worthy of consideration, since Reinhardt and Planchon are capital artists for a director to claim as predecessors.

With or without this addition, actors and directors will need to explore the nature of the marriage, that curious alliance between the bourgeois Dandin and his lady-wife. One question they may want to ask is: What has he done to improve the marriage, to make it work? The answer is apparently nothing. We can only speculate on what the marriage was like before Clitandre's intervention. But the opening speech offers some clues and the rest of the play sustains them, especially the two big scenes between the embattled partners. In the first of them, Angélique protests about the place of wives and how her marriage came into being:

> ANGÉLIQUE . . . This tyranny of husbands is outrageous. They want us dead to all diversions, alive for them only. Very kind of them. I refuse to die so young.
>
> GEORGE DANDIN Is this how you honor your public promise?
>
> ANGÉLIQUE I didn't give it willingly. You snatched it from me. Did you ask me beforehand if I wanted to marry you? You spoke to my father and mother only. Properly speaking, they're the ones you married, and that's why it'll always make sense for you to go griping to them when you feel hard done by. I never advised you to marry me, much less consented. You took me without asking about my feelings, and I don't see now why I need submit to your wishes like a slave. (II, 2)

Up to this point, Angélique has fought back by furtively rebelling against her cloistered and disciplined upbringing. In this outburst, she signals that henceforward she will direct her rebellion at her husband. But her parents' expostulations still intimidate her more than Dandin's indignation does. In their second big scene, after Dandin has locked her out of doors, she pleads over and over that she will reform if only Dandin will let her in before her parents arrive:

> You have every right to feel resentful. . . . But after all, you might pardon misdemeanors like these because of my age, forgive the eagerness of a young woman who has seen nothing and only just begun to meet people, the sort of liberties one can easily fall into without meaning to do wrong. . . .
>
> I'm not trying to excuse myself. I did provoke you. . . . This one time

spare me the ordeal of those angry reproaches from my father and mother. If you can be generous and merciful, this kind gesture of yours will win me over. It will touch me to the heart and plant a feeling for you there that my parents' power and the obligations of marriage couldn't awaken. . . . Because of this gesture, I'll give up all flirtations. I'll form no attachments, except to you. Yes, I give you my word that from now on you'll find me a model wife. I'll show you so much affection, so much affection, that it will be all you want or need. (III, 4)

By way of response, Dandin calls her a crocodile who licks her victim before she sinks her teeth into him.

It may be worth noting here that Angélique is probably under twenty, although there is no way of being sure. ("If you don't mind, I'd like to make the most of the few happy years of youth I still have, to take advantage of this precious, carefree age, see something of fine society, and enjoy listening to pretty compliments" [III, 4].) Dandin, played by Moliere who was forty-seven at the time, is very likely in his mid-forties. The exact ages hardly matter, but one can assume a difference of twenty years or more that may sharpen the incompatibility between them as much as the class difference or the clash of personalities does—the personality differences could result, as a matter for speculation, in part from the disparity in their ages.[3] Molière does not mention how long they have been married, but they are childless, unlike their counterparts in *The Jealous Husband.*

Gossman characterizes Angélique as a hypocrite. When she is locked out in the last act, she "alters her tactics," he says, from striking "an attitude of noble truthfulness" to entreaties and then to blackmail. Therefore, "at no point in this scene is the audience intended to take pity on Angélique or to believe a word she says about her youth, her innocence, her willingness to love Dandin truly, etc. She is bluffing all the time" (Gossman, 159). When looked at retrospectively, her speeches do appear disingenuous. So does her suicide threat, for shortly after uttering it, she is urging Claudine to get ready to slip into the house as soon as Dandin emerges. Every spectator will recall that early in the play she threw off one of those Molière speeches that consist of double-entendres. In front of her parents and husband, she says to Clitandre: "I'd like to see what would happen if you really were in love with

3. There is a similar age differential of twenty or more years between Arnolphe and Agnès in *The School for Wives* and probably between Alceste and Célimène in *The Misanthrope,* since these were also roles taken by the author and his wife.

me. Pretend, will you, please? You'll find out what kind of person I am. I dare you. Make the attempt. Practice all the usual lovers' stratagems. Send me messages for the fun of it. Write me secret love notes. Declare your passion when my husband is absent or when I'm out of the house. Just try, and I promise you'll get the response you deserve" (I, 6).

But is she equally disingenuous in the later scene with her husband? When we examine that scene moment by moment, as it must be played, we are bound to ask what it would be like if the actress makes her mean every sentence she speaks while she speaks it. Peter Brook has argued that there is no reason to suspect that Goneril's speech in the first act of *King Lear*, when she declares her love for her father, is hypocritical unless one reads her character backward, imposing the later complications on the exposition.[4] The same sort of consideration applies here. Angélique need not be a rigidly consistent (static) personality; the play will become more interesting if she is not. Her pleas have more conviction if she speaks them from the heart, and more conviction still if they sway Dandin, instead of evoking instantly negative answers from him. (Only if she *succeeded in persuading Dandin* in this scene would there be a justification—dramatic irony—for an overtly hypocritical reading of her lines.) Whether Angélique would live up to her promises to turn over a new leaf is another question, one that goes beyond the reach of the action. But she does try to break the impasse. She admits her guilt; she talks of putting the marriage on a new footing; and our final impressions of the play ought not to weaken the force of her concessions, any more than our first impressions should be allowed to govern our interpretation of Dandin's plight.

In the course of this same confrontation, Dandin faces an opportunity. He might still make something of his marriage, even salvage it. The play steers itself inexorably toward his decision—his, not hers. He may (and I think, should) contemplate this opportunity and hesitate over it. But caught up in self-pity and already reveling in his revenge to come, he is, unfortunately for him, no forgiving Sir Peter Teazle. He snubs her. He has determined to prove himself a cuckold in public, as the last line of act II tells us with its yearning for a psychic crucifixion: "Oh, God help me! Grant me the blessing of letting others see how dishonored I am!" He never tried to win Angélique; he wished only to own her. And he is not about to try winning her now.

Was she worth winning in the first place? As a woman, that is, and not simply for her rank or for Dandin's convenience in finding a wife-cum-

4. Peter Brook, *The Empty Space* (New York: Atheneum, 1968), 13–14.

housekeeper? Here we may take into account the motives of Clitandre, who is smitten with her, as Dandin apparently never was. In order to woo her, Clitandre has left the court and come to live in a country backwater. We might take a skeptical view of this *"damoiseau,"* as Dandin calls him, and infer that he is wooing her because she is married; that it suits him if she stays safely married and unattainable; but if we do we read something of Dandin into Clitandre's role. Angélique is attractive enough, seductive enough, to Clitandre, to have lured him away from his familiar haunts and made him take risks. He might even, with some reason, imagine he is rescuing her. Dandin, by contrast, takes no risks beyond peeking through a keyhole when he learns she is entertaining her lover at home. He doesn't think about his wife as a young woman being stifled by him and his way of life, following the former stifling by her parents. He doesn't consider that he was foisted on her. She has dishonored him; he must have justice, meaning the chance to triumph over her. He comes downstairs to investigate not for fear that she may have injured or killed herself but for fear that she has incriminated him out of spite.

Dandin is incapable of loving her, perhaps incapable of loving anybody. Lubin and his subplot seem to have been tucked into the play not only to keep Dandin informed of what is going on (and so aggravating his resentment) but also to include a figure who *is* able to offer a woman love, however cloddishly. When he proposes to Claudine, the *suivante,* Molière gives them the following exchange:

CLAUDINE Maybe you'll be jealous like the master.

LUBIN Not me.

CLAUDINE I hate possessive husbands. I want mine to be so trusting and so sure of my love that he wouldn't have a single doubt if he saw me surrounded by thirty men.

LUBIN That's how I'll be.

CLAUDINE It's dumb to distrust a wife and torment her. Doesn't do any good. It gives her naughty ideas. Husbands who make trouble like that have themselves to thank for what they turn into.

LUBIN Yes, I'll give you your freedom, let you do anything you like.

CLAUDINE That's it, you must, then you won't be deceived. When a husband gives us our own way we don't take any more freedom than we should. It's like having someone who opens his purse to us and says, "Help yourself." We'll treat him fair and square and be satisfied with what's reasonable. But the ones who drive us crazy with their meanness and nasty, suspicious ideas—we do our best to keep them worried. We don't show them any mercy.

LUBIN Listen, I'll be the type who opens his purse. All you have to do is marry me. Isn't that simple? (II, 1)

In Claudine's lines, we hear echoes of Ariste's and Lisette's from *The School for Husbands.* We cannot know whether Claudine is being sincere or whether she will ever accept Lubin. But we can have no doubt that he is genuinely smitten with her. In the darkness of the third act, he even grabs for her hand—finding Dandin's by mistake and fervently kissing it.

Dandin, his opposite number, offers not one word or gesture of affection, or even kindness, to his wife. Intent on challenging her timidly, he proves only that he is not her equal in wit, any more than in rank. Like the night setting of the third act, Dandin is in the dark. He will return to a cold bed—he talks of drowning himself, but how can we take him seriously?—as the night and the play draw to an end and daylight breaks in the sky, a mocking dawn, as in Ibsen's *Ghosts,* and the play has come full circle, almost. His mistake was not that he married Angélique but that he failed to consummate the marriage emotionally. Therein lies his tragic flaw, which is not lucidity but blindness to his defects, for he is no more enlightened now than he was at the beginning about what he did to ruin two lives. Bernard Shaw's comment to the effect that the tragedy of women like Hedda Gabler is that they do *not* commit suicide applies even more aptly to a meek grumbler like George Dandin. Diving head first into a river, as he proposes, is hardly a real prospect for him but more like a first-rate metaphor for that cold bed (and cold life). He will surely live on to continue bewailing his misery in lines like "The loser can't laugh" *(Marchand qui perd ne peut rire* [II,7]), which make it all the more difficult to laugh at him, and which leave an audience hanging between amusement and grudging compassion.

The Flying Doctor, 1982. American Repertory Theatre, Cambridge, MA. Artistic director: Robert Brustein. Translator: Albert Bermel. Director: Andrei Serban. Set designer: Michael H. Yeargan. Costume designer: Dunya Ramicova. Lighting designer: James H. Gage. Thomas Derrah *(left)* as Sganarelle; Tony Shalhoub as Valère. Photograph by Richard Feldman.

Sganarelle, or The Imaginary Cuckold, 1978. Yale Repertory Theatre, New Haven, CT. Artistic director: Robert Brustein. Translator: Albert Bermel. Director Andrei Serban. Set designer: Michael H. Yeargan. Costume designer: Dunya Ramicova. Lighting designer: James H. Gage. Michael Gross *(foreground)* as Sganarelle; *background, left to right:* Patrizia Norcia, William Converse-Robert, Joyce Fideor. Photograph by Eugene Cook.

The Forced Marriage, 1981. American Repertory Theatre, Cambridge, MA. Artistic director: Robert Brustein. Translator: Albert Bermel. Director: Andrei Serban. Set designer: Michael H. Yeargan. Costume designer: Dunya Ramicova. Lighting designer: James H. Gage. Cherry Jones as Dorimène; Jeremy Geidt as Sganarelle. Photograph by Richard Feldman.

The Doctor in Spite of Himself, "a dumb show," 1980. American Repertory Theatre, Cambridge, MA. Artistic director: Robert Brustein. Adapted and directed by Andrei Serban (and the cast). Set designer: Michael H. Yeargan. Costume designer: Dunya Ramicova. Lighting designer: James H. Gage. Choral direction by Patrizia Norcia. Jonathan Marks *(third from right)* as Sganarelle. Photograph by Richard Feldman.

Malpractice, or Love's the Best Doctor, 1984. Dell'Arte Players, Blue Lake, CA. Artistic directors: Michael Fields, Donald Forrest, Joan Schirle. "Inspired by the comedies of Molière" and adapted by Michael Fields, Donald Forrest, Michele Linfante, and Jael Weisman. Director: Jael Weisman. Set designer: Andy Stacklin. Costume and wig designer: Mimi Mace. Lighting designer: Michael Foster. *Left to right:* Michael Fields as Dr. Diafoirus, Joan Mankin as Dr. Patin, Donald Forrest as Dr. Currant. Photograph by Richard Duning.

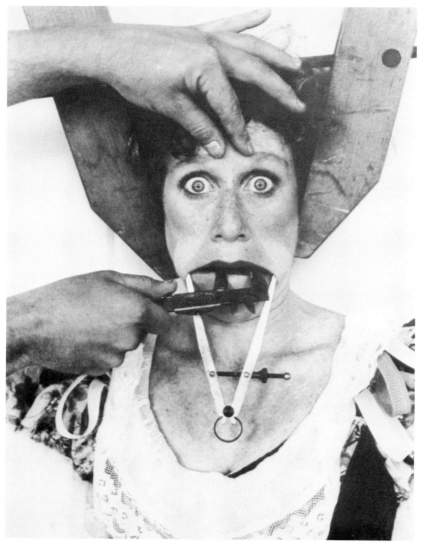

Malpractice, or Love's the Best Doctor, 1984. Dell'Arte Players, Blue Lake, CA. Artistic directors: Michael Fields, Donald Forrest, Joan Schirle. "Inspired by the comedies of Molière" and adapted by Michael Fields, Donald Forrest, Michele Linfante, and Jael Weisman. Director: Jael Weisman. Set designer: Andy Stacklin. Costume and wig designer: Mimi Mace. Lighting designer: Michael Forrest. Joan Mankin as Lucinde. Photograph by Richard Duning.

The Miser, 1988. The New Vic Supper Theatre, Flint, MI. Artistic director: Patricia E. Victor. Translator: Albert Bermel. Director: Patricia Victor. Set designer: Peter Bathum. Costume designers: Barbara Bautell and Patricia Victor. Original music by Attila Farkas. Ron Carter as Harpagon. Photograph by William Mackenzie, Jr.

The Miser, 1982. The Old Globe Theatre, San Diego, CA. Artistic director: Jack O'Brien. Adapted by Miles Malleson. Directed by Joseph Hardy. Scenic and costume designer: Steven Rubin. Lighting designer: Kent Dorsey. Composer: Conrad Susa. Sound designer: Roger Gans. *Left to right:* Paxton Whitehead as Harpagon; Tom Lacy as Master Jacques; John Tucky as the Commissioner; Gregg Bartell as the Clerk. Photograph by Robert Burroughs.

The Miser, 1987–88. Milwaukee Repertory Theater. Artistic director: John Dillon. Translator: Sara O'Connor. Director: Kenneth Albers. Set designer: Michael Miller. Costume designer: Charles Berliner. Lighting designer: Robert Peterson. Steven J. Gefroh *(left)* as Valère; David Hurst as Harpagon. Photograph by Tom Bamberger.

The Miser, 1987. Grace Repertory Theatre, New York City. Artistic Directors: Michele Harper, Rod McLucas. Translator: Albert Bermel. Director: Daniel Wilson. Set designer: William Engel. Costume designer: Sue Jane Stoker. Lighting designer: Paul Engel. Kevin O'Connor as Harpagon; Michele Harper as Frosine. Photograph by Joseph Clementi.

The Miser, 1987. London, England. Churchill Theatre and Yvonne Arnaud Theatre. Artistic director: Peter Coe. Translator: Albert Bermel. Director: Peter Coe. "Set dressings" by Jacqueline Pilfold. Costume designer: Annette Sharville. Lighting designer: Spike Gaden. Ron Moody as Harpagon. *Upper level:* Debbie Arnold as Élise; Collin Johnson as Valère. Photograph by Reg Wilson.

The Miser, American Conservatory Theatre, San Francisco, CA. Artistic director: Edward Hastings. Director: Allen Fletcher. Elizabeth Huddle as Frosine; Ronald Boussom as La Flèche. Photograph by William Ganslen. *(Other information not available.)*

Tartuffe, 1987. Portland Stage Company, Portland, ME. Artistic director, Barbara Rosoff. Translator: Donald M. Frame. Director: Michael Engler. Scenic designer: Christopher Barecca. Costume designer: Candice Donnelly. Lighting designer: Don Holder. Sound by Studio 3. Patrick Kerr as Tartuffe; Priscilla Shanks as Elmire. Photograph by Jenny Tuemmler.

Tartuffe, 1988. McCarter Theatre, Princeton, NJ. Artistic director: Nagle Jackson.
Translator: Richard Wilbur. Set designer: Robert Perdziola. Costumer designer:
Elizabeth Covey. Lighting designer: Phil Monat. Richard Risso as Tartuffe;
Kimberly King as Elmire. Photograph by Randall Hagadorn.

Tartuffe, 1985. Arena Stage, Washington, DC. Artistic director: Zelda Fichandler.
Translator: Richard Wilbur. Director: Lucian Pintilié. Set and costume designers:
Radu and Miruan Boruzescu. Harris Yulin *(left)* as Tartuffe; Harriet Harris as
Elmire; Peter Francis-James as Laurent. Photograph by Joan Marcus.

Tartuffe, 1985. Arena Stage, Washington, DC. Artistic director: Zelda Fichandler.
Translator: Richard Wilbur. Director: Lucian Pintilié. Set and costume designers:
Radu and Miruan Boruzescu. Richard Bauer as Orgon; Harriet Harris as Elmire.
Photograph by Joan Marcus.

Tartuffe, 1986. Los Angeles Theatre Center. Artistic director: Bill Bushnell. Translator: Richard Wilbur. Director: Robert W. Goldsby. Set designer: Karl Eigsti. Costume designer: Nicole Morin. Lighting designer: Toshiro Ogawa. *Left to right:* Jessica Walter as Elmire; Tom Rosqui as Orgon; Ron Leibman as Tartuffe. Photograph by Chris Gulker.

The Imaginary Invalid, 1983. Arena Stage, Washington, DC. Translator: John Wood. Director: Garland Wright. Set designer: John Arnone. Costume designer: Ann Hould-Ward. Lighting designer: Hugh Lester. *Left to right:* Christine Moore as Toinette; Richard Bauer as Argan; Marilyn Caskey as Angélique. Photograph by Joan Marcus.

The Learned Ladies, 1977. Williamstown Theatre Festival. Artistic director: Nikos Psacharopoulos. Translator: Richard Wilbur. Director: Norman Ayrton. Set designer: Hugh Landwehr. Costume designer: Rita B. Watson. Lighting designer: Roger Meeker. Elizabeth Parrish *(center)* as Philaminte, queen of the salon. Photograph by Jan A. Wein.

Scapin, 1984. Theatre of the Open Eye, New York City. Artistic director, adapter, and director: Amie Brockway. Set and lighting designer: Adrienne J. Brockway. Costume designer: David Mickelsen. Graeme Malcolm as Scapin. Photograph by Ken Howard.

Scapin, 1984. Theatre of the Open Eye. Artistic director, adapter, and director: Amie Brockway. Set and lighting designer: Adrienne J. Brockway. Costume designer: David Mickelsen. Rita Nachtman as Zerbinetta; Richard Henson as Géronte. Photograph by Ken Howard.

Don Juan, 1984. Denver Center Theatre Company. Artistic director: Donovan Marley. Translator: Christopher Hampton. Director: Garland Wright. Set designer: Douglas O. Stein. Costume designer: Ann Hould-Ward. Lighting designer: Scott Pinkney. Michael Winters as Sganarelle; Byron Jennings as Don Juan. Photograph by Nicholas de Sciose.

The Misanthrope, 1987. The Guthrie Theater, Minneapolis, MN. Artistic director: Garland Wright. Translator: Richard Wilbur. Director: Garland Wright. Set designer: Joel Fontaine. Costume designer: Jack Edwards. Lighting designer: Peter Maradudin. *Left:* Richard S. Iglewski as Acaste; *center:* Caroline Lagerfelt as Célimène and Richard Hicks as Clitandre. Photograph by Joe Giannetti.

The Misanthrope, American Conservatory Theatre, San Francisco, CA. *Left to right:* Carol Mayo Jenkins as Éliante; John Schuck as Philinte; Mark Bramhall as Acaste; Herman Poppe as Oronte; Michael Learned as Arsinoé; Mark Schell as Alceste. Photograph by J. M. Kucera. *(Other information not available.)*

The Misanthrope, American Conservatory Theatre, San Francisco, CA. Kitty Winn as Célimène; Michael Learned as Arsinoé. Photograph by J.M. Kucera. *(Other information not available.)*

The Miser
(*L'Avare,* 1668)

The characters in *The Miser* consist almost entirely of matching and contrasting pairs. We find two wealthy fathers, each a parent of a grown-up son and daughter: Harpagon, the central figure, one of the most unsparing and unspared misers in literature, and bountiful Anselme, who arrives on the scene late but in time to effect the climactic reconciliation; their respective daughters: Élise, Molière's most defiant *jeune première,* and Mariane, his most bashful one; the sons: Cléante the prodigal and Valère the astute; Maître Jacques, Harpagon's inexplicably loyal but slow-witted servant, and La Flèche, his son's moderately loyal and not altogether honest valet. To complicate the pattern, there are also cross-pairings: between two servants, Maître Jacques and Valère, and between Harpagon, the unloving father-widower, and Frosine, a matchmaker he has commissioned, who shows a motherly solicitude for his children.

This typically neoclassical balance sets up an arrangement of doubles, echoes, and dramatic interdependence, much as in other plays by Molière. As a further complication, the pairings overlay the author's specialized solo turns for his actors and himself. He has, however, integrated these so that his main plot and subplots fertilize one another. That main plot is itself a triple one. Harpagon feels fearful over a large payment he has received in gold coin and locked into a strongbox; he has endeavored to safeguard it by burying it in his garden; when it is stolen he panics. At the same time, he has unknowingly involved himself in a rivalry with his son over marrying Mariane. He has also involved Anselme in an unknowing rivalry with *his* son over marrying Élise, Harpagon's daughter.

This multiple main plot links up with four subplots. Each of them arises, directly or indirectly, from Harpagon's avarice. First, he gives his children such a measly allowance that his son is forced to seek a loan at an outrageous rate of interest from a lender who turns out to be his father. Second, Harpagon's suspicions and affronts incense the valet, La Flèche, who, on discovering the strongbox, vengefully hides it and so justifies Harpagon's suspicions of him, which at first seemed unjustified. Third, Frosine, to whom Harpagon will not advance any payment for her services, switches those services over to the two young pairs of lovers—also out of revenge. Fourth, Valère, the highborn youth who has taken on a job as steward of Harpagon's household, ingratiates himself with his master by protecting expenses so diligently that he provokes a squabble with Maître Jacques who—revenge again—falsely accuses him of having stolen the strongbox. Harpagon is thus the root and trunk of the play, as well as the feeder for most of its branches. But the tree draws sustenance from those branches. This is not the one-character comedy with interruptions from secondary characters that sometimes finds its way onto stages.

As one critic has shown, the play itself consists of "two series of mutually exclusive concepts and attitudes" (Hubert, 210), love and money. The author keeps borrowing financial words and terms, such as "debt" and "obligation," for segments of the dialogue that deal with nonfinancial matters. While this is true, such terms crop up in most people's everyday conversation: I used the words "deal with"—but not in a business sense—in the preceding sentence. And the number of plays that oppose loving characters to money-loving characters is uncountable. The opposition of love and money no more sets this play apart than it does *The Merchant of Venice* or *Volpone* or *All My Sons* or *A New Way to Pay Old Debts* or, in truth, almost any one of Molière's plays. *Don Juan,* for example, a play that dramatizes varieties of love, ends on the line, "My pay! My pay!" But the observation is well taken because it brings out the forcefulness of Harpagon in imposing his vocabulary, as well as his will, on the figures around him.

Among the dozen or so of Molière's central characters who conduct themselves with bizarre abandon, Harpagon is the most extreme—so morally degenerate at the age of sixty, so apparently devoid of warmth and kindness that he trusts nobody, least of all his children, as an early scene confirms, when he believes they have overheard him talking to himself about the strongbox and calls them his enemies. Almost everybody who has dealings with him wishes him out of the way. He is more misanthropic than Alceste, more callous than Don Juan, meaner than George Dandin, and self-devoted beyond the aspirations of Arnolphe. Harpagon is often said to be the most rigid, the most blinkered of Molière's creations. His passion for money can sweep him beyond the outer boundaries of self-control and into a psychotic condition. He breaks off conversations to run out into the garden and check on his strongbox. He assails La Flèche for trying to rob him and plumbs the man's pants pockets. He speaks endearingly to his strongbox, which is his beloved, and, in his tremors over possibly losing it, joins that line of Molière men who fear being cuckolded above all else. In the scene (IV, 7) in which he finds that the box has gone from its hiding place, one of the most celebrated soliloquies in the French theatre, he quarrels with his own arm, undergoes a mock death and rebirth, threatens to hang everybody in sight (and out of sight), himself included, and breaks out of the play to harangue the audience, as though he were too outrageous, too big, too monomaniacal for the stage to contain. Thus, Ramon Fernandez can call the play "a comedy unadulterated, a caricature that is nothing but caricature," and say of its antihero, "Cut off from his kind, deaf, blind, overwhelmed under his own fury, bombarding the world and unfailingly struck by every missile he launches, the comic protagonist in this play ends in insanity. Harpagon is a madman . . . he goes through the whole play in a state of hallucination" (Fernandez, 172–73). Arnolphe, we may recall, has also been called mad. Madness "through the whole play" would be too easy and flat an acting chore.

Of Harpagon's two dominant passions in the play, we accept the miserliness as a given, the play's prime motive. But his other passion, to take the young and timid Mariane for a wife, makes us wonder. Competition between a father and son for a bride predates the Italian comedy; audiences had loved it for centuries before Molière. But why would the playwright make Harpagon, who shows himself so eager to unload his daughter and son for gain, want to take on another mouth to feed, another body to clothe, another financial drain for the household, another money leak? He expects Mariane to bring a dowry with her, and passes along a message that her impoverished mother must strain her resources, "even bleed a little," to squeeze out the necessary sum. But if his objectives were strictly mercenary, wouldn't he look for a partner who did not live in poverty and was not young enough to be his grandchild? We might attribute his desire for Mariane to a surge of sexagenarian sexuality—she must be uncommonly good-looking, for Harpagon has resolved to have her after merely catching glimpses of her at her window. But his calculating nature encourages us to look further into what is, for him, a perverse motive.

When a character seems to behave "out of character," and we attempt to cope with the anomaly—so as to do justice to it onstage, not to explain it away—one useful source of enlightenment will be the interplay with other characters, already alluded to. We go beyond a study of that character as an isolated or self-contained personality, which no role or person but a lifelong hermit ever is, and examine the effects he has on others and theirs on him.

To begin with, Harpagon does not like, much less admire, his children. In insisting that Élise marry Anselme, a much older man whom she has not even met, he may be trying to justify his own marriage to a much younger woman, but he also wants to punish Élise by playing master of the house; and as she spiritedly resists him, his resolve tightens. In his squinted and spiteful view, and in one of the play's more impudently comic scenes (I, 5), he affirms that Anselme's superlative virtue and recommendation as a husband are that he is rich and does not ask for a dowry. Élise brings out his possessiveness with people, as distinct from his financial possessiveness.

As for Cléante, he has become a gambler, possibly by way of filial rebellion. Harpagon raises no objections to Cléante's gaming habits (so long as he does not lose), only to seeing the winnings go on clothes instead of being tucked away into investments. For this young wastrel, Harpagon has decreed another aged partner; her virtue is the opposite of Anselme's: she accompanies a generous dowry. Molière may intend us to assume that Harpagon's disgust at his son's elaborate garb is stimulated by certain youthful extravagances of his own, and that, like the old Argante or Géronte in *Scapin*, he forswears his earlier self by attacking in his son the very "sins" he himself once committed. But it is not easy to imagine a Harpagon of twenty who is much different from the Harpagon forty years further along in this play. So definitively has his author established him that he seems to have been born old and tightfisted and to have grown as chary of the younger generation as is Ibsen's master builder, Solness.[1] At one point, entering unexpectedly, he sees his son kissing Mariane's hand. Since Cléante had, shortly before this, purported to object to his stepmother-to-be, Harpagon decides to tease his son by offering to give up Mariane on the grounds that she may be too young for him and to let Cléante marry her instead. He speaks with such deceptive sincerity that, reading or seeing the play for the first time, one could hardly guess at his guile; but it takes this encounter with Cléante to reveal his skill as an actor.

His distrust does not extend to the other young brother and sister in the play, who learn that they are siblings only in the last act. Both win Harpagon's favor, for the simple reason that neither openly opposes him. Mariane is passive almost to the point of inertia. Although Cléante attracts her, she will not go against what she believes to be her mother's wishes, that she accept Harpagon, even after she has seen him for the first time and shivered at the

---

1. In *A Christmas Carol*, Dickens would later create an unconvincing transition when he flashed back to a young Scrooge as yet unspoiled by ambition and disappointment. But Dickens meant to reform Scrooge at the end of his story, and the flashback is a prefiguring of that reform. Molière has no intention of reforming Harpagon.

prospect of marrying him. Meeting her, he waxes poetic—a new mood for him—calling her the brightest star in the land of stars. By way of contrast to Mariane, Valère is an active plotter. Since losing his parents and sister in one of those shipwrecks that have conveniently divided families in the drama back to the days of Plautus, and perhaps before, he has searched all over Europe for them; saved Élise from drowning (bobbed miraculously to the water's surface, like a god, a Triton); won her devotion; and wormed his way into her father's confidence and the highest level of his employ by continually flattering him. At the start of the opening scene, he is swearing fidelity to Élise; by the end of that scene she has reason to doubt that sincerity when Valère embarks on a mischievous monologue about flattery as a ticket to success in handling intransigent people. He may even have already gone farther with Élise than promising to marry her.[2] But he feels—or suggests— that they cannot wed until he has recovered his family, his rank, and his fortune, after which he will be able to tell her father that he loves her and claim her honorably. Before long, however, Harpagon will threaten to put a stop to their marriage (without yet knowing about it) by introducing the strange Anselme who requires no dowry, and Valère will have to come up with a stronger expedient than ladling out further doses of flattery.

As yet, Harpagon has no notion that his daughter and steward are in love; therefore, Valère's disinclination to approach him on that score while still a servant and a poor man is a wise tactic, for to Harpagon a marriage within his family is another business deal and must promise a profit, notwithstanding his own wealth and his children's inheritance from their mother after they reach their majority. Until he learns of Valère's designs on his daughter, Harpagon exults in the young man's devotion to his own principle of exorbitant thrift. He would even like to have carved on his mantelpiece a motto quoted by Valère—"We must eat to live, not live to eat." His satisfaction with Valère, an employee and a stranger, points up his dissatisfaction with his son and daughter, and is third only to his attachments for Mariane and his

2. More than one critic has suggested that Élise and Valère have had sex before the play's action opens (see, e.g., Mander, 147.) If so, there is a analogy here between Élise and the pregnant daughter of Euclio in Plautus' *The Pot of Gold (Aulularia)*, which is the basis for much of Molière's play. Whether or not the author actually is implying premarital sex, that first scene in which Élise pleads that she does not know whether she can trust Valère's love acquires an added urgency, becomes more serious than a lovers' tiff, if the actors assume that she has indeed given herself to him and that his having saved her from drowning is a discreet sexual allusion.

strongbox, which becomes an invisible character in the action: one might say, the newest member of his family, his "infant fortune."

A man who does not give love, Harpagon does not expect to receive it. But he shares with certain other older men in Molière who plan to take a young wife (most notably Sganarelle in *The Forced Marriage* and Arnolphe in *The School for Wives*) the fear of young rivals. His misgivings come out during his interview with Frosine (II, 5), when he remarks that "a man of my age may not be to [Mariane's] taste." Frosine, lying shamelessly with the conviction that a natural swindler like Harpagon must be a natural mark, assures him that Mariane hates young men; she will not so much as look at anyone who is less than sixty and he must wear spectacles—she has already broken off one match with a callow fifty-six-year-old.

Later, planning to divert Harpagon's fondness away from Mariane so that his son can marry her, Frosine announces that she will produce a "lady of quality" who goes under the title of a marquise or vicomtesse, has a ready command of a hundred thousand crowns plus real estate, and professes to be wildly in love with the old man. This scheme never comes to anything.[3] Why, then, did Molière leave the speech intact? Carelessness? Possibly.

But then, most of the other plans in the play do not come to anything, either. Harpagon has picked marriage partners for his children and himself. Cléante has attempted to borrow money and Harpagon to lend it. Harpagon has buried his strongbox for safekeeping. Each of these plans goes awry. Each is defeated by the supervention of chance. Or synchronicity. Anselme, the miser's ideal choice for his daughter, turns up only to find out that he is now reunited with his lost children, thereby enabling them to choose their own spouses, so that Mariane can drop Harpagon in favor of his son and Valère can finally claim Élise—his father supplying the dowry for Harpagon. Harpagon and his son meet by accident before they can complete the loan. Only La Flèche succeeds in his plan: to unearth the strongbox. If *The Miser* were a comedy, the remaining plans would either take effect or be defeated because of the superiority of rival characters, for comedy relies as a rule on the deployment of the characters' will power, whereas fate in the form of coincidence, or synchronicity, the imposition of the *author's* will power, signals that a funny play is a farce. (If such a play is not funny, it is a tragedy, not necessarily a good one.) Because of this distinction, *The Miser* belongs,

---

3. The central character's love for a "lady of quality" does reappear, slightly modified, in *The Bourgeois Gentleman,* when Monsieur Jourdain falls in love with the comtesse Dorimène.

technically speaking, to one genre and a play like *The Bourgeois Gentleman* to another. Will the style of acting be affected? Probably not much, if at all. But a director who means to do justice to the play should keep in mind that the forces of fate loom over the action.

It would be misleading, if not patently false, to suggest that *The Miser* is farcical throughout. But the resolutions of the scenes are, and so is the overall action. While the performing thus calls for the extravagances and extremities of farce at certain critical points, the production as a whole calls for a broad, artificial style of directing that can encompass, on the one side, scenes such as Harpagon's insane, twitching monologue, which is addressed in part to the audience, and the duel between Valère and Maître Jacques and, on the other side, the impassioned opening colloquies between Élise and Valère and the recognition trio enacted by Anselme and his rediscovered children. The play constantly slips (and occasionally flips) from one mode to the other. Such artificiality runs deeper than mere stage aping of seventeenth-century manners, although it may well keep them in mind.

The direction also needs to take account of switches in personality, some of them abrupt, on the part of the secondary characters, most of whom are nearly as unstable as Harpagon is. Frosine, for example, lurches in her big scene from boosting Harpagon's confidence in his eligibility as a husband and in Mariane's eligibility as a husbandly wife to heartfelt entreaties as she tries to get him to advance expenses for an unexplained lawsuit. After her pleas are answered by nothing more substantial than Harpagon's frowns, she turns suddenly bitter and vindictive (II, 5). Valère, in introducing himself to the audience (I, 1), goes from protestations that are meant to reassure Élise of how sincerely he loves her to bragging of his lack of scruples when he flatters dogmatic souls like Harpagon. Cléante, who indulges himself by spending wildly beyond his means on his dress and who longs to give money to Mariane and her mother to help them in their poverty, thereby giving us the impression of a free spirit, can behave gruffly, at times despotically, toward his servant (II, 1). Even Mariane, that young beauty who conforms to a pattern of timidity, can turn as cunning as George Dandin's wife, Angélique, when she speaks to Cléante in front of his father in a run of double-entendres, seeming to repel him as she stealthily proclaims her love: "If you are repelled to have me as your stepmother, I am probably no less repelled to find you as my stepson" (III, 7).

But the most contradictory figure is Maître Jacques who admires his boss but tactlessly recites a long list of Harpagon's faults to his face (III, 1) and receives a beating for his candor; he resolves to tell lies from then on, but

the lies almost get him hanged. Harpagon's economy with his household help
has conferred two jobs on Maître Jacques: he is the miser's coachman and
chef, so that one can imagine him entering the kitchen to prepare a meal
while still smelling of the stable. He serves as the replacement for the pert
maidservant who appears in a number of Molière's other plays. He resents
Valère for being insincerely servile, his own servility having sprung from
genuine affection for his master, exceeded only by his affection for the aged,
unshod, underfed horses in his charge.

These and other oscillations in the personalities mean that the playwright
keeps us uncertain about who and what these characters really are and
what they may become. They allow generously for a variety of colorings in
interpretation. At the same time, they threaten the very notion of dramatic
character as a given quantity, even though Molière is often assumed, more
than most other celebrated authors, to have created "types." In the television
version directed by Michael Simpson and starring Nigel Hawthorne as Harpagon and Janet Suzman as Frosine, the characters, played by a generally
talented cast, had plausible motives throughout, made plain by cross-cutting;
by meaningful glances, bits of stage business and "shticks" (crocheting,
eating, changing chair positions); and by including in the action events from
the offstage story. These directing dynamics brought the farce tidily into line
with modern melodramatic realism, where it does not belong, at the same
time as they sacrificed the theatrical formality—the almost balletic duets,
trios, and quartets that proclaim its artificial nature.

And so we return to the conundrum of why Harpagon intends to marry
again.[4] His first marriage must have taken place relatively late, since he is,
by inference, some forty years older than his children. Or he might have
delayed becoming a parent until well after his marriage, an unlikely assumption about a period long before the discovery of inexpensive contraception.
I conclude that he wants Mariane to beget new children for him. He means
to expel his "enemies," Élise and Cléante, from his will. Like Orgon with his
passion to adopt Tartuffe, Harpagon regards his children as mistakes. When
he hears from Élise that Valère saved her life he answers, "Better if he'd let
you drown" (V, 4). There is no legal way he can rectify the mistakes; but he

4. One of Harpagon's dramatic forebears, the Venetian merchant Pantalone, wishes
in the different scenarios either to marry off his daughter to a crony of his own age
or else to marry a much younger woman himself, and so finds himself in competition
with one of her contemporaries. As a far more complex figure than any Pantalone
"mask," Harpagon means to do both.

can replace the children as heirs with the aid of a healthy young wife. (And as a Ph. D. candidate, Paul Somerville, has suggested to me, Mariane will be useful around the house as an unpaid servant.)

This supposition about Harpagon's desiring a new child or brood can be deduced but not conclusively proved. Our knowledge of Harpagon does not extend beyond what we see of him and hear from him in the action. He exists only in the present. The author provides no past, no background. Is he, for instance, a self-made man, or did he inherit wealth? Was he deprived in his youth? Or was he, like his son, a prodigal who paid, or failed to pay, his way by gambling, since gambling and investment are different sides of the same coin? If so, did he turn avaricious later, much as young libertines may decline into old guardians of public morality? What about his late wife? How did she influence him and the children? And what about the legacy Cléante says she left her children? How did her death affect him, if at all? A few—but not many—of Molière's plays supply earlier circumstances in a character's life that are useful to directors of the Stanislavsky stripe. Monsieur Jourdain's bourgeois origins and George Dandin's peasant upbringing help to account for the cheerful snobbery of the one and the regretful snobbery of the other. But Harpagon exists in the isolated pocket of time that represents the duration of the play. If his psychological origins are misted over, his literary origins have been carefully tracked down: Plautus' *The Pot of Gold,* the commedia dell'arte, the more intellectual commedia erudita, at least two plays by older seventeenth-century French playwrights,[5] and Molière's imagination.

The last agency has wrought notable changes in its sources, particularly in Euclio, the miser created by Plautus. A poor man on whom the pot of gold has been bestowed by his household god, Euclio cannot use it to allay his poverty, for he fears that if he breaks open the cache of wealth he will become the prey of thieves and prying neighbors. At the same time, he is terrified of losing it or having it stolen in its entirety. In the end, he gives it away to his daughter and her husband-to-be, gasping with relief at having escaped from the torment of being its futile guardian. Harpagon, though, would never dream of relinquishing his strongbox. A wealthy bourgeois, he acts out not only the conflict between love and money but also the frantic love of his class *for* money. He finally lets himself be blackmailed into consenting to the marriages his son and daughter wish for and into giving up his designs on

5. The playwrights in question are Chappuzeau and Boisrobert. For more information on these literary debts, see Philip A. Wadsworth, "From the Commedia Erudita to Molière," in Johnson, Neumann, and Trail, 451–52.

Mariane in order to regain the box, his darling, as a substitute for the new child or children he may have hoped for.

But unlike Euclio, he does not reform. As a structural close, the last act of *The Miser* amounts to a happy ending ordained by a fate that seems to have nullified much of the play's plaited strands of intrigue. Élise and Cléante are coupled with Valère and Mariane; the last two have found each other and their father again. Anselme will not remarry, for his wife is still alive. Harpagon, although denied Mariane, rejoices in the hope of again seeing his "dear strongbox." Yet, a somber note sounds amid the jubilation, precisely because Harpagon has unconventionally failed to reform; nor has he suffered any explicit punishment for his greed and tyranny.

Because of its flouting of poetic justice, the ending ought not to satisfy its audiences, and the play did experience a cool reception at first. Perhaps a hint in the opening scene of premarital sex was picked up by the public and offended them. Perhaps Harpagon's going unpunished and not even being forced to change his ways came in for disapproval. A third reason, cited by historians to explain the play's failure to appeal to intellectual spectators and readers, is that a five-act comedy was customarily written in verse, not in prose, although Molière had already broken with that custom three and a half years earlier with *Don Juan,* if that play can be called a comedy. Yet another reason for the dissatisfaction could be the plethora of sources from which the author lifted scenes, lines, encounters, character touches. Still, *The Miser* had its defenders, among them Boileau and Robinet. The latter wrote:

He speaks in prose and not in verse	*[Il parle en prose, et non en vers;*
Yet notwithstanding tastes diverse,	*Mais, nonobstant les goûts divers,*
So richly theatrical's his prose,	*Cette prose est si théâtrale,*
As trippingly as verse it goes.	*Qu'en douceur les vers elle égale.]*

Molière's craft has proved stronger than some of his contemporaries' notions of what a play ought to be. Henry Fielding's English adaptation of *The Miser* (1733) turned out to be his longest-running play.[6] The original has since

---

6. See Frank J. Kearful's "Molière Among the English, 1660–1737," in Johnson, Neumann, and Trail, 216–17. Professor Kearful remarks that Fielding wrote nearly thirty plays "and it is pleasant to record that the Molière adaptation which lasted longest in the eighteenth century was one of the best."

become one of Molière's most frequently performed works at the Comédie-Française and elsewhere; while Harpagon, little as anyone would like to cope with him in real life, if that were possible, has grown popular with both actors and audiences. Even if he does not behave self-consciously all the time, one cannot help noticing an air of detachment about him. He watches others, hardly ever granting them a smile or an unneeded word. But he is also watching the effects he has on those others, so that he is at times his own most intent spectator. Such sensitivity to nuances in a verbal exchange is a leading requirement for a businessman (as well as for a gambler, politician, teacher, or actor). Harpagon may talk in places as though distracted and unaware of the impact of his personality, but in other places in the text, he is alert to the repercussions of his words and dogmatic presence. Here we have more, much more, than caricature and unbridled insanity. He gives off rages and uncanniness, accusations and bluffing—opportunities for pyrotechnical explosions of acting.

Tartuffe, or The Impostor
(Le Tartuffe ou l'Imposteur, 1669)[1]

Seven and one-half years passed between two French productions of *Tartuffe* that visited the United States, but they appeared to be centuries apart. The first, brought by the Comédie-Française in early 1961 under the leadership of Louis Seigner, one of the company's veterans and *sociétaires*, presented a stolid revival, anchored in a convincingly seventeenth-century set and notable for its lashings of knockabout humor, especially on the part of Tartuffe himself, played as a greasy, aged, fidgety roué by M. Seigner, who also directed. The second production, directed by Roger Planchon and performed by his Theatre of the City of Villeurbanne, arrived here several years after it had aroused much admiration and critical speculation in France. Its scenic design, by René Allio, began as an intricately furnished room, but at the end of each act, properties and segments of the set vanished into the flies like inner carvings being lifted out of a Chinese puzzle box, until, near the fall of the final curtain, the audience watched the characters resolving the play against a wooden framework backed by three papered walls, as though the action had stripped itself down to bare truths.[2] The role of Tartuffe, assigned to the boy-faced Michel Auclair, broke with the convention of a patently hypocritical lecher who would fool nobody. Auclair put on display a dignified young cleric whose winning demeanor and voice could coax eggs from a rooster, and gold eggs at that. The critical brouhaha after Planchon introduced his version of the play in Villeurbanne, near Lyon, was provoked by the devotion shown by Orgon, the middle-aged homeowner and paterfamilias, to his guest, building at the end of act III to physical affection

1. This is the year, 1669, in which the play had its first performances in this third version. *The Hypocrite*, the three-act version, whose contents have led to much disputation among scholars, has been lost, so has the second version, *The Impostor*.
2. Allio's decor may have been commenting on a famous production mounted at the Odéon in Paris by André Antoine in which the five acts were for the first time given their own settings—a garden, a drawing room with a grand staircase, and so on—instead of sharing the one setting adduced from the play itself (see "*Le Tartuffe* d'Antoine, 1907" by James B. Sanders, in Johnson, Trail, and Neumann, 583–90).

158

that verged on caresses. At one point, for example, Orgon clutched at Tartuffe's arm to stop him from leaving, wept, knelt, and sank his head on Tartuffe's shoulder. Some reviewers expressed shock. To them, Planchon had answered one of the enduring questions posed by the play—why Orgon keeps overlooking Tartuffe's faults and remains determined not to part with him—in too obvious and dismissive a fashion by implying that the two men are lovers.[3] It is true that Orgon says Tartuffe is dearer to him than his wife and children are, and he misses no opportunity to lavish praise on Tartuffe for his saintly virtues. But Planchon's intention was not, I believe, quite so obvious. He conceived of a performance that made dramatic sense of the play's advances, retreats, and protestations, its climax, and its string of surprises.

For *Tartuffe* continually astounds its audiences. It opens with an attack by Orgon's mother, Madame Pernelle, on the rest of the family, a tongue-lashing leveled at her daughter-in-law, Elmire, who is Orgon's second wife; at her grandson, Damis, and granddaughter, Mariane; at Cléante, Orgon's brother-in-law; at the servant, Dorine, and finally at her own maid, Flipote, whose ears she cuffs in a physical release of the cruelty she has displayed throughout the scene.[4] After which, she storms out and does not reappear until the third scene of the last act.

Two more surprises follow rapidly. Orgon, back home after two days away from Paris on some mysterious business, steps into a hilarious exchange with Dorine. He asks after his family, but doesn't want to listen to news about his wife, who has been sick with a headache and high fever, lost sleep, and had to be bled; he is too eager to hear and worry about Tartuffe, who has been gorging himself on food and wine and is in the pink of health (I, 4). Soon after, he announces to Mariane that he is going to break off her engagement and marry her to Tartuffe (II, 1), to the amazement and horror of the rest of the household.

3. Molière could conceivably have proposed a gay relationship between Orgon and Tartuffe. Homosexuality certainly existed in seventeenth-century court circles. The playwright's first patron, the king's younger brother, known as "Monsieur," was homosexual, and his wife became the king's mistress without strong registrations of protest from Monsieur. But homosexuality is far from the only explanation for a close attachment between two men.

4. Jacques Scherer and Jacques Guicharnaud have noted that the opening of *Tartuffe*, in Guicharnaud's words, "lacks neither animation nor heat" (Guicharnaud 22, n. 1), by way of comparison with the more leisurely openings of most French classical plays.

Tartuffe's first entrance ushers in more surprises.[5] Molière has kept him offstage until the second scene of act III, while a reader or spectator has plenty of time to assimilate remarks dropped by the family, to form from them unflattering impressions of him as a glutton who nonetheless preaches aggressive self-denial, and to look forward to seeing how this counteractor acts. Instructing his servant to lock away his hair shirt and self-scourging whip (in case somebody tries to steal them?), while perceiving Dorine in her low-cut dress, he offers her his handkerchief so that her bosom does not arouse lustful thoughts. Lust? He means in others, surely, not in himself, never in this bluenose? But yes. He is a sexual as well as a gastronomic glutton. He has designs on the wife as well as the daughter. In an interview with Elmire (III, 3), he tells her that she haunts his thoughts, and asks her to forgive the demands of his flesh. Confronted by her beauty, he is, although a priest, "no less a man." Elmire replies that she will not report him to her husband so long as—she is about to say so long as Tartuffe doesn't marry her stepdaughter. But Damis, who has hidden in a nearby closet and overheard Tartuffe's advances, leaps out, confronts the hypocrite, and, within short order, tells his father about the attempted lechery (III, 5).

Yet more surprises are in the offing. Tartuffe brazenly confesses—not to the advances but, in a self-indictment that rivals Malcolm's in *Macbeth*, to being "the greatest villain who ever lived" (III, 6). Rather than putting Orgon on his guard or stirring his indignation, the confession satisfies him that nothing untoward happened between Tartuffe and Elmire. Tartuffe had already informed him that other men had been "making eyes" *(des yeux doux)* at his wife. From now on, he declares, he wants her and Tartuffe to be seen together all the time "to spite the world" (III, 6). He goes on to call his son a liar and a traitor, threatens to break his arms, banishes Damis from his house, and then wishes he had killed him. Tartuffe blandly defends the young man, asks Orgon to call him back, and offers to leave in his place, but Orgon pleads with him not to, because "my life is at stake" (III, 7). As a further inducement for Tartuffe to stay, he will instantly make over his house and other assets in the cleric's name.

In the next act, the big surprise happens when Tartuffe renews his courting of Elmire, on her initiative. She has persuaded her husband, against his better (that is, worse) judgment, to crouch under a table and witness Tar-

5. In Planchon's production, Tartuffe was announced but his valet preceded him and bowed oafishly to Dorine. Tartuffe then entered decorously and scored an extra point for gentility.

tuffe's treachery for himself. Tartuffe comes on strong. He is ready for lovemaking here and now. As he closes in on Elmire, and she accompanies her delaying tactics with increasingly desperate coughs to remind her husband to intervene, he will not budge from under the table. At last he emerges, barely in time to save Elmire from rape. Tartuffe does not deny the charges; he defies them, issuing a countercharge of entrapment. Orgon orders him out of the house, but the house has now been signed over to Tartuffe and he will do the evicting (IV, 7). As a closing surprise for act IV, Orgon says he must check right away whether a certain casket—hitherto unmentioned, but evidently significant—is still upstairs.

The final act ushers in more surprises as the fortunes of Orgon and his family dip further, rise, fall, and again rise. To begin with, they seem to be at the bottom of their luck, worse off than being homeless and penniless. It appears that Orgon has helped out a friend, an enemy of the king, named Argas, who fled the country and left a box of documents, the casket, in Orgon's charge. In a reckless moment, Orgon told Tartuffe about the casket and even gave it to him to divert suspicion from himself. Tartuffe may now use the box and its contents to incriminate his former host (V, 1). But Damis returns and swears he will chop off Tartuffe's ears or, better yet, slay him (V, 2). Madame Pernelle, even more fanatical than her son, marches back into the play, refusing to believe that Tartuffe has ever been less than perfection personified. When Orgon shouts, "I saw him, saw him, with my own eyes I saw him—or as good as saw him," she retorts that appearances often deceive (V, 3).

So they do. A law officer ironically named Monsieur Loyal, arriving to turn Orgon and his family out of their home with the aid of ten men, behaves in a suave and regretful manner unexpected in a figure who is in effect a public bouncer. But after all, as he says, he has his orders, an excuse our own century keeps hearing from soulless subordinates. Still exuding exquisite civility, he adds that the family need not abandon the premises until the next morning, and that his ten assistants will help them empty the house, after sleeping there overnight. He departs with a gracious wish: "May heaven keep you all joyful" (V, 4). After this further slump in fortune, Valère, the young man Orgon had rejected as Mariane's fiancé, hurries in to warn Orgon that Tartuffe will shortly return to have him arrested for harboring the documents. Valère offers Orgon a loan, assistance, and a coach to escape in, while there is still time (V, 6). But time has run out. To the family's dismay, Tartuffe reenters bringing another officer of the law, the "Exempt," from the palace. The play has now reached its comic peripeteia, and the closing moments generate its last and greatest surprise. The Exempt arrests not Orgon but Tartuffe, who has been recognized as a notorious swindler. Orgon's property will be restored: the king has annulled the contract and pardoned him for having aided a foe of the Crown, in recompense for the courage he once showed, presumably during his army service (V, 7). We can also assume that the Crown has impounded the box and documents, although nobody says so.[6]

Surprises form as much of a staple in Molière's mature dramaturgy as do exorbitant characterizations, with which they are usually allied. They derive from the revue format, which treats nearly every scene as a sketch in its own right (most of them popular, for this reason, among actors at auditions) and as an opportunity for a bravura solo, duet, or trio. But in no other play does he spring so many surprises. *Tartuffe* thrives on their jolts. The audience, recovering from one surprise by accepting the relief of laughter mingled with incredulity, grows less cautious and yields more readily to the next. The crowning surprise, that imposition of a royal fiat on the ending, has been prepared for and audiences go along with it. Many scholars in the past, coolly scrutinizing the text away from the playhouse, were liable to find it a "given," grafted onto alien stock, and to rationalize it as the playwright's effusive gratitude to his patron-protector for having permitted this draft of the script to reach the stage after five years of torturing doubts and pleas and despite opposition from the highest ranks of the court and the Gallican church. The surprises do more, however, than helping to justify the play's climax. Their farcical and melodramatic pounding of the audience distracts attention from the cryptic liaison between the two principals and from the question of why Orgon refuses for so long to see Tartuffe as anything but a paragon.

Did Orgon always play the despot at home or only since his discovery of Tartuffe? During the condensed day of the play's action, Dorine and the family are concerned for him and therefore even more puzzled than the audience is by his spurts of anger. In the fifth act, although it is true that their own interests are as much at stake as his, they rally around him. Damis, earlier expelled from the home, reappears to renew the family's solidarity.

6. Molière nowhere elaborates on the nature of the offense committed by Orgon's friend, the fugitive, Argas. He might have been one of the persecuted Huguenots, hundreds of thousands of whom successive French governments drove out of France, or a participant in the Fronde rebellions (1648–53), which had ended some sixteen years before Molière produced the final version of this play.

Elmire, Mariane, and Dorine have put aside Orgon's insults, complaints, and high-handedness; while Valère, after having been rejected as a suitor, comes with an offer to lend him a thousand gold louis and escort him out of danger—by doing so, Valère puts himself in danger.

Tartuffe's moving in may not have struck the family as being particularly unusual at first. Visitors and guests have always been welcome. Orgon and his wife enjoy being hospitable. In the drama, hospitality has been a token of good nature, rather than ostentation, as far back as Euripides' *Electra* and *Alcestis*. Mme Pernelle complains of the constant procession of carriages at the front door, the lackeys, the noise. She accuses Elmire of being a spend-thrift and going "dressed like a princess." Very likely she has been listening to Tartuffe, who also disapproves of extravagance at home, other than that expended on himself, as he watches the outgo of income that he means to inherit. During a part of the story that precedes the action, Orgon's two-day absence, Tartuffe too has hectored the family about its prodigal way of life.

As Dorine remarks, Orgon changed after he watched the impoverished Tartuffe praying in a church; gave him clothes, food, money, and a berth; and listened admiringly as Tartuffe professed scorn for "temporal things" (again in the story, not the action) in order to fix his ambitions on "eternal things." Tartuffe has even claimed that he is noble by birth but has been robbed of his entitlements. With a little help from his friend, he may rise out of his poverty and be restored to his estate. The others in the family feel threatened by these and other tales—with reason, as it turns out—as they watch Orgon go on making a fool of himself. Thus, for most of the first four acts, we have Orgon pitted against his wife, daughter, son, brother-in-law, and maidservant. But until he goes under the table to eavesdrop on the scene between Elmire and Tartuffe, they cannot dent his armor of confidence in his protégé. During the three middle acts, Molière deliberately keeps Orgon's mother offstage, so that he does not have an ally. (In the opening scene, she stands in for him as the family oppressor.) To ask, then, why Orgon does not reckon with Tartuffe's faults earlier in the play is equally to ask why he takes no notice of the others' barrage of protest. Does his family now mean very little to him?

Evidently, yes. They disappoint him. Cléante talks to Orgon with the candor of an old friend and a contemporary; he may even have introduced him to Elmire. As he treats his nephew and niece with sympathy and pleads with skill for consideration of their wishes, we could think of Cléante as an interested party, safeguarding his sister's future from Tartuffe's probable predations. But Molière presents him as a figure of integrity, serving as an interlocutor who offers a point of view opposed to the protagonist's, without necessarily becoming a spokesperson for the playwright. (The playwright's "spokesperson" is the entire play.) A conscience of sorts, Cléante appeals to his brother-in-law, in scrupulously fashioned alexandrines, for moderation, calmness, reason; but to the impeccable logic in which he, like Chrysalde, clothes his advice, Orgon lends an ear but no mind. Orgon hardly bothers to interrupt, precisely because Cléante purports to be objective. An obsessive like Orgon will heed only someone who agrees with him beforehand.

If Cléante cannot grapple orally with Orgon, Dorine can. Unlike a number of other servants in Molière, she doesn't concoct any schemes. Instead, she marshals and bluntly lays out her objections, irritating Orgon—getting to him—as she rips through his defenses. Toward her, he is unable to affect indifference. Why? Because she is a servant and he takes her reproaches as impertinence? Because in other words, she has no right to talk back to him, whereas Cléante, his social equal, does? Perhaps. She doggedly refuses to know her place and even takes pleasure in wounding him; but I find it more likely that he resents her ripostes to the point of continually losing his temper with her because she is a woman, and because her arguments hit home. She reminds him more forthrightly than Cléante can of his derelict behavior toward his children, and shows herself to be a more sensitive and approachable counselor to them than he is. Orgon resents her because she is his rival as a parental figure, and because he cannot match her honesty. He doesn't know how to articulate the underlying reasons for his being drawn to Tartuffe. He doesn't understand them. He must play evasive and bluster about his rights as master of the house, while she can openly declare her love and loyalty to the children and—harder to take!—to him. Dorine embodies one of the playwright's reminders that his women characters frequently know how to best the men in an argument and, thanks to the humane justness of their viewpoints, deserve to. Dorine does indeed outargue Orgon. She moves him to expostulations over and over. But she never weakens his fondness for Tartuffe.

Nor does Elmire, even though her name, an imperfect anagram of "Molière," might seem to qualify her as the author's voice in the play.[7] Why is

7. The perfect anagram for "Molière" (except for the change of accent) occurs in a satirical play *Élomire hypocondre* (1670), written by one of Molière's detractors, De Chalussay. The notion of Elmire as a transcribed Molière whom the Tartuffes of the time, the false *dévots*, are trying to assault is not indefensible, but it would take some doing to carry it through to a staging that was a not a travesty of the play in drag. In

Orgon not susceptible to his sincere, intelligent, tactful, and good-looking wife? Molière certifies her good looks by having Tartuffe endanger his standing with Orgon when he attempts to seduce her the first time and, then again, the second time, when Orgon has already promised him Mariane. Tartuffe may, it is true, trust Orgon's apparently unalterable trust in him; he may also rely on quick thinking and pious banalities to extricate him from an embarrassing situation. Still, Elmire's beauty does lure him on. As for her intelligence, we are struck by that during her verbal fencing, which succeeds for a time in keeping Tartuffe at a distance. She shows her sincerity and tact repeatedly, not least when she apologizes to Tartuffe after she has tricked him into renewing his importunities. Anything but the wicked stepmother (by way of contrast to Béline in *The Imaginary Invalid*), Elmire likes and gets along well with Damis and Mariane, who enlist her aid in approaching their father.

But this fascinating young woman no longer fascinates Orgon. Shortly after he first enters, inquires after his family, and learns that his wife has been ill, he asks impatiently, "And Tartuffe?" As Dorine elaborates on Elmire's illness, he continues to ignore it. Later, when Elmire neither confirms nor denies Damis' accusations about Tartuffe—she has given her word and doesn't want to trouble her husband—he obstinately believes she is trying to protect Damis. He is one of the rare older husbands in Molière who is not jealous of his wife and does not fear (or think about) being cuckolded. Some commentators have suggested that he is jealous, but of Tartuffe, not her: in the fourth act, he stays under the table seething because he thinks at first that she has become a competitor, and later, that she has displaced him in Tartuffe's affections. Now, if Orgon, not long before this, wanted a second, youthful wife, he may well have married her in the hope that she would give him another child, or even another brood, to replace Mariane and Damis, whom he finds unsatisfactory as offspring and wants to supplant as his heirs. Yet Elmire, the one family member who still has some slight influence over him, persuades him to let her go ahead with the plan to unmask Tartuffe, and it works, after bringing temporary ruin on the family. But Orgon never thanks her or gives any sign of revived love; he reserves his gratitude for the king.

His children have less chance than the other three of bringing him back to his senses. Damis is nearly as hotheaded, opinionated, and selfish as his

the original production the male actor Hubert played Mme Pernelle, who is a farcical character; but Elmire is not.

father. As he urges Cléante to urge his father to ratify the wedding between Mariane and Valère, he mentions that he has his eye on Valère's sister—one desirable match may lead to another. In dealing with Orgon, he is unable to function diplomatically on his own behalf or Mariane's. His sarcastic account of Tartuffe's preying on Elmire (III, 5) causes Orgon to round on him with a fury unmatched elsewhere in the play, to call for a cudgel, to drive him out of the house, and to bring forward the wedding between Mariane and Tartuffe to that very evening (III, 6). I put some weight here on these flaws in Damis in order to emphasize that Orgon may react with especial irritation to some of his own flaws writ young. Even so, he goes well beyond rage when he wishes he had killed his son.

With Mariane, Orgon is initially less brutal. She is engaged, but never mind that. He has heard that Valère is "inclined to gamble"—heard it possibly from Tartuffe—and suspects the young man of being a freethinker and not a regular churchgoer. Obviously Tartuffe, devout and of gentle birth, is a more fitting husband, and Mariane, he tells her, "will be able to make him into whatever you wish" (II, 2). By this he means whatever *he* wishes, for it is plain that he has a wildly exaggerated notion of Tartuffe's prospects in society. (My son-in-law the archbishop?) He does not say so, but a blood alliance with Tartuffe may produce a grandson as a substitute for the son Elmire has not given him. Failing the arrival of a little Orgon, he is more than willing to welcome a little Tartuffe. Since Mariane has always been a compliant, not to say subservient, child, Orgon can allay his disappointment in her by compelling her to actualize a Tartuffian image of himself. Mariane protests on her knees, and Orgon, in an aside, lets slip his misgivings over his callousness, allowing us to see that he is not absolutely coldhearted (IV, 3). But he has settled on Tartuffe for her and even more for himself. Mariane, to whom rebellion is unthinkable, doesn't openly refuse. Dorine takes her part, vigorously but unavailingly, and mocks her for not insisting on marrying the man she loves. Mariane feebly replies that it would be unbecoming for her to declare herself so passionately in love that she arouses a scandal; she mentions that she may decide to kill herself. When Valère comes to find out whether the impending marriage to Tartuffe is fact or rumor and whether she will go along with it, pride prevents her from confessing her love. She acts offhanded, gives no sign of caring one way or the other. Valère returns the same sort of punishment. A quarrel ensues. Once again Dorine has to cut in, this time to avoid a permanent break between the young couple (II, 4).

The lovers' quarrel, even when refereed by a lively Dorine like Lisa

Delamare in Seigner's production, becomes a sequence one usually hopes will end as soon as it begins. It looks like a clumsy, time-killing device for holding off—and, so, building up to—Tartuffe's entrance, which soon follows. But Planchon's staging developed an urgent question-and-answer game with the dialogue. From behind their frigidly polite lines the young actors gave us glimpses of thinly hidden and unmanufactured feelings of jealous anguish. The bickering, set to choreographed formal movements ("blocking" would be too lumpish a description of what was an unrealized mating dance), revealed something close to an animal attraction. Its purpose lay in the power Tartuffe must exert over the family. This Valère had cause to fear that he might lose this Mariane, that she might be genuinely attracted to this Tartuffe.

Now, a winning, youthful Tartuffe with a virile personality—not necessarily good-looking but certainly magnetic—represents more of a danger, to society as well as to Orgon's future and his family's, than an ill-mannered boor does or a wheedling wheeler-dealer. In the opening scenes Damis, Cléante, and Dorine mention that he is repulsive. But their need to say so should put us on guard; it could imply that he does not *appear* repulsive. Stray lines from Dorine tell us something, but not much, about his looks. "*Oui,*" she says, "*c'est un beau museau*" —he has a handsome mug, or possibly a fine snout. She also refers to his *oreille rouge* (red ear) and his *teint bien fleuri* (flushed or florid complexion, a probable allusion to his fondness for wine). When he hands her his handkerchief to cover her bosom, which "brings me sinful thoughts," she retorts that she would not be tempted if she saw him naked, a supererogatory remark if he were a repellent or farcical bum, as he is sometimes portrayed. In Planchon's production, the Dorine—played (theatrical synchronicity?) by Seigner's gifted daughter—even put on a slightly coquettish manner in her scene with Tartuffe. We can appreciate why Valère is jealous of an attractive Tartuffe, a plausible rival for Mariane's love, not merely for her hand. In addition, Mariane's reluctance to oppose her father, which baffles Dorine, makes more dramatic sense if she is toying with the prospect of marriage to a glamorous preacher whom her father reveres.

Similarly, Elmire, married to an older and (at this time) unresponsive spouse,[8] may be mystified by Tartuffe's initial advances but not quite displeased by them. She does not wish to report him. Nor is she required by anything but a fastidious sense of decorum—or an admission that she was to

8. Molière was forty-seven when he played Orgon. As Elmire, his wife, Armande, was about twenty years his junior.

some extent charmed by him—to say she is sorry for having summoned him to a second interview. Tartuffe was beggarly *(gueux)* when first brought into the house by Orgon, and it suited him then to be exactly that; but in the action of the play he looks prosperously fed, garbed, and outwardly groomed, a forerunner of today's television evangelists who sport custom-fitted suits and furnishings and meticulously blow-dried locks. Tartuffe requires at least a few of the lineaments of the original Tempter, as his name implies in its echoes of the infernal regions of Tartarus.[9] The French tradition that predated Seigner with spry, elderly Tartuffes like Lucien Guitry, Jean Yonnel, and Fernand Ledoux pushed ridicule too hard, even for the play's farcical sequences.

Tartuffe's engagement with different characters brings to light his different characteristics, his plasticity, much as the behavior—the acting—of a real person is to some extent governed by the nature of the people with whom he or she comes into contact. If the members of the family at various times find Tartuffe intrusively, insufferably free with his homilies and exhortations, sexually challenging, or a menace, Orgon has found a Tartuffe who corresponds to none of these: a son-in-law more to his liking than his natural children are. He sees Tartuffe wearing a face that does not in the least correspond to the ones they see. Here we reach what it is in Tartuffe that moves Orgon so profoundly, makes this middle-aged man his disciple, even his mænad. Tartuffe's initial poverty; his sharing the alms he receives with the poor or with prisoners; the breeding he claims as a gentleman born; his mien humbler than Uriah Heep's, together with his gentle and affectionate play of gratitude toward Orgon, his "brother"; and his zealous modesty in declining to interfere with heaven's command over human affairs—the whole exhibition put on for his patron's benefit—these make him more desirable in Orgon's eyes, more suitably *filial,* than the children are. Therefore, Orgon does what would-be fathers always had to do in the days before sperm banks and surrogate parents, and what some still choose to do—he adopts. Here is a ready-made son and heir, displaying—one might say, flaunting—qualities that he can admire. Orgon does not overlook Tartuffe's faults; he simply cannot recognize them. When the family draws his attention to those faults, Orgon attributes the complaints to their envy, bitterness, disobedience, and fear of having lost his favor. So loath is he to acknowledge Tartuffe's cant

9. Guicharnaud speculates on the origins of Tartuffe's name (19 n. 1) and also on the names of the other characters, some of which are "real," some "theatrical," with the implication that their acting styles may vary (19).

and fawning, so smitten with this new piece of human property he has acquired, that he will not come out from hiding to save Elmire no matter how much she coughs, or how hard and often she raps on the table top, or how insistent Tartuffe becomes in pressing her to "satisfy my desire" until—until Tartuffe makes a couple of reckless comments about *him*. Orgon, he says, is "a man you can lead by the nose . . . I've got him to the point where he sees everything and believes nothing" (IV, 5). That breaks the spell, shattering Orgon's hopes and ambitions. He is—the most apt word in English would probably be "floored." He crawls into view, fuming.[10] All of a sudden Tartuffe is an "abominable man" (IV, 6).

In the next and final act, his impetuosity has swung him to the other extreme. He will have no further truck with pious persons—he does not specify *falsely* pious ones; he means all believers—and will become "worse than a devil" in persecuting them. Having detested his son's flaws, he now switches to detesting his mother's. By the end of the play, he may have reformed, unlike some of Molière's obsessed heroes, such as Harpagon who doesn't emerge from his warped beliefs and desires, or others (Argan and Monsieur Jourdain) who get their way, are humored, and also remain encapsulated in their illusions. In the final couplet, Orgon accepts Valère as a worthy son-in-law. But Planchon's staging showed him standing isolated, disconsolate, and not altogether disillusioned during those last moments, as though to imply that Valère was no substitute for the Tartuffe he thought he had, the Tartuffe he only imagined.

Many recent critics believe that the play has resolved itself by focusing not on Tartuffe's gulling but on Orgon's gullibility. The play may then, according to W. D. Howarth, satirize true believers more sharply than it does hypocrites.[11] Lionel Gossman and Nathan Gross consider that Orgon attempts to

10. In most productions, Orgon is supposedly visible between the table legs throughout this scene so that the audience can laugh at his discomfiture; in practice he is not very visible to the audience, although he might well be spotted by a Tartuffe on the alert. Seventeenth-century tables, however, were covered with a cloth that draped down to the floor on all sides, and if the production was faithfully realistic, the original Orgon, Molière, would have been entirely concealed, hearing what was going on but not seeing even Elmire's and Tartuffe's feet. Being unable to watch Orgon during this scene or seeing only his feet and hands or ripples in the tablecloth might actually prove more stimulating to the audience's imagination than watching the whole man.

11. Howarth (195–204) contends that the original inspiration for the character of the false believer Tartuffe was the prince de Conti, once Molière's patron but later, after turning devout, his relentless persecutor.

use Tartuffe, even to play God to Tartuffe's Christ, so as to strengthen his own sense of superiority over other people.[12] This interpretation of Orgon may have some validity, but only so long as we do not project it back into that part of the story that precedes the action and thereby assume that Orgon has an *innate* craving to demonstrate his superiority. For the play tells us that the Orgon we see in the action is not the Orgon who always was. The craving for superiority and for religious upgrading of his lineage may not predate his discovery of Tartuffe and does not sum him up. Risking the king's wrath, he went to the aid of his friend, even managing to tear himself away for two days from his Tartuffe. Orgon may behave atrociously at times but to play him as a consistent atrocity is to damage the play. He is flexible, a character of many faces, like Tartuffe—like any character who is finally imponderable—and the face he reveals at any given moment depends on the reciprocity of the character he is confronted with. In the end, he has not reformed, only reverted more or less. The chastened and bewildered figure is still in the process of transition to a former self.

The interpretation offered here of a man who believes he has received the ideal son from heaven, as Xuthus does in the *Ion* of Euripides, of a man driven to replace his progeny, does not sum him up, either. It is no more than a guiding line through the performance and should allow for divergences from that line whenever the text calls for them. Is the line Freudian? To some extent. Freud, however, based many of his most striking deductions and inductions on myth, and *Tartuffe* does reach back to ancient myths having to do with diabolism and scapegoats, with the searches of parents for children, and with the likelihood that evil will bring upon a community both literal sickness (Elmire's) and the figurative kind undergone by Orgon. Orgon's violent rounding on Damis, followed by his supplicating of Tartuffe is reminiscent of Isaac, Jacob, and Esau.

Alfred Simon writes: "Modern psychology has in every way explored the conscience of the Liar, and psychoanalysis has demonstrated Tartuffe's. In vain, for Tartuffe is not a clinical subject, but a poetic crea-

---

12. Gossman, 100–144, and Gross, 13–38. The discovery of Christ figurations and Christ imitations, in life as in literature, continues apace. After the Tower Commission's report on governmental delinquencies during the Iran crisis, an unnamed "senior official" in the White House remarked a propos of the president's slump in public esteem and his chances of regaining it, "The media love crucifixions. But the American public loves repentance and resurrections" (*New York Times*, 27 Feb. 1987, p. 1).

tion."[13] A fair enough caution: it warns against false motives. But is there a better way for an actor to avoid false motives than seeking plausible ones? And "poetic creations," however unprescribable their boundaries, are impersonations performed by persons; they cannot avoid seeming motivated, even by self-defeating impulses. The disputes over whether Orgon or Tartuffe is the central character seem to me fruitless. For the action to make its dramatic points, the actors must play not separated roles but a complex interaction, a reticulum of responses among all the roles, with especial sensitivity between the two leading men. After Tartuffe has left the stage, no matter what motives we ascribe to Orgon, the last scene makes it clear to him that in transferring his allegiance away from the king, even temporarily, he sinned, and that in Paris, close to the king's person, one cannot live under the shadow of the king's displeasure, only in the glow of his favor. Not Orgon but the Sun King is master of this house.[14] Now, although Louis saves the day for Orgon and his family, much as he had saved the play from Molière's foes, the closing scene's imposition of a power above that of ordinary mortals still raises doubts among rational spectators and critics. And yet, it is consistent with his other endings. In almost every one of them, contrivances by the characters have to yield to the intervention, in one form or another, of fateful synchronicity, accident that is no accident. Further, the family's resistance to Orgon's desires miniaturizes Orgon's resistance, in whatever form it took, to the king's power.[15]

Planchon's closing tableau had a tragicomic flavor. Was this appropriate for a play that can be read as bustling, satirical comedy from start to finish, encroaching on farce in every one of its acts, and culminating in a happy wrap-up? I do not see that there is any way of answering that question with

13. Simon, 95–96; my translation.
14. A 1985 production in Washington, DC, by the Rumanian director, Lucian Pintilié, illustrated the granting of bounty (that is, the shedding of power) from above by introducing the Exempt from the flies, not the wings—and from a helicopter. It equally illustrated the distaste of some directors today for the literal stage treatments that prevailed for three centuries. Pintilié also had the inspired notion of giving "the role of the [Exempt] in the fifth act (the one who brings the news of Tartuffe's fall from grace) to Tartuffe's servant, Laurent, who appears beginning with the first act. When Laurent enters in act V, the audience realizes that he has been an in-house spy all along. 'That was my experience,' says the director. 'When one lives in a world of secret police, as I did, it is always your disciple who betrays you' " (*New York Times*, 31 May 1988, Arts and Leisure Section, byline: Daniel Selznick).
15. See Guicharnaud, 140–41, for a development of this point.

finality. The author's intentions, as we discern them from the dialogue and stage directions, still lie open to investigation. A spectator at Seigner's production would see the play as a straightforward tract with an all's-well ending, packaged faithfully with effects codified and justified for generations in the "House of Molière" and virtually devoid of subtext. It may have provoked more laughs than Planchon's, but even if I could prove that it did with the aid of a laugh meter on both occasions, I would not swear that it was funnier. Much of the laughter that greeted Seigner seemed of the guffawing variety that is automatically dragged out of some spectators by easy shticks, which annoy other spectators. In addition, Planchon's audience would be more likely to come away troubled by the incidence of Tartuffes, in one guise or another, on the societies they continue to poison with their insidious charm—and at least as troubled by the glad hands, laden with coin, held out to them by the Madame Pernelles and Orgons.

The Bourgeois Gentleman
(Le Bourgeois gentilhomme, 1670)

From a miser to a big spender: if Harpagon's secrecy and avarice have a sinister side to them, Monsieur Jourdain's eagerness to squander and flaunt his wealth does not strike us as being in the least threatening. If we laugh uneasily at George Dandin, the peasant who has abandoned his pretensions to social climbing, we laugh unreservedly at the pretensions of Jourdain who has no first name, the bourgeois who will not rest until the world recognizes him as a "gentleman," a man of "quality." Here we have the unmitigated snob aware of his weakness and glorying in it. After a tailor's apprentice wins successively bigger tips by conferring on him successively rising salutations (Your Honor, My Lord, and Your Grace), Jourdain confesses, "If he goes up to Your Highness, he'll have my whole purse" (II, 5). His father and his wife's father had modest beginnings: they sold cloth in an open-air market. Jourdain has either inherited his affluence from them or prospered independently as a merchant; the playwright does not say whether he stayed in the same trade. Now he watches and listens for news about how the upper echelons live, follows routes that lead to gentlemanly accomplishments, hopes to acquire all the culture that plenty of money can buy, and incidentally supports the arts and fashions. Who would oppose ambitions so worthy?

The three women in his household. Madame Jourdain deplores her husband's fees for teachers and his loans to a cadging nobleman. She has no desire to rise above her station; like Kristin, the cook in *Miss Julie*, she knows her place. Their daughter, Lucile, for whom he intends marriage to a man of rank, is in the process of landing a future husband without his aid or prompting. And the maid, Nicole, who makes a laughingstock of Jourdain, has plenty to say about the procession of dirtily shod strangers through the house.

The play's plotting is unorthodox to make room for the ballet portions of this comedy-ballet. Two brief acts give impetus to the main action, Jourdain's striving for recognition and his susceptibility to advice about how he can equate himself with "the quality people." He confers with music and dance teachers, takes lessons from fencing and philosophy teachers, and then undergoes a fitting of his preposterous new floral suit at the hands of a tailor and his apprentices. Subsidiary conflicts erupt between the teachers and between Jourdain and his tailor; but not until the lengthy third act does Molière set in motion the conflicts between Jourdain and his wife, his maid, his daughter, and her suitor. In that same act, we witness how vulnerable he has become to Dorante, a count, one of the playwright's smoothest scoundrels and his most uninhibited borrower. The late start of the main conflicts provides Molière with an opportunity beforehand to reintroduce his resident performers' specialty acts, among them comic *récits* that correspond to the tirades of seventeenth-century tragedy. The actors playing the teachers and their students do their turns in the form of demonstrations during the first two acts, interspersed by clashes, including a fist fight among the teachers and a squabble between Jourdain and the recreant tailor who has helped himself to a suit made from a length of material paid for by the customer.

But during the third act, as the main plot and subplots gear up, the revue format remains almost as obvious. Jourdain first encounters Nicole, who goes into a helpless fit of laughter at seeing him in his new suit; the part was originally conceived for and played by Mlle Beauval, an actress with a nervous giggle that sometimes infected the audience. His appearance next astonishes his wife, a part entrusted to André Hubert, who occasionally played comic older women, rather like the "panto dames" interpreted by male comedians in British Christmas shows.[1] The format persists: Jourdain mimics two of the teachers as he recapitulates what he has learned about swordplay and vowels for the benefit of his wife and Nicole, although he bungles it all or gets it back to front. When he tries to instruct Nicole in self-defense, she nicks him. Even a sequence of a lovers' recrimination between Lucile and her suitor, Cléonte, Nicole and her boyfriend, Covielle, is arranged as a formally patterned verbal and quasi-balletic quartet.

The Bourgeois Gentleman stresses its theatricality further by opening with a rehearsal, encompassing entr'actes of music and dance, building in the fourth act to a mock-Turkish ceremony of a play-within-the-play, and culminating in another of those international sequences of which the king was fond, the *Ballet of the Nations*, a spectacle that Dorante claims to have created.[2] In the *turqueries* ceremony, the Turks in their fezzes and curling-pointed footwear

---

1. Mlle Beauval played another laughing girl, Zerbinette, the following year in *Scapin*. Hubert later took on the much more substantial female role of Philaminte in *The Learned Ladies*.

2. The *Ballet des nations* is nowadays rarely, if ever, appended to the play.

are played by actors recruited for the occasion by Covielle, a character derived from Coviello, one of the zanies from the commedia dell'arte. Covielle himself puts on a white beard to play the role of an interpreter of phony Turkish. He once knew Jourdain's father who, he confides to a delighted Jourdain, was a gentleman—not a mere vendor of merchandise but a fabric fancier who bought cloth and gave it to his friends for money. Covielle's master, Cléonte, plays the "son of the sultan," who wants to marry Lucile but, in order to do so, must first appropriately ennoble her father. As a further theatricalist joke, in the original production the majestic part of the Turkish Mufti went to the composer Lully. Altogether, this is a play that openly proclaims the nature of theatre, good and bad impersonation. At the end, as its action gives way to the Ballet of the Nations, Jourdain has been promoted to the fictitious rank of mamamouchi. He thinks he *is* a mamamouchi; in truth he is enacting a role for everybody else's amusement. The strains of fantasy and performance are held, *sostenuto,* to the final curtain. Nobody disillusions him; he doesn't come down to earth but is left in ecstatic triumph, floating at mamamouchi height. What might happen later when the dream that keeps him aloft gets punctured; when Cléonte and Covielle abandon their impersonations—this is matter for another play, another performance. Jourdain's dizzy elevation has been a by-product of the plan to secure Lucile's marriage to Cléonte. The plan succeeds by playing on Jourdain's snobbery, and the action abruptly shuts itself off.[3]

Besides the theatricalism—theatre *as* theatre—the playwright has pulled his collection of separate turns together by means of another unifying theme, instruction. The action comprises one attempt after another by Jourdain to learn: how to appreciate music and dance; a "logical demonstration" of how to give and avoid receiving sword thrusts ("how a man who's no killer can kill his man without being killed"); how to mouth vowels and consonants; how to dress to the mellifluence of music; how to conduct himself in the company of blue bloods, such as Dorante, Dorimène, and spurious Mideastern royalty. These instruction scenes are supplemented by a few fumbled efforts by Jourdain to teach others—his wife and Nicole—what he has defectively learned. The "Turkish" business of act IV, which bamboozles him into sanctioning a marriage he has earlier spurned, underlies Covielle's

3. In a staging at the Comédie-Française in 1974, Jean-Louis Barrault kept the music from the *turqueries* of act IV going through act V and encouraged the normally staid Comédie spectators to sing the choruses, to stamp and clap rhythmically—all this in an intoxicating celebration of theatre as a communal event.

mischievous, contrary plan—to teach Jourdain a lesson he did not ask for. If Dandin is the snob-as-coward, Jourdain is the snob-as-child or, rather, an adult version of a spoiled brat. Perhaps that is why we indulge and relish him, even in his autocratic moments. It is appropriate for a childlike man to become everybody's pupil (as well as a mark for every sponger in town), the object of all the play's teaching, and at the end, to have taken none of it to heart. Yet, the good nature of the play and Moliére's refusal to preach a conclusive lesson either to Jourdain or to the audience signal that this is an extravaganza produced in order to laugh at extravagance; that in inventing a fake prince he can take swipes at the excessive servility paid a real prince; and that extremes of behavior, like Jourdain's, however irrational, are what makes the drama compelling. So much for criticism that has held this author up as the apostle of common sense and moderation, and Madame Jourdain, broadly interpreted by a male actor, as a repository of his wisdom.

I have mentioned that class-consciousness saturates Molière's drama. Among his gallery of roles written for himself, George Dandin, Monsieur de Pourceaugnac, and Monsieur Jourdain personify compromises between the upwardly mobile servant class and the master class. Jourdain displays some of the bossiness or even arrogance of the master while retaining some of the ingratiation of a servant. To his family, he presents himself as a final, dogmatic arbiter: "My daughter's going to be a marquise, in spite of everyone. And if you put me in a rage, I'll make her a duchess" (III, 12). Toward his teachers he maintains a deference that becomes one who admits to knowing much less than they do and offers himself as human putty into their hands while remaining conscious of his standing as the client who must be satisfied. But his most obsequious and (dramatically speaking) productive association in the play consists in his friendship with Dorante and, through this count, with the marquise Dorimène.

Jourdain is the French for Jordan. Molière evidently chose the name of the river in Asia Minor to consort with the *turqueries* and his hero's induction into the upper levels of the inscrutable mid-Orientals. The king had apparently ordered a spectacle in which Turkish fashions and mores would feature, in time to please (or embarrass?) a Turkish ambassador visiting the court.[4] The elaborate costumes and scenery cost Louis a fortune, but the monarch

4. It has often been remarked that "Turkishness," whatever that is or was, enjoyed favor with the king and the court in 1670 when the show was being written and prepared.

is said to have considered the work, including the *Ballet of the Nations,* one of the playwright's best, probably never realizing that he was playing Monsieur Jourdain to Molière's Dorante. For Jourdain serves as Dorante's backer or "angel." Whatever the count asks for, the merchant unquestioningly supplies. The friendship between unequals brings benefits to both parties. Jourdain thrills to the news that Dorante has mentioned his name in the king's bedroom during the royal *lever* that very morning. He wallows in Dorante's description of how ecstatically the marquise Dorimène, whom the count purports to be wooing on Jourdain's behalf, has received gift offerings of flowers, a fireworks display, a diamond ring, and the invitation to a banquet with entertainment, which is held later in Jourdain's house. Dorante neglects to mention that these bribes have contributed to his own campaign of winning the hand of the marquise. He has also borrowed eighteen thousand francs explicitly to cover his private debts, sums "I intend to pay back at the first opportunity" (III, 6). Jourdain does not forget to enter in a small book a reckoning of these sums, every sou he will never see again; but far from complaining about being mulcted, he considers himself honored to be the creditor of a nobleman, and one who is doing him so much kindness. In bringing these two characters together, Molière inverts the old relationship from Roman comedy between the wealthy citizen and the scheming parasite. Dorante is the parasitic aristocrat. His slogan might well be, "Roll Jordan!" Like Valère in *The Miser,* he advances by flattery but takes his blandishments to lavish and lavishly rewarding extremes beyond Valère's daring. The interaction between Jourdain and Dorante is also reminiscent of that between Orgon and Tartuffe. Orgon looks on Tartuffe as his (and everybody's else's) superior in virtue and sacerdotal zeal. For Jourdain, virtue is out of the reckoning; it is Dorante's rank, connections, and manners that move him.

Jourdain is often played by an actor in his sixties, perhaps to match the age of his opposite number, Harpagon, but the role seems more fitted to a man in his forties undergoing the midlife male crisis of pop sociology and remedial magazine articles that brings with it an infatuation for a young partner who will excite a hope of reliving one's youth. In this instance, he cannot have a crush on Dorimène's person, since he imagines he loves her before they meet. What seduces him is her "quality," as described by Dorante, his nascent sense of the power of money, and his impatience with his wife, all of which have made him susceptible to a love affair of some kind. They meet in the fourth act in Jourdain's home to consume the spread ordered by Dorante and paid for by his host. He does not seem to notice that both Dorimène and Dorante call him, and refer to him discourteously as, "Monsieur Jourdain" rather than the conventionally polite "Monsieur."[5] He is too infatuated, not exactly with the marquise but more with the fact of her presence and that of the count who have deigned to break expensive bread with him. Fumbling for compliments, eager to impress her with the "quality manners" he has begun to learn, and yearning to capitalize on the presents he has sent her, he blunders into one physical or verbal faux pas after another. Dorimène believes she is being regaled by Dorante. Jourdain's gushings and improprieties at first amuse her but later repel her (IV, 1), especially after Madame Jourdain walks in on them unexpectedly and upbraids her for making trouble between a husband and wife (IV, 2).

The dialogue Molière employs in his prose plays has the advantages for actors, spectators, and translators of being direct, active, and unobtrusive. He will occasionally retail a colorful list, such as the items of bric-a-brac in the loan offered by Harpagon and recited by La Flèche or the exquisitely tempting dishes that Dorante says his gourmet acquaintance would set before guests (IV, 1). But in *The Bourgeois Gentleman*, the playwright goes out of his way several times to play fanciful and farcical games with language that seem to predate the early, nonsense-juggling plays of Ionesco. As he practices the manipulations of lips and tongue-against-palate-and-teeth in mimicry of the philosophy teacher, Jourdain brays out arrays of vowel and consonant combinations: "A, E, I. I, I, I . . ." or "R, R, Ra. R, R, R, R, R, Ra!" As the lesson continues, he asks his instructor to rephrase a *billet doux* he wishes to address to Dorimène, using exactly the same words, "Fair marquise, your beautiful eyes make me die of love," but in a more presentable order.

> PHILOSOPHY TEACHER First, you could try what you said. Or there's, "Of love die me make, fair marquise, your beautiful eyes." Or, "Your beautiful eyes of love me make, fair marquise, die." Or, "Die your beautiful eyes, fair marquise, of love me make." Or even, "Me make your beautiful eyes die, fair marquise, of love."
>
> MONSIEUR JOURDAIN Which of those is best?

5. Nathan Gross writes of Dorimène as "a giver," with a name derived from Greek, by way of contrast with Dorante, whose Latinate name suggests "a gilder." Gross deals interestingly with Dorimène's role (144–46). But it is worth remembering that more limited meanings can be attached to these names than he finds in them because they were both used elsewhere in Molière and in other authors. The giddy young fiancée in *The Forced Marriage* is also called Dorimène, and Dorante is a much less selfish character in other plays, such as *The Criticism of the School for Wives*.

PHILOSOPHY TEACHER The one you said: "Fair marquise, your beautiful eyes make me die of love." (II, 4)

In the fourth and fifth acts Jourdain has progressed from French gibberish to mock-turkey soup.

COVIELLE . . . When I told [the sultan's son] I knew you and I'd seen your daughter, "Aha," says he to me, "marababa sahem," meaning, "Oh, how I love her!"

MONSIEUR JOURDAIN "Marababa sahem" means "Oh, how I love her!"

COVIELLE Correct.

MONSIEUR JOURDAIN I'm glad you let me in on that. I'd never have thought "Marababa sahem" could mean, "Oh, how I love her!" It's a clever tongue, that Turkish.

COVIELLE Cleverer than you'd imagine. Do you know the meaning of "cacaracamouchen?"

MONSIEUR JOURDAIN Cacaracamouchen? No.

COVIELLE "Cacaracamouchen" means "beloved." . . .

MONSIEUR JOURDAIN That's a miracle. Cacaracamouchen, beloved. Who'd have guessed? (IV, 3)

He goes on to perplex his wife with fragments quoted from his initiation as a mamamouchi, "Dara dara bastonara" and "Hou la ba ba la chou ba la ba ba la da," and to hail Dorante with a back-to-front version of a "Turkish" greeting: "Monsieur, I wish you the strength of a snake and the cunning of a bull" (*Monsieur, je vous souhaite la force des serpents et la prudence des lions . . .* V, 3).

In these and other episodes in which Jourdain falsifies what he was taught or told, Molière touches on questions that trouble every artist. Since art is a form of enlightenment, and sometimes of instruction, how is it possible for artists to make their work clear without its becoming painfully obvious? Where does subtlety end and obfuscation begin? Can one guard against misunderstandings and accidental distortion by a public (as well as its representative critics) that unavoidably includes some Messieurs Jourdain? He encroaches on these questions during the opening scene in a passage worth an extended quotation.

MUSIC TEACHER We've found the patron we both needed. Our Monsieur Jourdain is the softest touch. Your dance and my music could use a world full of people like him.

DANCE TEACHER Not quite like him. I'd be happier if he had a keener appreciation of the things we do for him.

MUSIC TEACHER True, he doesn't properly appreciate them, but he pays beautifully. That's what our arts need the most.

DANCE TEACHER But I like my little share of glory. Applause stimulates me. It's agonizing to play to dummies and clods and hear their vulgar responses. There's pleasure in extending yourself for people who can detect the subtleties, who give a knowing welcome to the finer passages. Nothing repays our labors better than that.

MUSIC TEACHER Agreed. But honeyed words won't keep you alive. Pure praise requires something solid stirred in. The most heartfelt applause is delivered not with two hands, but one. Our man gets everything jumbled. He claps at the wrong moment and for the wrong reason. But he has perception in his purse. His compliments are worth their weight in gold.

DANCE TEACHER There's crude commonsense in what you say, but money is such a sordid thing that a self-respecting artist should never show it any affection.

MUSIC TEACHER I notice that when our man hands you your money, you manage to accept it.

DANCE TEACHER And with a smile. But I only wish that, with all his wealth, he also had a modicum of taste.

MUSIC TEACHER That's my wish, too. In the meantime, he'll compensate for our other clients who do have taste. What they praise, he'll pay for.

The slightly more cynical (or more frankly cynical) music teacher gets the last word.[6] But music, like the dance, has to be sifted, prior to the public's reception, through performers. So does theatre. The opportunities that only arise for misunderstanding, deformity, misinterpretation at both stages—and after! When he wrote this theatrically self-conscious play, Molière had endured more than his share of misinterpretation, some of it willful. Yet, his

---

6. But the dance teacher's opinion had already found support in *The Criticism of the School for Wives*, when a different Dorante says: "It infuriates me to see those persons who . . . have a fixed view of everything, which they voice boldly, without knowing a thing about it. At a play they shout their applause for the awful items and don't react to the good ones. When they look at a picture or listen to a concert, they similarly misplace their blame and praise, pick up at random any critical jargon they can find, and never fail to misuse and misapply it" (sc. 5).

script holds onto its buoyant good humor throughout, thanks largely to the delicately drawn portrait of Jourdain.

That philistine resembles the upwardly mobile "me first" people who splurge on clubs, cults, and other types of association that deliver exclusivity (keeping some people in by keeping others out), on therapy that promises self-fulfillment and self-improvement, and on nameplates in opera houses and theatre complexes. (The late Charles Ludlam neatly caught this aspect of the play in his modernized adaptation several years ago.) Today we are inclined to look on Monsieur Jourdain as a quaint dispenser of wealth and amusement, as a counterpart to Alceste, as Molière's Philanthrope. But there is a sharp, hard edge to him. He does not really like or behave decently to others he encounters in the action. If he gives money to Dorante or scatters it elsewhere, he does so for show. If he defers to his teachers, he does so out of ignorance, not respect. Like his model Mascarille in *Two Precious Maidens Ridiculed,* he is a servant decked out as a master. He fawns over Dorante and splatters Dorimène with clumsy sexual innuendoes. He reminds Nicole of her humble origins but shies away from his own and bawls his wife out when she recalls them. His most agreeable qualities are his wonder at being taken, as he believes, for the son of a gentleman and thus an eligible father-in-law for the son of a sultan, and his astonishment at the thick veins of knowledge that offer themselves to a conscientious prospector. Inside the buffoon dwells the child who will go to any lengths for the toys he wants, even when he is in a momentary dither about exactly how to proceed. His saving grace is that Molière has made him, if not lovable, laughable, and never more so than when he drifts off at last into a never-never land of nobility.

The Imaginary Invalid
(*Le Malade imaginaire*, 1673)

Did Molière's last work kill him or keep him alive until he had brought it to life? After writing, staging, and playing the demanding lead in the three-act farce-comedy with spectacular trappings, he collapsed and died only four performances into the run of this anything-but-crazy quilt, sewn together, while he was gravely ill, from bits of his earlier comedies and farces, with the addition of swatches of new merriment, irony, and caustic observation.

Of the staple figures the author adapts from his repertoire, as though pulling favorite old garments from a wardrobe, Argan belongs with the other masters of the house: he explicitly claims the right "to do what seems good to me" in his family (III, 3); this right includes offering his daughter the option of wedding the man of *his* choice (in this case, a young doctor) or going into a convent. The daughter, Angélique, like the nubile daughters in earlier Molière, has her heart set on somebody else, a scrupulous young man named Cléante, who resembles other *jeunes premiers* in finding himself compelled into trickery in order to woo her. Argan's brother, Béralde, is the last in a line of interlocutors who are generous to a fault with their advice and, unless assigned to vivid or even eccentric actors, tend to disappear into their lines and become transparent. Toinette, the maidservant, has the motherliness of Nicole and Dorine, together with a dash of the wiliness and agility displayed by the playwright's conspiratorial male servants.[1] A notary, an apothecary, and several physicians, all derived from the pedants of the earlier writings, especially the ones in *Doctor Love*, round out the cast of

---

1. A number of Toinette's lines in act I, scene 5 are directly lifted from those of Scapin in the play presented less than two years before, and Argan's responses correspond closely to the lines of Argante in the earlier play (I, 4), the gist of both scenes being the impertinence of the servant in assuring the master that he will *not* marry his child to an unknown, unloved partner. The similarity between the names Argan and Argante suggests that, in the later plays, the antagonism of the fathers toward their families is emphasized by an *agôn* (contest) or a variant of it, as the root syllable of their names, e.g. in Harpagon and Orgon.

familiar faces. Argan, like Orgon, has a young second wife, Béline, but she does not resemble Elmire or the other wives; she is more of an analogy with Tartuffe: an object of affection and, at the same time, a sweet-talking, malicious hypocrite.[2] Above all, Argan shares with other would-be masters of the house a hunger for something he does not have, which looks attainable but proves elusive. The Sganarelles of *The School for Husbands* and *The Forced Marriage*, Arnolphe, and Harpagon want a young and malleable bride; George Dandin hopes for the dissolution of an indissoluble marriage; Orgon seeks a spiritual son and heir; Monsieur Jourdain would break away from the mediocre middle; and Argan yearns for triumph over disease, a form of yearning for immortality. The only strict novelty in the dramatis personae is a significant child's role, that of Argan's eight-year-old daughter, Louison (played in the original production by the daughter of Mlle Beauval, who took the part of Toinette).

But as always, Moliéresque mannerisms and full-blown idiosyncrasies give a blunt or fine freshness to each character, and most strikingly to the role designated for himself. Argan does not quite qualify as an *imaginary* invalid, despite the play's title. He lives in a state of anxiety as he wavers between constipation and diarrhea. These he brings on by engorging a chemical banquet intended, in alternation, to scour and restabilize his bowels. In the play's opening soliloquy, as he queries the charges on the bills submitted by his apothecary, he recites a catalogue of seventeenth-century purgatives, laxatives, softeners, hardeners, emollients, internal cleansers, and other agents that correspond to the items hawked during today's dinner-hour television—only here they accumulate in an incantatory poetry-by-listing reminiscent of the one declaimed by Volpone as he plays the charlatan Scoto of Mantua—or of the delicacies that Dorante in *The Bourgeois Gentleman* says he would have liked to prepare for the dinner party given by him and paid for by Monsieur Jourdain. Argan's speech reveals a devout attitude toward medicine, a preoccupation with the expulsion of dirt, wind, and disorder, a vision of the body freed from the impurities of intrusive matter, a perfectly

---

2. As though to refute those critics who, then and later, would argue that Molière contrives to dramatize his private life, he cast as Béline not his wife Armande, who played Angélique, but Catherine de Brie.

A character described as "the eulogist" in Philip Roth's novel (or anti-novel) *The Counterlife* asks rhetorically, "Isn't it true that, contrary to the general belief, it is the *distance* between the writer's life and his novel that is the most intriguing aspect of his imagination?"

lubricated and impeccably organized organism that is the counterpart of an immaculate soul. To Argan the notion of health, the ideal that is an absence, has its own mystique and can be attained only by a fervor that almost mounts to a belief in witchcraft. Like Beckett's Krapp and Hamm, he spends much of his time awaiting the next internal spasm, his nearest equivalent to a sign of grace from on high.

Molière only slightly tempers this dedication to medication. Just as Harpagon can, so to speak, step outside himself and pretend to become the loving father as he offers to give up his prospective bride to his son, and just as Monsieur Jourdain "lends" Dorante all the cash he asks for but keeps a notebook with a reckoning of the total debts, so Argan shows a streak of practicality as he cuts as much as two-thirds off the apothecary's asking price for certain medicines. He is never altogether submersed in his fanatical devotions. By plotting the scene as a monologue, Molière shows us Argan at odds with himself, an eager imbiber of medicine pitted against a manager of the household accounts—like a millionaire, he plays Mr. Frugal when it comes to small expenses. The internal conflict finally erupts into anger, a flow of bile, which generates fear. What harm will the bile do him? He realizes he is alone and vulnerable; he calls for help. And by the conclusion of the play's first speech we can diagnose his sickness as not imaginary but real, a chronic (and comic) terror that he may suddenly die unattended.

This husband and father has his blind spots. The most obvious one, after his unbounded faith in physic and physicians, is his wife. He believes she loves him without reserve even in his supposedly ailing condition, while the others in the family have already taken her for the "gold-digger" she is.[3] He confides that he wants her to bear his child (his doctor has said it can be done!) and that he means to disinherit Angélique and Louison in her favor and presumably the baby's (I, 7). By contrast, Harpagon and Orgon never openly declare their similar intentions of acquiring new offspring to replace the present ones as legatees, although these intentions can be deduced from the plays. No doubt Argan expects to enroll the child as soon as possible in a medical school, but in the meantime he can bring a doctor into the family

3. The term "gold-digger," according to David Robinson, "was coined in honor of Peggy [Hopkins Joyce] around 1920" (*Chaplin: His Life and His Art*, [New York, McGraw-Hill, 1985], 303). Peggy married five millionaires in a row, and although Argan's bourgeois resources may not extend into the millions, Béline has her future set on them.

for free consultations by giving Angélique to Thomas Diafoirus, a recent medical graduate and another of Argan's blind spots.

Dr. Thomas and his father arrive for formal introductions (II, 5). Cléante, rejected as a suitor for Angélique, has already presented himself in the guise of a substitute for her music teacher (II, 4), and is invited by Argan to watch the proceedings, that is, to witness Argan's pride at having lured a medico into the family. As often happens in Molière, no mothers take part in the marriage arrangements or, indeed, in the play, only Toinette as a pseudomotherly but skeptical presence. She has previously registered her protests about the alliance. Angélique, she says, is not ill and therefore doesn't need to marry a doctor (I, 5).

After an exchange of greetings, during which both fathers speak at once and do not hear each other or comprehend that this means they are at odds from the start, the senior Dr. Diafoirus (the name is a play on the French word for "diarrhea") boasts that his son holds tenaciously to "the old school of medicine"; that he never changes his opinions; and that he vigorously disputes any new theories that come up, such as Harvey's proposal that blood circulated throughout the body, not exactly a recent discovery, since it was published fifty-four years before *The Imaginary Invalid* but remained in contention among French medical practitioners. Young Thomas may lack imagination and enterprise—did not begin to identify alphabetical letters until his tenth year—but now, according to his father, he has a reliable mind and the required *temperament* for fathering well-made children. The young doctor more than lives up to some of these boasts. His *physical* potential for fatherhood is not tested in the play, but he shows off his reliable mind as he recites by rote some speeches, balanced in their rhetoric, hackneyed through and through, and evidently composed by his father. He follows his father's instructions all the way, despite several lapses of memory and after he has directed the address meant for Béline to Angélique. He offers an engagement gift to his fiancée-to-be: a copy of his thesis attacking the "circulationists"; he then invites her to a performance, not of a play, but of the dissection of a woman's body, on which he will discourse. According to a stage direction, this mechanical monster programmed to appear human "does everything with bad grace and at the wrong moment," an example—perhaps exaggerated only a little, if at all—of the new graduate who has capitulated to the rules banged into his head and calls his calling an art while regarding it as a literally prescriptive science.

We soon learn the author's purpose in keeping Cléante onstage during this scene. Argan retained him as a reciprocal measure: after one father has shown off his son, the other must show off his daughter. She will sing for the guests, accompanied by the tutor. Cléante sets up a pastoral duet in which a shepherd and shepherdess exchange vows. Argan grows displeased with the content of the song, especially when he peeks at the sheets of music and sees there are no words written on them. Cléante replies that a new form of notation, just invented, incorporates the lyrics in the music; but to the audience it has by now become obvious that he and Angélique are openly improvising (in rhyme) as they seal a secret love pact.

This continuous, two-part scene (II, 5) lies at the heart of the play, not only in its structural placement, but also in its juxtaposing of the two types of wooing. The rigidity of the Diafoirus doctors, *père et fils*, relying on unfelt, rehearsed sentiments, contrasts with the spontaneity of Cléante and Angélique as they give vent to their outbursts of feeling. Diafoirus senior speaks of treating patients by "following the current" and going "according to the rules," but the method applies also to his and his son's conduct in life beyond their professional practices. The bleak young graduate has dragged himself through his training by obedience and obduracy. In order to qualify as a candidate, he was forbidden to trust his own thoughts and feelings; his father and teachers have trained him to suppress any glimmer of initiative.

Since *The Imaginary Invalid* is a *divertissement*, the three acts spill over into a balletic prologue, two intermissions, and a finale. But the drama itself can be broadly visualized as two connected parts. Part one consists of a demonstration of the follies and deficiencies of physicians and the foolish credulity of this one patient-victim; part two grows into an extended debate over whether medicine has any value at all, whether indeed it does more harm than good. The demonstration reaches one climax with the appearance of Dr. Diafoirus and his son. It rises to a second climax with the arrival of the apothecary, Monsieur Fleurant, syringe in hand, to administer an enema, which Argan declines to take after being pressured by Béralde, although he has strong reservations about giving it up (III, 4). With hardly any delay, Argan's personal physician, Purgon, strides into the house and because of his patient's refusal to follow orders, works himself up into a lather culminating in a curse: He wills Argan to sink into a succession of sicknesses (from bradypepsia to dyspepsia to apepsia to lientery to dysentery to dropsy) and thence, within four days, into death (III, 5). This second climax reduces Argan to a state of terror.

As a third climax, Toinette impersonates an itinerant male doctor who claims to have lived for ninety hale years by following his own miraculous cures and has now sought out this "famous invalid" to be his patient. When Argan tells of his symptoms (headaches, blurred vision, heart pains, and the like), "Doctor" Toinette repudiates Purgon's diagnoses, attributing all the maladies to Argan's weak lungs. She pooh-poohs the remedies and diet decreed by Purgon and advises Argan to have a leg amputated and an eye put out, advice he is reluctant to follow but can't quite bring himself to discredit, either (III, 10). The second climax and, even more, the third climax with its outrageous suggestions, push the action out of farcical satire and into the world of fantasy in which medicine sometimes operates, in both senses of the word, as they prepare us for the fantastic sequence of the finale.

The other part of the play, the debate that punctuates these climaxes, takes place, on and off, between Argan and Béralde, and it too leads into the finale. Béralde asserts (III, 3) that Purgon would never dream of questioning the dogmas he lives and works by; that he bears his patients no ill will (this statement is strategically placed, shortly before Purgon utters his curse), for he would despatch them all, Argan included, no more remorsefully or malevolently than he would, if need be, kill off his own wife and children, or even himself, for the sake of going the limit with a "cure." Argan counters weakly by accusing his brother of thinking he knows more than all the doctors put together. He protests that it is easy to argue against medicine when one is in good health and (as a smattering of his own malice pops out) wishes his brother were ill; then he might change his tune (III, 4). Béralde says that the only effective remedies are rest and the workings of nature without interference from the medical profession; Argan must have an uncommonly strong constitution for it to have withstood all the enemas, laxatives, and other drugs he has taken.

In the course of the debate, Béralde proposes a visit to "a comedy by Moliére on this subject." Argan badmouths Molière for making fun of doctors and patients. This touch of theatricalism reminds us that Argan enjoys robust health—physically, at any rate—but that his creator, while speaking the lines, is dying. How many "cures" had Molière been subjected to in the effort to preserve those organs "Doctor" Toinette blames for all Argan's symptoms, the lungs? In the play's ultimate scene (III, 14), Béralde, realizing that no argument can sap his brother's faith in medicine, closes the debate by suggesting that Argan become a doctor and learn to cure himself. Toinette supports him by adding that there is no illness rash enough to attack a doctor. Béralde has hired some actors for the finale, as Covielle did in *The Bourgeois Gentleman*, to induct the hero into a new mode of being, only this time they dress up not as Turks but as members of the doctoral faculty, as the play's two parts come together.

In expressing his disgust with Molière's plays, Argan complains that the dramatist makes fun of "decent people like doctors" (III, 3). Béralde replies that he does not make fun of doctors; he ridicules medicine. Even if this claim truly expresses the author's intentions, and I am not at all sure it does, he or any other writer would have the utmost difficulty in separating out the practitioners from the practices, because of the nature of drama. Certainly, his mockery of doctoring and doctors begins early, with his second play, and continues intermittently to the end of his life. For several centuries, critics and biographers have been asking why. One obvious answer is that medicine repeatedly failed him. Ariane Mnouchkine in her televised version of the playwright's life implied another cause. In her first episode, the boy Molière watches a clutch of doctors attending his mother while she is dying; they seem indifferent to her plight and her family's, more concerned with their fees and professional squabbles than with saving her. The memory of their callous behavior stays vividly with him for the rest of his life. Mikhail Bulgakov, in his bouncing, dancing, slightly fictionalized biography of the playwright, refers similarly to the "succession of doctors" who attended Madame Poquelin; they came "mounted on donkeys and wearing sinister tall caps" *(The Life of Monsieur de Molière,* 11). There are other plausible explanations: that in oral, written, and improvised plays, doctors were a traditional object of mockery; that in purporting to effect cures, they play God and therefore deserve to be cut down to size, as overweening heroes always were in Greek myth and tragedy, among them the "first physician," Asclepius, the son of Apollo, cruelly punished by Zeus.

Without discounting any of these possibilities, one can hypothesize that Molière would not have mocked doctors who *a)* attempted "natural" healing, without the aid of drugs and paraphernalia; *b)* scorned rules and mechanical reasoning. What he appears to find most objectionable in the doctors of his day—at least, the ones he made fun of—was their dogmatism. Memorized learning that leads to false certitudes and masquerades as science (while calling itself an art) is a sign of stasis, mental death in life. Hence, Thomas Diafoirus' machinelike behavior. This character is often played as an idiot. The role might seem more persuasive in performance if the actor begins like a well-ordered machine that runs with admirable smoothness—it makes one early blooper in mistaking Angélique for Béline—but gradually runs down, as if its power were cut off. The Diafoirus dogmas then give way to the improvised love duet, inspired by impulse and passion, which are signs of humanity and life. Such an interpretation flatly contradicts the old view of

Molière as the apostle of rationality, but that view, in all its variations, was educed from favoritism, preferring some of Molière's characters and their arguments to others, rather than gauging the meanings of the *clash* of characters and of their ideas.

Molière's comic and farcical assaults on medicine are of a piece, then, with his assaults on the absolutist (and sometimes insincere and grasping) theologians of his time, as in *Tartuffe* and *Don Juan;* on amorality in the legal profession, as in *Scapin;* on secondhand scholarship, as in *The Learned Ladies;* and on the unbending personal traits evinced by his "masters of the house," from Arnolphe to Harpagon and Argan. The latter is nearly as dogmatic as his doctors are, and they in turn are nearly as miserly as Harpagon, in that they cling possessively to their bits of prejudice, which they look on as priceless possessions. Even so, the doctors in the play, who believe themselves repositories of the conventional medical wisdom of the age, prescribe differently. Diafoirus traces Argan's illness to the spleen and recommends roast meat for it; Purgon, who blames the liver, recommends boiled meat. When told of these conflicting causes, Diafoirus protects the profession by closing ranks quickly and says the spleen and the liver are "in sympathy" and that roast and boiled meat are "the same thing" (II, 6). Later, Toinette, playing the ninety-year-old quack, scorns all the previous medical advice Argan has received (III, 10). Doctors, in other words, exemplify blinkered attitudes, and Molière's spectators are more likely to have been familiar with—and adversely affected by—medicine than by other professions.

The doctors in this play may come across as figures of fun, but they are too humorously treated for us to regard them as willful villains, people who intend harm—even the incensed Purgon as he launches his curse. The action, however, does throw up one unmistakable villain, Argan's wife, Béline, who aims to dispossess Angélique and Louison, the daughters of the earlier marriage, and would like to see Angélique sent to a convent. In the same scene (II, 6) in which Thomas Diafoirus hopes to win over Angélique by pointing out that "the ancients" used to seize their prospective wives by force in order not to give the impression that the young women went eagerly into their arms, Béline, also speaking to Angélique, appeals to the "old times" when daughters obeyed their fathers without question. She thereby aligns herself with the dogmatic doctors.

But she has more medical discernment than they have. She has accurately diagnosed Argan's complaint as a desire to be fussed over and cajoled like a small child: when he feels bilious, she calls him "my baby boy" (I, 6). His addiction to medicine confirms that he "needs" such attentions. Because she plays up to his desire to be babied, much as Tartuffe plays up to Orgon's desire to be considered a man of great moral worth, Argan trusts her more than he does the others. Béralde even compares Argan's excessive fondness for medicine with his excessive fondness for Béline (III, 11). Bringing her insincerity into the open requires an old ruse suggested by Toinette, that Argan pretend to be dead so that he can hear how she will grieve over his body. As we expect, she sees him lying inert, is overjoyed, and looks forward to her inheritance. When Toinette then tells Angélique her father has died, she, by way of contrast, is stricken with remorse at having flouted his wishes.

But an actress who plays Béline as a villain from her first appearance on betrays the role. If she convinces Argan that she loves him, she should be able to convince the audience, or at least keep them in a state of uncertainty about her aims, until Argan is induced to play dead and show her up for what she is. Until that late switch, the *character* puts on an act, but her performance should not appear crass when we notice her on the same side of the conflict as the doctors. Much as Toinette impersonates a doctor and Cléante a music teacher, Béline impersonates a loving wife.

As for Argan, after impersonating an invalid, he will impersonate a doctor in the "third interlude," which serves as the ceremonial finale. Molière based this ritual on the secret, almost masonic, solemnities at the University of Paris, held when the Faculty of Medicine submitted candidates for questioning and approval. He brings onstage a chorus of surgeons, other doctors, and apothecaries who dance and chant their verses in a hodgepodge of rhymed pidgin-Latin, French, and Italian. The candidate, Argan, promises the identical treatment for wildly varying ailments: he will administer a clyster (or enema), then a bleeding, and last a purgative. He swears to obey the faculty's rules, never to swerve from "the opinions of the ancients," and to apply only the remedies prescribed by the faculty members, even if the patient is dying. As the degree is conferred amid balletic caperings, a chorus repeatedly congratulates Argan and wishes him an uncommonly long life ("a thousand, thousand years") in which to "eat, drink, bleed, and kill." This farcical rendition, undertaken by the actors recruited by Béralde, must have gravely offended those doctors who heard about it; probably only a few saw the staging, since most of them considered it below their dignity to attend the theatre at all, and the title of the play provided sufficient warning that Molière had once again attempted to lance their profession.[4]

Medicine and theatricalism may dominate the action and themes of *The Imaginary Invalid,* but like all of Molière's plays, it contains a love story: Cléante wins Angélique; Argan loses Béline (the Béline he loved and trusted), although whether they remain married is unresolved in the action. Molière sustains the love motif in the prologue and the first and second interludes, intricately rhymed pastoral ballet-operas with music composed by Charpentier, which are often dismissed as having no bearing on the play and omitted from some translations. There are actually two alternative prologues.[5] The first, an elaborate gathering of nymphs, shepherds, shepherdesses, the goddess Flora, and the god Pan, pays tribute to Louis XIV for the courage he showed during his recent wars in Holland, welcomes him home as "the greatest of kings," and implies that his triumphs in battle have made France (and the prologue's Arcadia) safe for lovers. The second prologue, a lament in four verses by a shepherdess, frets that conceited doctors with "their little knowledge and big Latin words" cannot cure her heartache: "Your idle chatter would be accepted only by an IMAGINARY INVALID." Curtain up for act I.

A slender thread ties that act to the first interlude. Almost at the end of the act, Toinette remarks she will seek the help of her suitor, Polichinelle, to take a message to Cléante about the threatened marriage between Angélique and the young doctor. In the interlude, Polichinelle, the ancestor from the commedia dell'arte (Pulcinella) of Punch, comes to the house but doesn't mention the message, and doesn't seem equipped to halt the marriage, anyway. The old fellow stands outside and chides himself for being in love with a female dragon, neglecting his business (moneylending), missing food and sleep, losing his mind. He serenades Toinette in Italian; but his beloved does not appear at her window, only an old woman who answers him mockingly with a matching Italian song, as though he had addressed his fervor to

---

4. It is believed that Molière may have learned about the actual proceedings at the university from one of his personal doctors named Mauvillain, who was subsequently attacked as a traitor by many of his peers.

5. Mesnard, the editor of one of the great editions of Molière's plays, argues that the two prologues were originally part of one.

her. Polichinelle has more serenades in store but, like Lyciscas in *The Princess of Elis,* he is interrupted—by violinists and then by watchmen and archers, who threaten to arrest him for creating a disturbance at night. He mollifies them with bribes, and the interlude comes to an end with the bribe takers ecstatic and Polichinelle as lovelorn as the shepherdess in the second prologue. Perhaps we are meant to assume that Polichinelle did deliver the message, after all, because the next act opens with the prompt arrival of Cléante, who poses as the substitute music teacher.[6]

If that first interlude takes place in a new setting, with the exterior of Argan's house in the background, the second interlude, which follows act II, goes on in the same setting as the play, as Béralde leads into view four gypsies in Moorish costume who dance and sing. The burden of their song compares with Feste's *carpe diem* advice to Olivia *(Twelfth Night,* II, 3): Enjoy our young years while they last, it recommends—the springtime of our life; love brings anguish but also pleasures; "beauty passes,/ effaced by time,/ The ice age / Takes over." The gypsies dance and display some performing monkeys they have brought with them. Once again the theme of spontaneity is sounded, the gypsies' songs reinforcing Cléante's pastoral duet with Angélique.

Does Argan heed such sentiments? As the gypsies go off and the third act takes over in the drawing room, Béralde asks his brother, "Wasn't that as good as a laxative?" and Argan replies with a line that has become a familiar French quotation, "Hm, nothing's as good as a good laxative" *(Hon, de bonne casse est bonne).* Argan is incurable, even after his eyes are opened to his wife's deceits. That is why, for the last interlude, or finale, Béralde will arrange for him to believe he has locked himself into the ritualistic rigidities of medicine. The occasion for the finale, according to Béralde, is Mardi Gras, although Argan has no idea, once it is over, any more than Monsieur Jourdain does, that he has taken part in a carnival, a pretense. As the actors troop out of the drawing room in their medical robes, they leave behind an incontestable master of the house, the imaginary doctor.

6. It seems that the action runs continuously between the acts and the interludes, without intermission. Molière and his collaborators evidently provided nonstop entertainment.

2. Mistresses of the House

Amphitryon, 1668

Those Molière heroes who play, or fear to play, the roles of cheated husbands in the form of Le Barbouillé, the Sganarelles of *The Forced Marriage* and *The Imaginary Cuckold,* Arnolphe, George Dandin, and Alceste are laughable figures (and also pitiable) because of their pugnacious indecision. By way of contrast, the Theban general, Amphitryon, occasions no laughter, even though the play named after him carries the subtitle "a comedy." Molière's plotting keeps him onstage for only about five-ninths as much time as his batman, Sosie, the principal source of the play's laughter and the role the author reserved for himself.[1] It seems then that Molière meant to subordinate Amphitryon's plight to Sosie's, which is nevertheless no more than a partial reflection of his master's. The general's newlywed wife, Alcmène, does deceive him, but by being deceived herself, for when Jupiter, in the guise of her husband, seduces her, she can conclude only that Amphitryon has become a more ardent and loquacious lover and probably, all of a sudden, more practiced. But Sosie, after being impersonated by Mercury, is not cuckolded, only alienated further from a wife who has henpecked him for fifteen years. As a further curious feature of the action, Amphitryon insists that the deception costs him his honor, while Sosie collects bruises all over his back before temporarily losing his name and, by implication, his identity; yet little is made of the loss to Alcmène, the most abused victim, who does not even appear in the last act.

The most likely explanation for the uneven parceling-out of woes is that the playwright lays a coat of comic and farcical varnish on an essentially serious drama and equips it with mechanical marvels in order to gloss over a satire of Louis XIV's exploitation of the women around him at court. Did the play's action successfully distract attention away from its target or at least cover its satirical scratches? Evidently it did at first. The king watched it at the Tuileries and did not obstruct it from going public several days later for

---

1. The order of importance of the five main roles, estimated by the length of time they each spend onstage, rather than simply by the number of lines they speak, is as follows: Sosie, Amphitryon, Mercury, Alcmène, Jupiter.

twenty-nine showings. But many commentators since 1668 have remarked on Molière's audacity and wondered how he got away with it.

As his only full-length play heavily dependent upon a classical myth,[2] *Amphitryon*, though considerably in debt to two known versions (the *Amphitruo* of Plautus, ca. 186 B.C.E., and Rotrou's *The Sosies*, produced some thirty years earlier), moves significantly away from them, especially in proclaiming Jupiter's purpose in seducing Alcmène. In the earlier plays, and possibly in a Middle Comedy by a Greek dramatist that may have inspired Plautus, the monarch of the gods intends to use Alkmena as a womb for Hercules, who will rid the world of monsters and confer a benefit on humanity. In Molière, the annunciation of the heroic demigod comes late in the action, almost as an afterthought or a sop, leaving an audience to assume that Jupiter did not mean to extend an eventual benefaction from heaven but simply to take advantage of a beautiful and virtuous young woman.

One way to analyze the play is to observe how the characters change, or more accurately, how their clashes and abrasions force them to reveal themselves. The prologue to the three acts consists of a colloquy between Mercury, who dallies on a cloud, and Night, a female presence who enters in an airborne but horse-drawn chariot, an encounter recalling Puck's with the fairy *(MND* II,1), that prelude to strange nocturnal druggings and brain-washings in the wood outside Athens. Mercury wants Night to slacken the reins of her horses, that is, extend the hours of darkness, so that Jupiter, who has already gone to bed with Alcmène, may prolong his pleasure. He took on the shape of the husband, Mercury adds, as a stratagem that does not always work, since some husbands are unwelcome in their wives' beds. But in this case, the god had been struck by "the young heat and tenderness" of love between the newlyweds. Here we have Jupiter as jealous voyeur, as well as rapist, while his messenger and the goddess Night must serve as panders. She gallops off—slowly, as requested—and he alights from his cloud. The Mercury we see on earth will now go from being playful to spiteful.

In the longest scene (I, 2), he appears to Sosie as the latter's double and lets him overhear how "I'll enjoy myself by stealing his name and his likeness" and how "my arm shall very shortly punish his insolence," before it grows weary from lack of practice, for it has not broken any bones for more than a

---

2. There are mythical traces or themes in some of the other plays, such as *The School for Wives*. The five-act spectacle *Psyche*, written, like *Amphitryon*, in rhyming free verse, also uses classical myth but was the result of a collaboration between Molière, Corneille, and Quinault.

week. Mercury is as bad as his word. He slaps Sosie around and compels him to renounce his identity until Mercury chooses to be "no longer Sosie." In his most disheartening act, he proves that he "is" Sosie by recalling events and feelings from Sosie's recent past that no other human being could have known about. He then drives the baffled servant away from the house to the harbor, where Amphitryon is expected.[3] Soon after, having already confused Sosie's past and present, he proceeds to complicate the batman's future, by telling his rough-tongued wife, Cléanthis, that he can't be bothered to greet her or show her any signs of affection. Far from acknowledging her fidelity for not trafficking with other men while her husband is away—she expects thanks and praise for her self-denials—he would not object if she did. She irritates him when she keeps dinning her claims to loyalty in his ears. He wants "less honor and more peace"; he prefers "an appropriate vice to an exhausting virtue." Whereupon, he leaves her fuming, "enraged at being an honest woman" (I, 4), and intent on taking out her rage on him (that is, on Sosie). Mercury's nonchalant dismissal of the value of (somebody else's) honor stands in contrast to Amphitryon's later cherishing *his* honor, which becomes virtually an obsession that recalls Harpagon's cherishing his gold and Argan's his imaginary diseases.

Mercury remains offstage during the middle act of the play, allowing the fears and bad feelings that he and his master have planted to take root and ramify. In the last act he reappears three times. First, he turns his malice on Amphitryon. He leans out of an upstairs window in the guise of Sosie, refusing admission to the house, and accuses the general of being drunk for thinking he is Amphitryon, when Amphitryon is indoors with Alcmène (III, 2). Next, he frightens the famished Sosie away from the house at the dinner hour (III, 6). In the penultimate scene, he reveals that the Amphitryon impostor is Jupiter. Before taking off on his cloud, he avers that Sosie can feel honored at having been drubbed by a god and that he is fed up with wearing Sosie's ugliness (III, 9). If the play were not a farce at its heart, and therefore heartless, one would have to say that Molière has, during the action, developed a portrait of a pretty unsavory attendant god, whose amorality recalls that of the author's other antisocial stage beings.

In the *Amphitruo*, Plautus puts a feather and a tassel on Mercury and Jupiter to distinguish them from their human counterparts. Molière does not bother with this badge of distinction. We cannot be sure whether he found,

---

3. Molière has picked up from Plautus the howler that Thebes, an inland settlement, was situated on the Greek coast.

or enhanced, any natural resemblance between himself and La Grange (Mercury), who was about thirteen years younger, and between Hubert (Amphitryon) and La Thorillière (Jupiter). But here, as in other plays of muddled identity, plausibility for the spectators depends not on what their eyes tell them but on what they see the other characters see. The look-alikes need not look identical. A spectator will notice that the two pairs of actors are not doubles, but can assume that if the gods can press the pause button on their VCR of night, their descent can cast a spell on the other characters to make *them* unable to differentiate between human victims and godly oppressors. Because of the farcical situation, Jupiter and Mercury might even appear as stylized imitations or caricatures of Amphitryon and Sosie, wearing similar costumes and perhaps broadly mimicking their vocal mannerisms, stance, and gait. This effect would be particularly telling in the mirror-image scenes between the four roles. It would also make plain the inability of the gods, who are short on human feelings, to become altogether human.

Like Mercury, Jupiter is a bully. He shows no more scruples than Mercury does in deploying his powers, although he does not inflict any corporal chastisement, only the agonies of uncertainty. As the most consistent figure in the play, he comes across as a winning, unflappable masher who makes the most of his *droits de seigneur.* And why not, when he is the Omnipotent? This play does not specify, as in Plautus, that Jupiter initiated the war between Thebes and Athens in order to remove Amphitryon to the Boeotian plains, but he does make the most of the general's absence by reining in the steeds of Night. To get his way with Alcmène, Jupiter will wheedle, lie, browbeat. He even indulges in some quasi-suicidal heroics (II, 6), threatening to do away with himself in case he has offended his "heart's adorable object." (What might happen if he tried to make good on the threat? Could he die, and if so, would Amphitryon and the rest of Creation die with him? A question not to be asked.) In the short run, he wishes Alcmène to separate, in her mind and responses, the husband to whom she owes her duty from the lover to whom she owes her affection, in other words to love him, Jupiter, for himself and for his superior lovemaking techniques, leading up to a celestial orgasm,[4] and to do all this somehow without knowing that he is not her

---

4. In this respect he is not unlike the poor little rich girl who does not want to be loved for her money, for instance, the Grace Kelly character in Hitchcock's *To Catch a Thief.*

Whether under the influence of *Amphitryon* or not, a number of twentieth-century works have developed Jupiter's notion that a husband and lover could be like two

husband (I, 3 and II, 6). For the long run, he promises to repair or reinstate her compromised virtue by showering "a thousand prolific benefits" on her household and to "let it be known that I am [Amphitryon's] support," the benefits to include the birth and deeds of Hercules. In this closing scene (III, 10), the equivalent of the traditionally combined dénouement and reconciliation, there actually is no reconciliation. Molière's plotting keeps Alcmène offstage and Amphitryon, although present, silent. The closing words are assigned to Sosie: "In matters such as these, it is always best to say nothing."

Amphitryon, the last of the main characters to appear, although a general and now a cuckold, is a young husband, a warrior probably no more seasoned than Rodrigue in *The Cid*, but he has grown accustomed to seeing his orders instantly translated into action and receiving intelligible answers to his questions. He demands a straightforward report from Sosie, who preceded him home; he does not receive it (II, 1). He expects a conqueror's welcome from his wife; he does not receive it (II, 2). He has not yet given his wife an intended gift of some diamonds acquired as spoils from the enemy's leader, but they have been presented to her, miraculously and infuriatingly abstracted from a sealed casket. He believes he has escaped from the insanity of war; but he has just walked into a maddening world in which, he is told, he arrived the day before. So addled is he by one unexpected reaction after another that if he noticed how elastic the previous night was, he does not remark on it. To this no-nonsense youth, his valet-batman and his wife make no sense. Time, space, the personalities of others, and the order of things have gone awry, started to spin. Perhaps they will right themselves if he can only keep his head and become the still center of the whirling events. But he cannot. He is human. He grows furious and stamps off in search of his wife's brother, who had been with him until that morning and can witness that he had not been home before. When he returns, his servant, impersonated by Mercury, keeps him locked out of his own house because "Amphitryon" is already there making love to his wife (III, 2). But this same servant now invisibly whisks himself from the upstairs window to the wings, bringing onstage Amphitryon's brother-in-law and another Theban officer, and casually saying, "I've just invited them to dine with you."

"Who gave you that order?"

"You" (III, 4).

At this point, Jupiter, having heard the fracas or divined what it was about,

distinct characters in one personality, among them Pinter's one-act *The Lover* and Nino Manfredi's film *Nudo di donna.*

comes out of doors to investigate. Amphitryon, in this moment of his most acute confusion, is at last face to face with the figure who has supplanted him. What he must now do is disprove this man's authenticity and so prove his own. But once again, he cannot hold his temper in check; his officers have to restrain him. While the impostor remains majestically reasonable and therefore convincing, he, Amphitryon, a self-styled "martyr," must stand with his arms pinioned, as though in a straitjacket, expostulating like a crazy impostor. All he can think of is that he must slay this other Amphitryon likeness and heal his bludgeoned honor. Sosie's and Alcmène's perplexities make no impact on him: he is entirely wrapped up in his own troubles.

Later, he seeks out two more of his officers, who swear to avenge him (III, 7).[5] But his vehemence again peters out, this time overcome by Mercury's and Jupiter's unanswerable elucidation and promises, to which he can find no reply. In plotting this Amphitryon, Molière relentlessly sketches a retreat from blustering, victorious commander into silenced, acquiescent plaything of the gods.

In the original myth, Alkmena gives birth subsequently to twins who are stepbrothers, one sired by Amphitryon, the other by Jupiter; in other words, she was already pregnant when Jupiter seduced her. Molière spares his Alcmène this additional indignity. He also gives her a part that is even more reactive than Amphitryon's. During her first scene (I, 3), played with Jupiter, she expresses conventional, wifely fears for her husband's safety during the fighting. Jupiter, who is not engaged in any fighting, diverts the conversation to his love for her, which "exceeds a husband's." She cannot understand what he is getting at. How could she? Nor can she understand Amphitryon's indignation when he turns up. Like Alceste and Orgon before him, he has been away for some days and has left her mistress of the house. He had looked forward to her "eagerly desiring" his return. But then, he hears her say merely, "What! back so soon?" She protests that she showed him on the previous night how welcome he was, and that he "had never before seemed so tender and passionate." He questions her closely about what happened during that night, much to her vexation, because he behaves as though in

5. Here, in the play's final moments (III, 7), Molière introduces and establishes with a single speech of nineteen lines a character based on the braggart soldier or the Spanish Capitano (or, come to that, Dorante in Corneille's *The Liar*), a bully with the Plautine name of Argatiphontidas, who wants no further discussion, only to rush into action with his "head lowered" and to put his "sword through a body." His eagerness to kill whatever opposes or vexes him substitutes him momentarily for Amphitryon.

less than one day he had forgotten the lovemaking, forgotten even the "knot of diamonds" he gave her. And when he tells her that he was not the one who made love to her, this is the last straw: she is "determined that our bonds shall be broken this very day" (II, 2).

Alcmène will have only one more scene, and that not with her husband again but with Jupiter, still in disguise and ready to argue his way into another night of pleasure. Denouncing him at first as a cruel, frightful monster of a husband, she goes on to rail at his "subtleties," his "frivolous excuses," and to affirm that he deserves her hatred. She relents, but not much, after he offers to stab himself. He knows that she loves Amphitryon (and what there appears to be of Amphitryon in him); that her husband's death would punish her; and that his threat is unconscionably nasty. But Jupiter takes what Jupiter wants. Besides, he has a golden, forked tongue. He carries everything before him, Alcmène included. As they go inside together, she cuts short his blandishments as she speaks her last words in the play: "Enough: I loathe myself for being so weak" (II, 6). As her sadness cuts into the farcical maneuvering, the joyous bride gives way to the resigned sexual quarry. In Molière's story, nobody informs her what has taken place. She learns only that her husband is capable of disbelieving her and of acting duplicitously. Will he ever let her know why? Probably not, if he thinks that doing so might impugn his precious honor.

A number of Molière's servant-heroes, their souls transmigrated out of the wily slaves of Plautus, play the activator as they manipulate love matches against parental opposition. Sosie is different, a pawn of circumstances who suffers simply for being who he is. His final, meager reward consists in an end to his discomfiture when the gods allow him to take back his own place in the universe. More bitterly than any other Molière valet, he begrudges his servitude and degradation. The part might almost have been conceived by a modern socialist (or Sosiealist?), who has been a postal worker: "The great . . . want everything in nature sacrificed for their sake. Day and night, through hail, gales, danger, heat, cold—the moment they speak we must fly. Twenty years of hard service bring us no reward from them" (I, 1). In the first scene after the prologue, he also functions as a narrator when he rehearses his master's greetings to Alcmène. He steps outside the action again in the last scene when he advises Amphitryon and his assembled officers that "the great god Jupiter has greatly honored us" and that now "we should each retire quietly into our homes." The concluding sentiments either reek of sarcasm, if they are consistent with Sosie's earlier lines, or reek of sincerity, since Molière spoke them at the first performance before the "Sun King."

Between these bracketing speeches, Sosie undergoes enough thwarting, mishaps, and poundings to content an addict of television wrestling. For a start, he never gets to deliver his greetings to Alcmène and his account of Amphitryon's success on the battlefield, which we have seen him rehearsing, thoroughly satisfied with his own eloquence,

> Madame, my lord Amphitryon, your mate . . .
> (Great! Beautiful opening!)
> His spirit overflowing with your charms,
> Chose me above all others to relate
> The story of his triumph under arms

and improvising her replies:

> Oh! Is that true, dear Sosie?
> I am so delighted to see you again. (I, 1)

But Mercury will not let him enter the house, let alone deliver his battle description (a skit on the messenger speeches of contemporary tragedies) to Alcmène, who is busy in bed with Jupiter. He is also deprived by Mercury of his name and person and roundly beaten until he cries out, "If you really are [Sosie], then tell me who you want *me* to be, for after all, I must be someone" (I, 2). When Amphitryon arrives on the scene, Sosie keeps alleging that he was prevented by *himself* from entering the house and speaking his piece to Alcmène. After hearing this inexplicable explanation more than once, Amphitryon wonders, "Is it a dream? Is it drink? A mind gone astray? Or a nasty joke?" Sosie gamely elaborates: "For quite some time I treated this other me as an impostor; but he finally forced me to recognize myself. . . . He's like me from head to foot: good-looking, a noble air, well set-up, charming manners; two drops of milk are not more alike. I'd be quite satisfied with him if only his hands were a bit less heavy." His master orders him to stop mouthing this nonsense, whereupon Sosie mutters, "Talk is always nonsense when it comes from someone humble. If an important man said the same thing it would be an exquisite utterance" (II, 1).

Not long after, he must cope with his sour wife, made more crotchety than usual by Mercury's coldness. He refused to go to bed with her, she says between insults and reproaches. Sosie, pleading that he must have eaten garlic or been drunk at the time, argues that doctors don't recommend sex while one of the parties is drunk because it begets dull-witted children who cannot survive. He is not displeased to find that one of his tormentors talked back to the other; we can appreciate why when Cléanthis says that doctors should mind their own business (which is sick people, not healthy ones) and goes on to refer joylessly to the "*duty* of conjugal love" (II, 3). In a couple of subsequent scenes, he halfheartedly attempts to "make a little peace" with her, but she spurns him, tells him to leave her alone, and declares that "a woman sometimes grows tired of being honest." After this final line of act II she reappears only in some crowd scenes in act III and speaks a few words but has no further conversation with her husband. We are bound to deduce from the stand-off, this absence of a reconciliation, that the servants' marriage has become as iced over as that of the master and mistress.

Sosie's experiences and lines have led many critics to view the play as another thematic conflict between appearance (illusion) and reality.[6] Such an interpretation does not quite hold up because Sosie is never mistaken for Mercury nor Amphitryon for Jupiter. There is no two-way confusion, as in *The Comedy of Errors*. Both Amphitryon and Sosie know who they are; what baffles them is the materializing of their respective clones and the blame they must shoulder for acts they did not commit.[7]

Sosie stays in the forefront of the action in order to cope with further imbroglios in the last act. Jupiter (as Amphitryon) has sent him to round up some of "my" officers for dinner (II, 6). Returning with them to find an Amphitryon who gave him no such order, and who has been kept out of the house by Mercury, and who blames this insolent batman, Sosie cannot comprehend what the general is talking about, just as the general was unable earlier to make any sense of what the batman said. Sosie fears more undeserved punishment ("Before they hang a man, they tell him why") and calls on the officers for protection. He enjoys both a reprieve and a partial revenge on his master when Jupiter appears and he can identify the god as "the true Amphitryon . . . the Amphitryon who invites you to dinner" (III, 5). But his appetite speaks too soon. Once again, Mercury stands in his way. Sosie offers a truce ("Let the two Amphitryons squabble over their jealousies while the two Sosies co-exist in pleasant peace"); he is even prepared to become the subordinate Sosie by analogy with the laws of inheritance: "I'll be the younger and you can be the older"; and then, in an ultimate concession, "At least, let me be your shadow." The god will not budge, and when Sosie hisses to himself that this creature is a "double son of a whore," Mercury's mind-

6. Please see Introduction for a discussion of what are often called "tensions between opposites."

7. For a detailed discussion of the supposed appearance-versus-reality conundrum, see Gossman, "Amphitryon," 1–34.

reading intelligence picks up the remark and Sosie gets another thrashing. After this he kneels in commiseration before his master, for a servant exists to be the butt of punishment, an object on which a master can take out his wrath: "Strike, beat, pile it on, overwhelm me with blows; kill me in your anger. . . . I deserve it. . . . The same pitiless fate dogs us both. Result? I was de-Sosie'd, just as you were de-Amphitryon'd."

Once the complications are (only partially) unraveled, and Mercury sails away on his cloud, a relieved Sosie yells after him, "I never in my life saw a god who was more of a devil than you." Jupiter takes his leave on another fast-moving cloud, and Sosie then unburdens himself of the sixteen-line speech that calls for, and achieves, silence all around.

The silence is hardly a comfortable one. Jupiter, rather than settling everyone's affairs, has brushed aside all the misunderstandings plaited into the action. Two of the principal characters did not take part in the dinner arranged by Jupiter and presumably paid for by Amphitryon. Alcmène did not hear Jupiter's last speech, and he does not say that he told her about the questionable privilege she will have in bearing Hercules. What happens after act III—whether, for example, Sosie and Amphitryon will or will not make the effort to patch up their marriages—is one of the questions left open. It could provide matter for the director and actors to chew over during rehearsals. They may decide to impose a closing tableau that amounts to some sort of celebration, but the play itself implies that the gods' intervention has driven both couples apart. Sosie's remarks about having been honored by Jupiter's visits and by the "infallible happiness" his blessings have conferred ring false and sound like the reticulate double-entendres found in many other plays by Molière, just as the closing moments recall the comic despair that crowns the end of Molière's next play, George Dandin, written that same year.

The Seductive Countess
(*La Comtesse d'Escarbagnas*, 1671)

Following the examples set by several Molière characters who preceded her, the Comtesse d'Escarbagnas has bloated aspirations: she wants to be recognized for what she is not. A native of Angoulême, she deplores the provinciality of her servants, neighbors, and surroundings, expecting, after a two-month visit to Paris, to be taken for a lady of quality who is *au courant* with the latest in fashionable manners. The plotting of this one-act is deceptively simple, a run of entrances and some exits by awkward servants, who cannot keep up with their lady's airs and artifices, and by three suitors, one humble, one rude, and the third a sham. Once again, the author, as manager of his troupe, provided opportunities for some of his actors to rely on their best skills, but he gave Marie Ragueneau, who played the comtesse, her first leading role. The play also worked as a departing point for another of the spectacular events commanded by the king, and could therefore be cross-listed here with the diversions. But the script of the accompanying *Ballet of Ballets* has disappeared. As with *The Bourgeois Gentleman,* the play's text is open-ended so as to lead into a performance within the performance.

Molière introduces several sources of conflict. The first proceeds from the sham suitor, a vicomte named Cléante. He loves a young woman, Julie, whom the comtesse treats as a confidante but who uses the comtesse's home to meet Cléante—surreptitiously, because they are waiting for a quarrel between their families to mend before they can openly declare their love. Cléante justifies his visits to the house by pretending to be in love with the comtesse and paying her ironically rich compliments. She welcomes his attentions and the possibility of a match with a genuine aristocrat,[1] her own claim to nobility being questionable, since she remarks that her late husband "took the quality of *comte* on all the contracts he signed" (sc. 2), but she nowhere specifies that he actually held that rank.

The second conflict arises among the suitors. Monsieur Tibaudier, a councillor who believes he doesn't stand a chance with his beloved because

1. Mlle Ragueneau, who played the comtesse, was married in that same year (1672) to La Grange, the man who took the role of her sham suitor.

of the competition from Cléante, writes her atrociously imitative love poems and sends her unripe pears as a morose tribute to what he considers her hard heart; while Monsieur Harpin, an irascible tax collector who has evidently showered her in the past with money, throws off unexciting oaths with every sentence he spits out.

The third conflict opposes the comtesse and her notions of fastidious etiquette to a maid, who appears when the mistress summons her "ladies," and a pageboy she calls her lackey, both of them innocent of the more groveling service the comtesse observed in Parisian drawing rooms. The maid has never learned to place a saucer under a glass of water. The page brazenly announces a visitor instead of whispering news of the arrival to the nearest "lady-in-waiting," that is, the chambermaid. Such acts of negligence (which, it is safe to say, the comtesse was unaware of before her stay in Paris), pain her and scar her sensitivity.

The play's movement is generated less, though, by the conflicts than by the speech and manners of this rural pretender, a dramatic sibling of Magdelon and Cathos, Madame de Sotenville, Argan, Monsieur Jourdain, and Monsieur de Pourceaugnac, and something of a trial run for Philaminte and Armande in *The Learned Ladies*. The other characters exist to humor her, rather than irritate her, as she attempts to show off her gentility, knowingness, the household help, and even her child, "my son the count." The play itself exists to display her, to give rein to her conceits and frustrations:

> I realize that I am capable of inspiring a powerful passion in men; you must blame that on my beauty, my youth, and my quality, for all of which I thank heaven . . .
>
> It's so disconcerting in these small towns. They simply do not know a thing. Whenever I return to the bucolic life I throw up my hands at the lack of respect for my quality . . .
>
> I swear there wasn't a gallant in the city who didn't come to see me and make pretty conversation. I still have all their notes in my purse, and they would give you some idea of the number of proposals I rejected. (sc. 2)

As her final frustration, an unsigned note comes for Cléante informing him that the quarrel between his family and Julie's has been settled but only on condition that the two young people marry. The comtesse, feeling abandoned now that two of her suitors have fallen away, declares that she will marry the one left, Tibaudier, to spite everybody else, as though she has some choice other than to remain the unpartnered mistress of a rural house.

The Learned Ladies
(*Les Femmes savantes,* 1672)

Owing, probably, to its alliterative *L'* s and *d* 's, this English title has become almost officially established for at least 250 years. A more accurate name would be "The Scholarly Women" or possibly "The Learning Women." But insisting pedantically on the distinction would be like marching into Molière's trap, for his satirical comedy takes its aim at pedantry rather than at women; and my intent is to defend it once again against the charge to which it appears more susceptible than do any of his other plays: misogyny.[1]

In recent years, feminist criticism has moved swiftly beyond the analysis of neglected female subjects and authors in literature and the drama; it is now calling on the arts to explore the inner and outer "experiences of half the human race" as those arts seldom do. But in the three centuries since the play's first showings, distinguished women and male advocates of women's rights, among them Stendhal,[2] have been disapproving of it, while its cheerleaders have claimed that the play is more "balanced" than a first encounter with it might suggest. For instance, against the learned or learning or scholarly women in question —the strident mother, Philaminte, her vengeful older daughter, Armande, and Philaminte's dotty sister-in-law, Bélise— the author has arrayed a trio of male buffoons—the meek father, Chrysale, and the two poetasting cult heroes, Trissotin and Vadius. The scale of opinions voiced in the play tips, however, because the four remaining characters have generous opportunities to speak their minds, and they all take issue with the three *savantes,* not always effectively. They are Chrysale's brother, Ariste, the cook-cum-maid, Martine, and the young lovers, Henriette and Clitandre. In addition, the two male *savants* indulge in a verbal scrap during

1. Palmer has a short, excellent segment on this play, 461–69.
2. According to Gita May, Stendhal took Molière "to task for indulging in ridiculing serious-minded women and for treating in a flippant manner a theme worthy of more serious attention. Stendhal's sympathy for women and their difficult lot in society is clearly evidenced by his harsh remarks on Molière's play" (from "Molière and Stendhal," in Johnson, Trail, and Neumann, 132). Stendhal's critiques of Molière are collected in *Molière jugé par Stendhal* (Paris: 1898).

one of the most entertaining and therefore definitive scenes, positioned at the very heart of the comedy (III, 3). In undermining each other, they pile more ridicule on the women who idolize them. Thus the conflict does suffer from imbalance as an intellectual debate. But what about its balance as a dramatic action?

In his plotting, Molière has created five substantial male and five substantial female roles—more of the latter than in any of his other plays. The distribution of these roles is almost symmetrical in its matching of opposites: weak husband and strong wife, contrasting sisters, contrasting sisters-in-law and brothers and suitors for Henriette and poet-pedants and servants. The formal doubleness carries through into the language as its smooth progression of rhymed couplets harbors outbursts of euphuistic gallantry and colloquial anger. His main plot is also double. It turns on whether Clitandre will succeed in marrying Henriette. He has the support of her father but faces the antagonism of her mother, who has destined her for the pedant Trissotin. Henriette's older sister also wants Clitandre, but to keep him on tap as an admirer, as she previously did for two years, rather than to give herself to him as a wife. This love conflict meshes with a marital conflict, which determines whether the mother or the father is the operative head of the household. Uncle Ariste, Aunt Bélise, and Martine, the maid, each take sides in this main plot. As slight complications, there are two subsidiary conflicts, the dispute between the pedants and a disagreement between husband and wife over whether Martine shall be kept on as a servant; but both of these fit tidily into the bifurcated main plot. The play thus has almost intact unity of action, as well as conforming to the artificial unities of time and place—everything happens within twenty-four hours in one of those ambiguously neutral settings so favored by the neoclassical playwrights; in this case, a drawing room.

Chrysale vows over and over that he is the power in his "own house." But he lacks the psychological wherewithal. A comfortable and indulgent middle-class citizen, he has evidently contributed little to the running of the home up to this point and now feels he must assert himself when it comes to his daughters' husbands. In all likelihood, he would argue that the dowry will come out of his, the breadowner's, pocket: money entitles one to power, doesn't it? He is also prejudiced in favor of Clitandre as a son-in-law, because he and Clitandre's late father once spent time together in Rome, where "we strenuously wooed the Roman ladies, and everyone talked of our exploits: we made the men jealous" (II, 3). These heartbreakers were then twenty-eight, and so Chrysale married fairly late, unless he was already married, a doubtful supposition. At that time, if he is telling the truth rather than tinting the past, he looked on women as playthings. But in Philaminte he met more than his match. With all his professions of asserting mastery over his family, he backs down as soon as he runs into her resistance, even when Ariste and Martine are egging him on to take and hold the initiative. Although Clitandre is not very rich, Chrysale counts it a pleasure to have this man of "honor, intelligence, heart, and refinement" as a son-in-law, not considering that he may be committing his daughter to a chip off the old wolf. In the last act, he stands ready to concede Henriette to Trissotin and Armande to Clitandre, as if that arrangement were a compromise, when it is exactly what he was trying to prevent. As a sonless father, he has few exchanges in the play with his daughters; when he does talk to them it's to issue orders—"Remove that glove; take this gentleman's hand" (III, 6); "Submit to your father's will" (V, 2)—or shrill protestations—"Do you take me for a idiot? . . . Am I a pushover? . . . Would I be weak enough to let my wife lead me by the nose?" (V, 2). Here and in other scenes, he reveals traces of Gorgibus, the blustering parent of Molière's early plays, and of that impotent braggart, the capitano from the commedia dell'arte.

His wife insists that Martine be dismissed because her verbs do not agree with her subject nouns; he contends she is a good cook, the one servant in the house who has no ambition to be a scholar, only devotion to his meals, and should therefore be kept on. At one point he is about to explode at Philaminte: he will "snatch off the mask" of civility and "unload his rage," but when Philaminte snaps back, "What was that?" he turns hastily to his sister with: "You're the one I'm talking to" (II, 7) and proceeds to rant at her in a fifty-seven-line monologue, a litany of the injustices he must put up with in a house infested with servants who dare to read and dream, womenfolk dedicated to writing and astronomy, and their books, which ought to be burned. Molière reserved this broadly comic role, which *could* be invested with moments of pathos, for himself.

His bachelor brother, Ariste,[3] another of those close relatives and friends who have little to do but hang around the house dispensing common sense and serving as tireless interlocutors and intermediaries, is probably younger than Chrysale. Despite his geniality, the worm of sibling rivalry gnaws at him, as it does Armande and Henriette. In prompting Chrysale to stand up for his rights and to his wife, he accuses him of being effeminate and cowardly (II, 9), hard words, especially when aimed at a fellow who thinks of himself as a

---

3. Some of the character's traits, like the name Ariste, come from *The School for Husbands*.

retired philanderer. But he has an excuse for his harsh urgings, namely, a childhood and later years with Chrysale for a brother and Bélise for a sister. Perhaps this upbringing, allied to his sense of fair play, is what makes him take Henriette's side against her older sister, although the playwright nowhere brings Ariste and his niece into direct conversation. In the fifth act, he takes over as the equivalent of the scheming servant or playwright-within-the-play when he fakes messages to Philaminte and Chrysale telling them they are financially ruined. As he hoped, the trick causes Trissotin to withdraw from marriage to Henriette ("No dowry!" whispers the memory of Harpagon) and gilds Ariste's final image as Chrysale cries, "Praise heaven!" and Philaminte declares, "My heart is joyful."

Ariste acts in effect as a substitute father for Clitandre as he pleads his case, doubtless seeing in him a younger version of himself—cultivated, level-headed, sincere, sociable—with one obvious difference, that Clitandre is love-struck. After entertaining for Armande a drawn-out passion that was almost unavailing—but not quite, because she did not turn him down as an admirer, only as a husband—the young man cooled toward her and turned his attentions to Henriette. As a skilled tactician, Clitandre knows he must win her by wooing her mother, since her father's assistance is at best a hope-shattering liability. Therefore, he must debate Trissotin with the latter's chosen weapon, literature, and cut his pretensions to ribbons. He nearly succeeds in this (IV, 3), but is forestalled by a note that suddenly arrives from Vadius with documents testifying that Trissotin has plagiarized quotations from Horace, Virgil, Terence, and Catullus. The note warns Philaminte not to let her daughter marry Trissotin, but it has the opposite result. Philaminte rightly ascribes it to envy, and she not only settles firmly on the marriage but also brings it disastrously forward to that evening, brushing aside the proof of Trissotin's dishonesty and Clitandre's proof of his capability as a *littérateur* (IV, 4). In the end he does win Henriette, but by an act of chivalry (very similar to Valère's in the last act of *Tartuffe),* when Trissotin hastily retreats and Clitandre proclaims himself eager to take this daughter, rich or poor, and to put his own income at the disposal of her parents. Honor wins out, backed by that competing bourgeois value, cash, which Philaminte, if she remained true to her principles, should despise.

Clitandre personifies the difference in genre between *The Learned Ladies* and *Two Precious Maidens Ridiculed.* In that earlier farce, the two vengeful plotters, La Grange and Du Croisy, walloped and humiliated their servants for lying and taking on airs; in this stately verse comedy, Clitandre engages his adversary in a thoroughgoing, pre-Shavian duel of wits. Molière intro-

duces no knockabout business here and no broadly humorous undressing
sequence, like Jodelet's. Instead, Clitandre tightly pursues an argument that
pits imaginative thinking against mechanical learning, the discernment and
taste of the court against those of the academy.

His rival, Trissotin, is sometimes played as a bumptious and egregious ass.
Any actor who perpetrates such a portrayal, giving his audience a version of
Sir Benjamin Backbite, burlesques his role, anticipates the final scene, draws
the play's sting, and obstructs its gathering drama as soon as he appears,
much as happens with a repulsive Tartuffe. The character's verbal conceits
need physical blandishments and the women's adoration of him needs strong
attributive backing from the performers; he should come across when he first
appears as being young, charmingly histrionic, even spellbinding, or, if older,
as nonetheless captivating.[4] He may lose his temper with Vadius during their
set-to but recovers it to become all earnest suavity while he and Clitandre
debate over literary merit (and indirectly over Henriette). Like many an
author today who reads aloud some stanzas from an epic poem in progress
or the first chapter of his forthcoming novel at a colloquium or club or in a
chain bookstore, sometimes at the coaxing of his publisher, Trissotin exempli-
fies the yearning on the part of writers, those isolated toilers, for recognition,
approbation, praise. That his poems are husks, scrupulously conventional
forms but juiceless, void of the feeling that makes poetry live, lends added
irony to his pride in them, and to his calling a new one his baby; but his
reading, which amounts to a self-induced ecstasy, brings forth rapturous
squeals from his three comic bacchae (III, 2).

Molière prefaces this scene with an accident. The lackey, L'Épine, trips
and falls while moving a chair. The women berate him: he should know
better than to misplace his center of gravity after he has studied the principles
of equilibrium. This brief episode has sometimes been accounted a stumble
on the playwright's part into rowdy farce, but surely it predicts that, while
they pant over Trissotin's offerings in the episodes to come, they too will lose
their equilibrium; and that the pace and tone will move into verbal farce until
near the end of the act.

When Trissotin brings Vadius into their parlor, the *savantes* feel privileged
to watch two great minds, as they believe, hurling superlatives at each other
for their madrigals, odes, chansonettes, rondos, and ballads composed with

4. Voltaire once played Trissotin in an amateur performance in 1763, when he was
sixty-nine years of age (see "Molière and Voltaire" by Emilie Kostoroski-Kadish, in
Johnson, Trail, and Neumann, 90).

a dash and a wit that exceed those of the ancients, until the pair of mutual puffers have elevated their ranking to the tip of the peak of Parnassus. This portion of the scene (III, 3) has already overstepped the boundaries of comedy and into farce; but when, without knowing who wrote it, Vadius condemns Trissotin's "Sonnet on Princess Uranie's Fever," which the women (and we) have already heard recited, and the barrage of compliments gives way to a cross-screeching of such epithets as hack, scribbler, plagiarist,[5] the action has shifted wholly into the farcical realm. During the course of this switch, in other words, the two men display a *range* of characterization. So do the women. From an active onstage audience that matches Trissotin's effusions with their own, they decline into a baffled silence, broken after Vadius' furious exit and Trissotin's recovery of his suave manner as he explains to Philaminte that he could not allow the taste of his hostesses, their approval of his sonnet, to be called into question.[6]

Into this sequence Molière has introduced a third element. Besides the two performers and their onstage audience, he has kept Henriette present as an uncomfortable observer. She makes two attempts to get away, but her mother will not hear of it and keeps checking to see whether Henriette is as impressed as she is with the visitors, but particularly with Trissotin. He may have been wounded during the debate, but not decisively, and Philaminte is stubborn. Having got her hands on this paragon of letters, she means to keep him in the family.

As we turn from the men in the play to the women, we find two voices of moderation to match those of Ariste and Clitandre, and three excessive personalities who correspond to Chrysale, Trissotin, and Vadius. The ungrammatical Martine bobs in and out of acts II and V, getting to speak a total of only forty-eight lines. But they align her firmly on the side of her master and against the mistress, who wants to fire her for her solecisms. She doesn't follow academic jargon and defends plain talk in which the parts of speech may not agree so long as the listeners understand what is being said (II, 5, 6). In her big scene (V, 3) she says what is on Chrysale's mind and preempts his role. The man should be boss of the house; his wife should study his desires, not her books; he should, when necessary, bring her into line with

---

5. Among other insults traded, the two men bicker over whether one or the other of them was more effectively targeted in the *Satires* of Boileau, Molière's friend.
6. Molière, it will be recalled, used a similar defense for *The School for Wives*. The king liked it, therefore the playwright's critics are aspersing their monarch's taste.

a few whacks; and Philaminte has no business sticking her daughter with a word-spinner like Trissotin, who "never stops carping," when Clitandre is a more suitable spouse. Chrysale thankfully utters little exclamations of approval at these appeals to traditionalists in the audience, and it would be no wonder if women, then as now, took umbrage at Martine's zeal in calling for the preservation of male superiority in the home.

Martine is unmarried. So is Bélise, who imagines that men are secretly infatuated with her.[7] She has answers ready for Ariste when he asks why, of the men she names as her helpless admirers, one stays away from the house— he is bashful—and another speaks harshly about her—to disguise his passion—while a third went off and got married—out of disappointment (II, 3). The delusions save her from being little more than an echo of Philaminte. She remains caught up in them until the end of the play, when she warns that Clitandre's unspoken love for her may cause him to regret for the rest of his life his marriage to Henriette. The role is not an easy one. Bélise is a farcical female invention and therefore unique in Molière's drama: he keeps her, even more than he does Martine, visible onstage during a number of scenes to which she has few lines to contribute. If she is not to intrude her farcical presence too blatantly and yet to act as more than mere decoration, she needs a scenario of blocking that brings her forward on occasion as a pleasing surprise and then lets her withdraw without altogether resigning from the action.

Her niece, Henriette, shines with normality. Thanks to that negative radiance, she looks very much like a sensible goody-goody. An even-tempered youngster, a "whole" person who seeks bodily satisfaction as well as mental satisfaction (in contrast to her sister's professed horror of physical love), she is capable of responding in kind to Clitandre's magnanimity at the end of the play by declining to marry him now that she has no dowry; she says this *because* she loves him and because nothing chafes a marriage more than lack of money (V, 4). Apart from this premarital caution, which reveals a shade of cold practicality in an otherwise conventionally romantic heroine, Henriette has a comparatively dull personality, intelligent but sober, prickly only when provoked, unaffectedly and tenaciously loyal, and for that reason all the more attractive to Clitandre, to whom she must be a restful haven after his two

7. For a probable antecedent of this character in Hespérie, *"qui croit que chacun l'aime"* (in *Les Visionnaires* by Desmarets de Saint-Sorlin, 1637), see Howarth, 82. The type has often returned with many variations, notably in several plays by Labiche.

years of trying to stay afloat on the stormy surface of her sister's whimsicality.[8] But character differs from role. Some critics who find Henriette colorless have handicapped themselves by assessing her as a person rather than as a complex theatrical device. She functions at the core of the double main plot, yet her future hangs on how its uncertainties are resolved. These uncertainties form the subject matter of the first and last scenes and many of the intervening ones, but she will have almost no say in their resolution. She does make one direct attempt to persuade Trissotin to look elsewhere for a bride (V, 1); it does no good so long as he can count on her mother's backing. She must mostly hope and urge and rely on the good will and purposeful behavior of her father, uncle, and lover. At the same time, she is enough of a tactician to advise Clitandre that the safest plan is to win her mother over and to seem to go along with her notions and those of Bélise. As a role then, Henriette has reason to fret and appear agitated throughout the action—all the more so since she is at the mercy of others. But there is a further consideration. If Molière had approximately type-cast the first performances, his wife would have played her namesake, Armande. But he gave that part to Mlle de Brie, while Mlle de Molière played Henriette, doubtless lending it a note of piquancy, or even asperity.

If Henriette resembles her uncle, Ariste, more than she does either of her parents, Armande invites comparison with her aunt, Bélise (and with Arsinoé in *The Misanthrope*), more than with her mother—not in her behavior but in her motives. The opening scene sets her up as a vindictive older sister who wants to prevent Henriette's marriage out of jealousy, resentment, and the fear of appearing spurned. She later inflames Philaminte by tattling that Henriette obeys their father sooner than their mother (IV, 1) and that Clitandre remained icily indifferent to Philaminte's reputation and to her writings when they were read to him; why, he even had the nerve and stupidity to criticize them. She makes it look as if she is not prepared to give Clitandre up, yet in slandering him to her mother, she works against her own interests, expecting perhaps that she will be able to repair the damage later. She does offer herself to him again, at first stipulating that she is seeking a pure marriage of hearts, unsullied by "filthy desires" and "with no awareness of

8. One author, taking a heavily ironic view of the character and of the play, calls Henriette "hateful" and "a little viper" (see Antoine Adam 3: 392). Such a personal interpretation is not out of the question. But a performance that announced itself as, say, an unapologetically feminist tract would require rethinking of the other characters, too, and turning them upside down or inside out by playing against the lines and, I suspect, by cutting quite a few that no longer fitted.

the body," though she subsequently wrings from herself the concession of submitting as well to "ties of the flesh, corporeal chains" (IV, 2), but by then, he says, it's too late.

Like her aunt, Bélise, Armande practices pre-Freudian sublimation. In spite of her several speeches that are virtual hymns to chastity, before and while Trissotin unburdens his musty commonplaces, she and the other women break into gasps and expostulations that have distinctly sexual overtones. She "burns" to see his poems; they have "an unparalleled sweetness"; to one expression (which happens to be *sleeping prudence)* she "surrenders her weapons." Her "heart is smitten" by the innocuous line filler, *no matter what is said,* which she begs to have repeated. On hearing another stanza, she is "dying of pleasure." There is one clause in the poem personifying a fever as an invalid's "ungrateful and insolent" guest; Armande says she cannot get it out of her head, as though she fastens onto any words, however trite, that seem to speak to her about herself.

Armande thinks of marriage as a man's opportunity to exploit a woman's body, and so do—and did—many men, as well as women. (Magdelon, we may recall, in merely entertaining the idea of marriage in *Two Precious Maidens Ridiculed,* says she could not abide the prospect of being in bed with a naked man.) As the daughter of a philanderer who is now the weak partner in a marriage, without brothers to foster in her some understanding of men of her own age, Armande may have come to believe in the fiction of sexless love between two brains—an exalted camaraderie. But her family situation can hardly explain her peculiarities, for how would one apply it to Henriette, who also has Chrysale for a father and no brothers? I surmise, partly from the casting of Mlle de Brie and partly from Clitandre's persistent courting of Armande for two fruitless years, that we are meant to see her as extremely good-looking or in some other manner alluring. For this reason, she might well feel she could have him on her terms. After he closes out that possibility, she believes that, as the more submissive daughter of the parent who holds sway, she deserves him. In her last line, she asks whether she is to be sacrificed to the marriage between Clitandre and her sister. Philaminte replies cryptically, "You're not the one I'm sacrificing to them"—who is, then?— and adds that Armande has philosophy to support her in regarding "the crowning of their passion with a satisfied eye." A meager reward, this answer, and no consolation at all. It may even be tinged with sarcasm. Amid the general rejoicing as the play closes, Armande stands as a forlorn figure, bitter and wasted.

Philaminte, like her daughter, has often given the impression of being one of Molière's most unrelieved assaults on those women who want to invade territory men claim as their hallowed own. But there is another way of looking at this far-from-admirable personality who is yet an admirable characterization. By 1671 the playwright, nearing fifty now, had created a gallery of outstanding roles for men but few for women (among them Agnès, Célimène, Angélique in *George Dandin*, and Elmire), and those as subordinate partners of the male characters for whom the plays were named.[9] In any case, Philaminte resembles the large male parts in being obsessed and therefore warped as a persona, a counterpart in some respects to Orgon in that she has set her mind on a son-in-law who she imagines will glorify her house. She makes an entrance (II, 6) almost as pushed forward into the action as is Tartuffe's and well after the first appearance of her husband (II, 1). He in turn fills a lesser place in the play, not unlike that of the leading women in the earlier works. She has become the autocrat because nature and the household gods abhor a power vacuum. In other words, she is less unnatural than some of the other figures in the play, such as Henriette and Ariste, would have us believe.

Philaminte's sighs and joyous cries over Trissotin's verses denote her determination not to be wrong in having chosen (very nearly appointed) this hack to be Henriette's mate. Maybe he can convert the stubborn child. She doesn't contemplate marrying him to her other daughter, who practically swoons over his lines and would seem a more suitable wife:[10] Armande is already in her camp, and will even be a cofounder of her ambitious academy.

As Philaminte begins to describe her academy-to-be, she makes it sound like a justified and overdue institution, an extension of the one proposed by Plato in *The Republic,* and a rendezvous for female scholars excluded from male preserves. But it rapidly degenerates as we listen to the elaborations.

9. One might speculate widely and wildly on this matter. Perhaps the dramatist reproached himself for unfairness or for not having (or not having shown) the requisite talent. Perhaps his wife or Catherine de Brie or another woman in his troupe or of his acquaintance challenged him to write a big role for a woman or for two women or a comic portrait of a woman that would measure up to the great tragic roles for women composed by Corneille and lately by Racine (Hermione, Andromaque, Bérénice). Perhaps he thought back to Cathos and Magdelon as youthful mimics of the salon women and asked himself why he should not turn his attention to the less youthful women they had tried to imitate.

10. In the absence of the mother, Henriette directly asks her sister, "If [Trissotin] is such a fine choice, why don't you take him?" Armande replies, "He's been offered to you, not to me," and brushes away the suggestion (III, 5).

She calls it an act of revenge. Odd tag phrases and disconnected inanities fall from the lips of the three *savantes* as they show off their scant knowledge of Epicurus, Descartes, the Stoics. They then mention the academy's "rules" and "laws," which are reminiscent of Philaminte's and Bélise's petty, syntactical reasons for wanting to get rid of Martine and also of the artistic petrifaction associated with Trissotin and Vadius (III, 2).

Like a religious convert, Philaminte feels driven to proselytize. Everyone in her purview, servants included, must share her faith in grammatical rectitude and her absolute observance of decreed forms. She sees herself as an arbiter of behavior, an Emily Post.

Philaminte does not hate men. She adores her pedantic visitors. When Vadius arrives and she learns that he "knows Greek as well as any man in France," she invites kisses from him "for the love of Greek" (III, 3) and possibly seizes him in a rib-endangering embrace. But although she is not as frigid as Armande, she has inculcated in her daughter an ideal of chastity that goes well beyond the spiritual zones (and is reinforced by the fluttery example set by Bélise). I picture her, trading on her charms, as an exceptionally attractive woman in her late thirties.

If she is, why did the playwright as director hand the role to a man? This decision has occasioned some meditation among Molière specialists. He might have hoped to play down the idea that she represented all women scholars. The casting of Hubert as a bossy wife may have ridiculed the part even further and so appeased audiences in those paternalistic times.[11] A drag interpretation may have edged the comic effects away from satire and toward more palatable farce throughout. But any explanation that requires Molière to have blunted his own work seems unconvincing. My guess is that he conceived the role for his theatre partner, former mistress, and inspirer. Madeleine Béjart was an obvious choice. After having excelled in a succession of parts, the most significant being Elvire in *Don Garcie of Navarre*, Frosine in *The Miser*, and Dorine in *Tartuffe*—but none that carried a play for lengthy stretches, as Philaminte must do—she had earned this female equivalent of the roles he had undertaken. But Madeleine had been ill; as it happened, she died less than a month before *The Learned Ladies* opened. There was evidently no other actress in the company whom Molière thought eligible. André Hubert, however, had taken over as Madame Pernelle and also performed the original Madame Jourdain and possibly Madame de Sotenville. Whether he and the author chose to portray Philaminte realistically or

11. See, e.g., Richard Wilbur's introduction to his translation, p. ix.

broadly or with alternations of the two modes, on paper she remains as persuasively funny a figure as are the two pedants, whose poems and portraits are said, on reliable evidence, to have been drawn closely from life.

The five female roles, diverse though they are, cannot constitute anything like a spectrum of feminine attitudes and personalities that might stand for all women in the later part of the seventeenth century. Most conspicuously missing is a woman of accomplishment, a genuine scholar or poet or mover-and-shaker. Does her absence mean that Molière did not believe that such a woman existed in his time? That he had a poor opinion of such achievers as Mlle de Scudéry, Mme de Rambouillet, that formidable political influence, Mme de Maintenon—and Madeleine Béjart? That any woman who tried to break away from an accepted sex role must be a pretentious fraud? Or does he mean us to accept Philaminte and her followers simply for what they are and to make no broader deductions about them and their assertions?

Well, literary salons, famous and infamous, in court circles and elsewhere among the upper crust did provide models for women at the bourgeois level inhabited by Philaminte, Bélise, and Armande, and so we are forced to assume that Molière was to some extent recording as well as reinventing his time. The three women (and some of the other characters) are, at once, *sui generis* and caricatures of actuality; they are individuals *and* types. Their outlines resemble the bands of facial makeup put on by some Kabuki actors.[12] One edge of each band is firm; the other edge shades off to blend with the skin, as though to resemble the coloring of the peony's petals. So, these figures shade off into the real world, their features blending with those of certain people in life who also seem to be caricatures.

Like the women, the men in the play do not represent a cross-section of the attitudes and opinions of their sex. They too lack an outstanding achiever. While two of them, Clitandre and Ariste, come down on the side of sturdy reason, two of the women, Henriette and Martine, do the same. Only if we insist on narrowing down to the contest between the sisters can we detect an authorial imbalance in that he has supplied Armande with a sour personality, which ricochets her between febrile jealousy and affectation. Even so, these characteristics combine to make her one of Molière's vital roles, certainly more stimulating to play (and watch) than Henriette's.

---

12. This type of makeup for ferocious characters, the *kumadori*, is used in the more vigorous Kabuki plays known as *aragoto*. See, e.g., pls. 42–47 of *The Kabuki Theatre* by Earle Ernst (New York: Grove Press, 1956).

But isn't the play "unfair" to the three *savantes?* Hardly. Not one of them comes out of the marital conflict or the sibling rivalry damaged. Philaminte will go on ruling the household and her academy. Armande loses Clitandre, but has shown few signs of wanting him, only of wanting to deny him to her sister. Bélise remains incidental to the goings-on, a clownish family appendage and possibly a rough portrait of Armande in the future. A sort of poetic justice finally prevails, and without any retribution. Even Trissotin pulls out of the action unscathed.

Martine and Chrysale do put the case for women's domesticity (and domestication), but they are intellectual primitives whose sentiments arise from *partis pris*. Several of the characters also fault the women's scholarship—but because it consists of gush, name-dropping, opinion flinging, and the aping of ritualized, institutionalized learning, which stunt the initiative of teachers and pupils. True learning, the play unmistakably implies, has nothing to do with the exchange and accumulation of compliments and honors and invocations of the great dead, all recited as a sort of comparison shopping. It has everything to do with the risks and labors entailed in a search for a keener appreciation of others and ourselves. Such an implication, or warning, suggests no antifeminine bias. One of the more memorable thematic lines in the play, spoken by Clitandre, is couched in masculine gender in French: "A foolish scholar is more of a fool than a foolish ignoramus" (IV, 3).

It may be worth adding that throughout his years in the theatre, Molière collaborated with women who were artists, and married one.

3. Loners

Don Juan
(*Dom Juan ou le Festin de pierre*, 1665)

The alternative title of this play literally means *The Feast of Stone*. It harks back to Tirso de Molina's *The Trickster of Seville and the Stone Guest*, published in Spain in 1630. But it became promoted to the full title of two derivative dramas later performed in Italy, both called *The Stone Guest*, and the modified title of two French dramas of the late 1650s, in both of which the Guest of the title turned into a Feast: *The Feast of Stone, or The Criminal Son*. Within a few years of these last two, in 1664–65, Molière's adaptation retained the French *festin* but returned it to the status of alternative title. He thus took advantage of the fame of the story and of the ironic notion of a "feast" at which an inhuman host, incapable of eating, first freezes his human guest into paralysis and then heats him to death in flames that lick up from hell.[1] Some critics and historians have spotted a possible wordplay on *Pierre* (because of the capital *P*), which may have been the name of Juan's late father-in-law, the commander, transmogrified into the animate statue. It now serves in its diminutive form as the name of Pierrot, the peasant in the second act, whose fiancée Juan tries to steal.[2] The roasting of Juan in the fifth act would then avenge both Commander "Pierre" and Pierrot. It is in line with the condign punishment found in Molina's and other moralistic drama of the Spanish "golden age," as well as being reminiscent of the fiery hell's mouth in a medieval passion play.

If Molière hoped that renewing the damnation of Juan found in the earlier plays would blunt the wrath of foes in and out of the Church, the hope was

1. English cannot reproduce the French words "the stone feast" without implying a meal consisting of rock, and translations have therefore resorted to meaningful analogies. Some examples: Baker and Miller, "The Feast of the Statue"; Wood, "The Statue at the Feast"; Frame, "The Stone Guest"—a reversion to Tirso's Spanish; and my "A Statue to Supper."
2. For the connection between the "Pierre" and the "Pierrot" see James Doolittle's study of the play, "The Humanity of Molière's *Don Juan*" in *PMLA* 68, no. 3 (June 1953), reprinted in the first volume of *The Great Playwrights*, ed. Eric Bentley (New York: Doubleday, 1970), 944–67.

an unreal one, and quickly dashed. His play offered too many other spiky provocations. In revamping the Spanish legend, he switches the genre from a *drame sérieux* to a comedy with flecks of farce—offense number one. His Juan goes beyond the libertinism in Molina's and other plays, which by itself would have been enough to earn the hero capital punishment for adultery; Juan does not deny that he is a "freethinker," a word that was more or less a synonym among Catholics for "atheist."[3] But though he never openly calls himself an atheist, he gets in some powerful digs at religious hypocrisy (V, 2)—offense number two. The character who most frequently protests Juan's beliefs is Sganarelle, his valet, whose rebuttals consist of confused and misquoted lumps of pious platitude;[4] and Sganarelle, played by Molière, was therefore assumed to be the author's purposely ineffectual mouthpiece— offense number three. During the action, the scandalous Don and his quakily reproachful servant are hardly ever offstage, as though to rub the ears, if not the noses, of Molière's detractors (and targets) in the dirt—offense number four. The author has also compromised the remoteness of the play's settings in Sicily; he brings them closer to home by the appearance in the second act of peasants with French names and by the presence throughout the play of the familiar Sganarelle, the fifth in Moliere's line of seven Sganarelles, as though to signify that this, like *The Sicilian*, which followed two years later, is an irreverent drama not about a real or even an unreal Sicily, but about France—offense number five. As a matching adjustment, the period has changed from Molina's thirteenth century to a not-quite-definite seventeenth century with the aid of a few contemporary references—offense number six. Far from being a churl or baseborn criminal, the Don is and behaves as a gentleman, at times as a mockery of one—offense number seven. Other

---

3. The usage has lasted. In "The Boarding House," one of the stories in *Dubliners* (1905), James Joyce writes of a Mr. Doran: "As a young man he had sown his wild oats, of course; he had boasted of his free-thinking and denied the existence of God to his companions in public-houses."

4. The most telling attacks were launched in a pamphlet signed by an unidentified sieur de Rochemont and in the *Sentiments of the Fathers of the Church on Comedy and Spectacles* by the Prince de Conti, who had been one of Molière's grudging patrons for a time. The play had its defenders, but they were not sufficiently effective to save the playwright from having to cut certain scenes and tone down some speeches. After his death, the play was tamed and versified by Thomas Corneille and did not revive in its original form until after a lapse of some 170 years.

offenses to religious propriety occur, but these seven sins sufficed to damn the author nearly as heatedly as he damns his hero.[5]

Don Juan is an anomaly among Molière's works and introduces some striking novelties that he did not repeat.[6] It has an epic structure, opening in a room in an unidentified palace that looks onto a garden. The next act moves to the countryside by the seashore. Act III goes into a forest and then into a mausoleum, the commander's tomb, which gives way to a fourth act in Juan's living room. Finally, Juan and Sganarelle venture out again into the countryside, which will open up, swallow him, emit flames and noise, and leave Sganarelle alone in the open, masterless and unpaid. The text does not specify the settings; they have persisted by stage convention. In their shiftings there are two constants: the varied scenes all take place on the island of Sicily, to which the legendary Juan had fled to escape retribution in Spain; and Sganarelle appears onstage whenever his master does. One might say that the different locations enable the playwright to give us an epic tour around and inside Don Juan and his servant.

In most of his plays with a principal servant's role, male or female, Molière observes the tradition of the intriguer who is smarter than the master, honored since the days of Plautus and sustained by the commedia *zanni*, the Spanish *graciosos*, and the gallery of valets and domestics in his own comedies. *Don Juan* effects a reversal: the master determines what shall be done, while the poltroon of a servant meekly objects to his master's escapades at the same time as he envies them.[7] The third act seems to comment on the reversal when Juan tries to fool a search party of enemies by dressing in Sganarelle's clothes. (In the meantime, Sganarelle has put on a physician's cloak to become a preliminary doctor in spite of himself, and even dispensed medical advice.)

5. *The School for Wives* may have earned Molière physical mistreatment at the hands of the duc de la Feuillade, but *Don Juan*, together with *Tartuffe*, brought him grievous threats and anguish while he lived and, after he died, a denial by the parish priest of the last sacrament and a burial with "no ceremony" and "no solemn service."

6. In addition, "no other Molière play contains such a variety of institutional conventions. No other Molière cast contains representatives of so many classes and professions" (from "Human Nature and Institutions in Molière's Plots" by James Doolittle, in Demorest, 157).

7. Molière may have picked up the notion of a weak servant from the character of Catalinon in Molina's play (although Catalinon does save his master from drowning) and the apposition of two contrasting principals from another Molina play, *The Man Condemned for Being Faithless* (*El condenado por desconfiado*, 1635).

A character, and the hero at that, dies onstage. No deaths occur in the action or story of Molière's other plays, and a visible death like this one went against the grain of the French neoclassical theatre.[8] It conforms more with the Seneca-shaded endings of Jacobean drama. The death incorporates supernatural effects. As its preamble, a statue nods, speaks, walks. A ghost materializes, so does Father Time. At the climax, the ground opens up into a flaming furnace and consumes Juan. Other Molière principals—Arnolphe, the Sganarelle of *The School for Husbands,* Harpagon, Orgon, and Alceste—face sentences no worse than isolation and disappointment, debilitating as those conditions can be; Dandin will have to put up with the continuation of his marriage, more of the same; even Tartuffe is only arrested. Juan's penalty, however, is the extreme and final one: damnation bespoke crimes that were barely mentionable and that merited a more durable punishment than mere execution. What are these crimes? And their extenuating circumstances, if any?

– As his first "minus," he has killed the commander—in the story, which we never witness, not in the action—but in a fair duel.

– Also in the story but not the action, he has lured Doña Elvire out of a convent, seduced and married her. As the play begins, he has fled from her; she overtakes him in the third scene and swears revenge. But by a later time (IV, 4), she has worked out her own salvation, declares that she forgives him, and tries to save him before he is damned.

– He tries to bribe a poor man to utter a blasphemy (III, 2). When the man refuses, Juan hands him a gold louis "for the love of humanity"—itself a blasphemous neologism that mocks the traditional "for the love of God." But he does give the man alms.

– He woos the peasant girls, Charlotte and Mathurine, promises to marry them both, turns their heads, and is obviously bent on deflowering one or both (II, 2 and II, 4). But he does not reach consummation in either case—at least, not as a part of, and not hinted by, the action.

– He pushes Pierrot around (II, 3), hitting Sganarelle by accident but not Pierrot, and causes a rift between the peasant and his fiancée, Charlotte, this after Pierrot and his friend have saved Juan from drowning. But the affection between Pierrot and Charlotte is one-sided, emerging only from *his* mouth;

8. Technically speaking, we see Juan enveloped by the flames and disappear, not shrivel up and expire. Similarly, Racine's Phèdre is said at the end of the play to "be dying," and Orestes at the end of *Andromache* to be "losing his senses" or "sensations."

and Pierrot did win a bet with the friend and so make some money out of the rescue.

— By overwhelming his creditor, the merchant, Monsieur Dimanche ("Mister Sunday"), with effusive compliments and questions about his wife, children, and dog, Juan verbally duels him out of his cash in a scene (IV, 3) that prefigures Dorante's "milking" of Monsieur Jourdain.[9] But Sganarelle, that right-thinking citizen who is also in debt to Dimanche, repeats the exercise more brusquely and finishes by pushing the man out of the house. Two wrongs may not make a right, and Juan's elaborate civility does not narrow the gap in rank between him and his social "inferior"; rather, it intimidates Monsieur Dimanche, undermining the civility with a patronizing tone that typifies the disdain of a young aristocrat. But he does admit the creditor to his house and acknowledge the debts, rather than keeping him waiting outside indefinitely, as Sganarelle proposes.

— Juan vexes his father, Don Louis, by his misbehavior or, more likely, by the scandal it causes and, after the father lectures him and leaves, wishes him dead (IV, 4). But he later delights the old man by promising to reform. He makes the promise "out of pure expedience, as a useful trick, a posture to win over my father, whom I may need." In a society where good appearances count for more than sincerely good acts, the promise becomes a perverse act of kindness.

— Juan announces to his valet that henceforward he is going to wear a hypocritical mask; then, when Don Carlos, Elvire's brother, asks him to return to Elvire and remove a slur on the family name, he keeps pleading "heaven's will" as his pretext for not doing so (V, 3). His cant is blasphemous, but it averts a swordfight and the perpetuation of an ill-advised marriage. In any case, as we have repeatedly seen, Sganarelle is at least as hypocritical as Juan is. For instance, after Don Louis goes, Sganarelle says Juan should have turned the old bore out of the house and then, in an aside, condemns himself for being so craven.

— All through the action, Juan startles, rattles, belittles, and threatens Sganarelle. But he seems to be constantly testing him, daring him to be a man and talk back, challenging him with the opportunity to say or do something unorthodox, if not rash.

— Juan dies without having paid his valet's back wages. But his death does

9. Like Dorante, Juan does not address the merchant courteously; he calls him "Monsieur Dimanche" instead of "Monsieur" (or in English, simply "Dimanche"). That name, the sabbath, may have further annoyed God-fearing spectators.

happen unexpectedly, and Sganarelle's grieving for the loss of his pay, rather than the loss of his master, doesn't show *him* in a very favorable light.

These crimes of Don Juan's do not add up to outright criminality, only to a succession of misdemeanors, private declarations to Sganarelle, and unfinished intrigues. They convey an insinuation, which must have disturbed devout people of the time, that this "wicked nobleman" *(le grand seigneur méchant homme)* is no more evil than other members of the aristocracy and, in some of his actions, more virtuous. Against his assorted "minuses" we can set a short catalogue of his "plusses":

+ He risks his life when he saves Carlos from a band of robbers and defies Alonse who has brought with him several men to outnumber Juan.

+ He brings some excitement into the lives of the young peasant women and momentarily relieves the tedium of their village.

+ By declining to marry Elvire, he unintentionally sends her back to her true vocation—if she is sincere when she professes it.

+ Elvire considers him worth warning and saving—if, again, she is sincere.

+ He is disarmingly frank with Sganarelle.

+ He unleashes some memorably satirical comments about society, medicine, and honor.

+ He remains unafraid to the end, braving the Statue and the supernatural omens without blenching or retreating.

+ Sanctimonious persons might have bridled at his tongue and exploits, but sanctimonious persons would not (and still will not) admit to themselves that Don Juan is every man's secret dream of utter independence at the same time as he is every man's secret dread of feeling utterly alone, nor will they admit that it takes an extraordinary personality to cope so brazenly with the dream and the dread.[10]

Why, then, does the Don suffer the extreme penalty? Critics have wildly disagreed in their responses to this question. Molière was tired, ill, busy, distracted by the *Tartuffe* imbroglio or by administrative and artistic pressures and the need to keep providing material for his company. He did not have time or could not bother to invent a new ending to replace the climax he took over from earlier playwrights. That final scene builds to a crowd-pleasing spectacle with splendid and fearsome mechanical effects; while the tacking-

10. Jean-Marie Teyssier contrasts Juan with the mythological hero, such as Prometheus or Sisyphus, who is not "presented as a man sensitive to every beauty and weak in front of women. From this point of view, Don Juan is a modern hero, the representative of the inclinations of his time and ours" (Teyssier, 183).

on of Sganarelle's final brief soliloquy, bracketed by cries for his lost pay, makes farce out of calamity and neutralizes the Don's evil. In other words, the conclusion seems not only cowardly, designed to placate the religious community, but also morally arbitrary, designed to placate some of those spectators who came to the Palais-Royal in search of laughs. Thus, the ending must be a joke—Juan carried off by the supernatural, which he does not believe in. One theory has it that Juan as the Tempter, the devil on earth, receives the only fitting punishment, even though his being consumed by fire at the end suggests that he was anything but the devil, who, after his many eons in hell, ought to be what our advertisements call fire-resistant, if not absolutely fireproof.

Some commentators interpret this Juan as a not-unsympathetic figure who dares to reprehend the medical profession, religious dogmatists, superstition, marriage, commerce. The earlier Juans played at exploiting women and soiling the family name. Molière broadens his Juan into a social rebel, a critic of contemporary civilization, a lone soldier carrying the banner of truth, who goes boldly to his death refusing to apologize or backtrack in his beliefs or to plead for mercy. Doolittle remarks that the instrument of death, the stone Statue, cold and inhuman, symbolizes the institutions Juan tilted at.

The Church and its devout followers should in theory have found the ending inevitable and therefore satisfactory. A firm unbeliever, a supposed atheist, presented them (and society) with a threat almost as grave as that posed by the irruption of a heretic. They could imagine no more rightful outcome for heretics than a rousing vengeance, either wrought by heaven and accompanied by supernatural manifestations of displeasure—or, if heaven would not deign to grant their wish (the same wish some of us still express as a helpless dismissal, and not always in jest, "Go to hell!"), the vengeance would have to be imposed here below. When suasion proved unavailing and the unbeliever would not reform, why, burn him. Or her. Juan does burn. In this case, heaven obliges. But Molière's foes wanted more. Why should he have any virtues to display? Why should Elvire consider him worth saving? How could they take seriously the vengeance of a Statue pompously got up in a Roman emperor's toga and laurel and speaking in the name of heaven? They pressed for the removal of the holy terror from the boards before he could begin to propagate imitations of his swaggering life among those who would not see death by scorching as enough of a deterrent.

Members of the clergy could have borne with Juan's death (and stage life) only on condition that he was outpointed in debate before he died. But to have suffered a doctrinal defeat, Juan would have had to engage in debate.

He chooses not to. The plotting makes him a formidable and surprisingly patient listener who waits through attacks and condemnations from Elvire, Don Carlos, Don Alonse, Don Louis, as well as directly and indirectly from Sganarelle *without refuting them.* He tosses out some amusingly unctuous excuses for not doing what they say he should have done, but unlike John Tanner or Tanner's alter ego, Bernard Shaw's Don Juan, he avoids ratiocination that has to do with his principles—with a couple of exceptions, when (in I, 2 and V, 2) he explains his motives to Sganarelle, who finds them meaningless. But otherwise, Juan remains noncommittal or silent and maddens Molière's foes not alone by his iconoclastic acts and assertions but also (and perhaps more) by his refusal to defend himself or enunciate his "philosophy of life" and thereby expose chinks in his armor. When, for example, Elvire asks him to justify his running away from her, he answers, "Here's Sganarelle, madame. He knows my reasons," and pushes forward the bewildered and barely coherent servant. Soon after, he does provide a sort of answer—he was stricken by his conscience at having enticed her from the convent; God must have been jealous, and so on—but it reeks of falsehood (I, 3). This don is intellectually a slippery figure. The frigid attention he accords the other characters as he lets them ramble on through sentiments so stale they might have been rehearsed beforehand makes them look ridiculously windy; his very restraint forces us to watch them with something akin to his aloofness.[11]

But the first of the two exceptions is worth looking at more closely. When Juan first confides in Sganarelle, he seems to reify the thick-lined likeness of him sketched by the latter in the preceding scene, which introduces the play. In trying to explain his master's flight from Elvire, Sganarelle has told her valet, Gusman, that Juan is

> the most shameless sinner ever born, a madman, a demon, a brute, a heretic. He doesn't believe in heaven, hell, or werewolves. He lives like a wild beast, like an Epicurean pig—as debauched as Sardanapalus. He shuts his ears to all reproaches; mocks everything people like us believe in. You say he married your mistress: so what? To glut his passion he'd go on to marry you, her dog and her cat. A marriage costs him nothing; it's his usual way of trapping beauties. He'll marry them all. Older women, younger women, middle-class or peasants—they're never too

---

11. D. C. Potts discerns a pre-Brechtian alienation in Molière's treatment of the speeches and situations in the play in "*Dom Juan* and 'Non-Aristotelian Drama'" in Howarth and Thomas, 61–72.

hot or too cold for his taste. If I told you all the women he's married in different places, I'd be reciting the list till this evening. (I, 1)

Sganarelle has depicted himself in this scene as a decent fellow who shares his snuff with all comers and has genial pretensions to acting like a gentleman; an audience will probably trust his word. When Juan walks onstage, his lines confirm the first impression delineated by Sganarelle. He refers to a woman as an "object." He doesn't believe in marital fidelity. Every beauty he runs across tempts him—until he has overcome her scruples and made a conquest of her. Then he shucks her off; the adventure has passed, the thrill evaporated. "Passion is over. Beauty has turned stale. We lull ourselves to sleep unless some new object awakens our desires and holds out the challenge of a new conquest. In the end, nothing is more exhilarating than wearing down the resistance of a beautiful woman. In this respect I'm like those empire-builders who flit from victory to victory: the only thing they can't conquer is their ambition" (I, 2).

He has "a heart large enough to yearn for the whole earth" or even, as Alexander did, for "other worlds," but he would subdue those other worlds "with love."[12] He invites Sganarelle's opinion of what he has said. Sganarelle longs to reply but doesn't quite know how to—"You twist things so that you sound right; yet you're not"; and admits that a new marriage every month "is enjoyable and entertaining. I could go for it myself if it wasn't wrong." The exchanges in this scene can be read in at least two distinct ways. Juan has taken some time off between beauties either to review his life reflectively and find out what somebody else thinks of it or to tease Sganarelle by scandalizing him, giving him the chance to prove himself unequal in argument because he is less alert, less sure of himself, less articulate, and a servant. In either case, this introduction to Juan will make the audience mentally echo Sganarelle's harsh judgment of him. Whether candid or sardonic or both by turns, Juan fits anybody's definition of what British colonels, landed gentry, and their mimics used to call a cad or a bounder. Or worse: his certitude, far from being admirable, will play havoc with the lives of inexperienced young women as "I confer on each [object] the most suitable, natural compliments and tributes" in order to "wear down her resistance."

Such an "object" happens to be the next order of business. She is

engaged, the loveliest thing you ever saw. Her fiancé has just escorted her here [and Juan has followed them] . . . . I caught sight of them three

12. Any mention of Alexander the Great (or of Julius Caesar) was generally taken by people at the French court to allude to the king (see Couton I: 745).

or four days before they left. Never have I seen two people so happy with each other. They radiated love. And aroused the same emotion in me. I was struck to the heart: it all began with jealousy. I couldn't stand seeing them so much in love. My desire was multiplied by spite. I thought about the joy it would give me to break up this tender arrangement, which jarred my sensibilities.

A bounder? This is a monster, more vile even—to a solid citizen (and his wife)—than Sganarelle had intimated. He dares to speak of love and sounds as though it's one emotion he is incapable of.

Before Juan can exert his wiles on the fiancée in question by luring her into a boat he has hired, and away from her husband-to-be, Elvire catches up with him. As he sees her approach, his first reaction of surprise that his wife has put herself out sufficiently to pursue him "all the way here" (but from where? another part of Sicily?) gives way to a swift second reaction as he asks Sganarelle, "Is she mad to travel to the city without changing her country clothes?" Even in a crisis the social rebel conforms with the fashion, what one should wear and when. He then succeeds in driving Elvire away by assuring her that he lacks "the ability to dissemble" because "I have a sincere heart." In disgust at his open mockery, she promises "that God will punish you for your wickedness, and if the thought of God doesn't frighten you, then beware of the fury of an insulted woman."

Sganarelle wonders whether his master is now ready to repent, but the moment Elvire leaves, Juan is ready for something else: to "consider how to put our boating plan into action" and conquer the other man's fiancée.

Molière has piled up incidents and dialogue in the first act that ratify and extend Juan's callousness. Sganarelle closes the act by summarizing what the audience has been brought to feel: "Oh, what an abominable man!"

But as the second act unrolls, attentive spectators notice that Juan's intentions meet questionable fulfillments, if any. The boat overturns and his latest plan of conquest with it. Pulled from the water by Pierrot and dried off, he woos and proposes to Mathurine and then her friend, Charlotte, Pierrot's fiancée. The other "object," the one he tracked down, his reason for venturing into this unnamed city where he killed the commander, is forgotten or dropped. Nor does he carry through to a conclusion his flings with Charlotte and Mathurine, who embarrass him by demanding at the same time that he make good on his conflicting proposals to them. He has to leave the resolution up in the air: "You'll see, when I marry you, which one I love." Exactly: he loves neither, will marry neither. And so the scenes proceed, revealing one default after another. He does not persuade the Poor Man to swear or to forswear God and his calling. The dueling "satisfaction" he offers Carlos never comes about. He does not get to eat supper with the Statue, as Molina's Don Juan does—tarantulas, vipers, and fingernail pie, among other delicacies. Whatever he may have accomplished (or perpetrated) *in the story*, in the action Molière's plotting continually undoes his plans. In this respect, if in no other, he shares the fate of Arnolphe, Orgon, Harpagon, and George Dandin.

The pattern of the play thus differs markedly from the murderous rise and fall that underpin the drama of such an unarguable, epic villain as Tamburlaine, Richard III, or Macbeth. Don Juan does virtually nothing in the play that could be unhesitantly classified as being wicked. His fall falls on us abruptly; and since he has hardly misbehaved, he goes unharmed through to his closing moments. One might even say that the scene with Monsieur Dimanche illustrates that Juan does not pay; and Sganarelle's last words, "My pay! My pay! My pay!" reinforce the assumption. He does, of course, figuratively "pay" with his life; but in an unrepentant act of bravado, not in the spirit of giving anything up. He regards himself as unencumbered. It takes "other worlds" to destroy him. As one critic observes, he remains free until the final moments, when he gives the Statue his hand (Scherer, 13), though even that gesture flaunts his unmaimed self-confidence, his gentlemanly trust and *politesse.* To be punished, he has to be obliterated. The punishment comes upon him with unexpected speed. There have been warnings, omens, but he has dismissed them so blithely that the audience feels confused, sent home with mixed feelings. It is possible to play the role as an unmistakably evil character, but the most notable performances created in the past half century, those of Louis Jouvet (1947) and Jean Vilar (1956), have explored Juan's positive attributes as well as his defects.[13] One can imagine (although I have never seen it done onstage) a final scene that transfigures Don Juan, treats his last words (literally: "Oh, Heaven! what do I feel? An invisible fire burns me, I can do no more and all my body is becoming . . .") as a curtailed cry of triumph and his death as an awaited and ecstatic crucifixion, an apotheosis.

13. For an account of Jouvet's stage interpretation, see *Louis Jouvet* by Bettina Knapp (New York: Columbia University Press, 1957), 234–43. Dr. Knapp's endnotes provide a list of reviews of the performance and other sources; the frontispiece of her book has a striking photograph of Jouvet in one of his two black-and-white Don Juan costumes designed by Christian Bérard.

Sganarelle, Juan's companion in life, serves as the only living witness of his death. A strange bond unites these wanderers, the young seeker-and-seducer and the (probably) middle-aged, softhearted sidekick. The author has made them a study in contrasts, "and yet," says Scherer, who sees a resemblance to Beckett's Didi and Gogo, "they love each other" (99). I am not so sure about that. Nor do they correspond to Beckett's master and slave in the same play, Pozzo and Lucky. "Love" is too strong a word for an attachment in which each of the two parties seems at times scarcely able to tolerate the other. Their affiliation is not in any sense a partnership, much less a "marriage," although they remain *theatrically* interdependent. (In the original production, the omnipresence of Molière, long accustomed to holding a stage, must have given reassurance and support to La Grange who, as Juan, had come into the largest Molière role in his career.) Sganarelle, the slave-clown, metaphorically samples the master's dishes beforehand and dips his elbow in the bath water to test the temperature, but less to ensure Juan's comfort and safety than to supply him with entertainment. His master in turn fascinates him by scorning the code of duty and getting away without a penalty. They are each other's spectators and performers. Sganarelle closely watches the Don's drama, convinced that retribution ought to come, *must* come as a tragic end, self-summoned (it does—and leaves him destitute); while Juan coolly takes in the comedy of Sganarelle. But why?

J. D. Hubert looks on Juan as a fugitive who keeps on the move, and whose plight is unenviable,[14] a reading possibly deduced from the interpretation by Jouvet and from our priding ourselves, since the advent of popular psychoanalysis, on scrutinizing the unconscious motives of the philanderer. As he "flits from victory to victory," he is fleeing from himself and not recognizing that he fears commitment to a long-term affair, in case he falls in love; doing that would be a form of surrender, never a victory. But a mounting of the play that shows Juan on the run from himself requires defensive playing throughout; he becomes a sort of pathetic parolee who keeps looking over his shoulder. André Villiers takes a more positive (and suggestive) view, namely, that the play represents Juan advancing rather than retreating, on "a quest, more or less consciously."[15] Following this lead, one can take Juan to be an existential adventurer, a playboy who has missed no opportunity to gratify his senses but has always, "more or less consciously," sought some-

---

14. Hubert, chap. 11, "The Seducer as Catalyst," 113–29.
15. In the chapter of Villiers' book Le *"Dom Juan" de Molière: un problème de mise en scène,* translated by Beth Archer in *Molière,* ed. Guicharnaud, 85.

thing further, a function, a purpose, a better life rather than better living, as he explores the margins of conventional freedom and, whenever he can, oversteps them.

His discoveries are not encouraging. Winning Elvire from the convent has, provoked the bothersome pursuit by her brothers. Chasing the unnamed fiancée led to his near-drowning. Courting Mathurine and then Charlotte let him in for an embarrassment of riches—and an ultimate gain of nothing. Tempting the Poor Man shows him that piety can result in poverty and reliance on the generosity of others, but that the piety stubbornly survives. The encounters with his father, Carlos, and Alonse remind him that the code of honor has petrified them in life as the Statue is petrified in death, but their encounters with him do not soften them. The quest takes him not only over the boundaries of freedom but also, as the quest of Heracles or Theseus did, across the border of life itself; unlike them, Juan does not come back. Shortly before his end, he appears to have reached a point of change: farewell to the audacious rebel—from now on he will turn respectable hypocrite. The resolution does not quite herald a new mode of life. In the action, we have already seen him practicing hypocrisy when he tells Elvire he left her because he did not wish to make God jealous and when he swears he loves Charlotte and Mathurine, so that the change was superficial, if a change at all—more like an affirmation of his customary technique in presenting himself to others.

Nor does his second visit from Elvire (IV, 6) bring him any satisfaction, sexual or otherwise. As she begs him to repent and save his soul while there is still time, she reawakens his lust. He offers to put her up for the night; she declines. Copeau and other commentators assume that her real motive is to win him back because she still loves him. In *Don Giovanni*, the Elvira does sing of the persistence of her love for the Don, in her act II recitatives and the arias "Mi tradi quell'alma" and "Ah, taci, ingiusto core." But if the Elvire of *Don Juan* is still infatuated, why does she not take up his invitation and stay? Because she fears a renewal of the liaison and then a second betrayal? In that case, why did she come at all? I would suggest that her ostensible, beneficent motive, his salvation, is more convincing—and more dramatic—for the actress to play and for the actor to play up to.[16] It sounds the first

---

16. The remarkable coaching by Louis Jouvet of a young actress at the Conservatory of Theatre in Paris during 1940 as she struggled to find a convincing way of playing Elvire's second scene is recorded in Jouvet's book and in Brigitte Jaques's dramatiza-

warning for Juan, who makes plain his determination to defy the warning, even to trivialize it.

But his explicit yielding to the advantages of hypocrisy marks his surrender. When it arrives, the role of Don Juan has played itself out. It is just as well that he has little time left to turn into merely another full-blooded hypocritical nobleman; he can die with his evil but individual reputation intact.

The hypocrisy already lurking in Juan's temperament does not, however, make him a character with a fixed set of opinions and intentions. That notion of the role would be a static one, incompatible with his flitting among the flower of womanhood. As he tells Sganarelle, "I follow the line of least resistance toward whatever appeals to me" (III, 5), and shortly after saying that and catching a glimpse of the commander's tomb, he decides to visit it. He strays in any direction that may open up self-possibilities, his "conquests." If the Statue, when it accepts his invitation to supper, takes him into "other worlds," he has said in the first act that he looks on them as his legitimate stamping grounds. Don Juan is another example in Molière of the character who acts on impulse—as he does even when he proclaims his forthcoming hypocrisy—and not by meeting the requirements of encrusted codes. As he wanders across the landscapes of an abstract space known here as Sicily, from a palace with no name or features to the country setting that will open up and engulf him in flames, he goes downhill, reaffirming that reputation of his by doing irreparable damage en route to the reputations of the Spanish and Spanish-derived heroes conceived of by his contemporaries. It seems to me essential that a production not neglect the act of feasting (implied in the subtitle) as part of Juan's rebellion. To close the fourth act, he has sat down to supper after delays occasioned by the visits of Monsieur Dimanche, Don Louis, and Doña Elvire. He makes fun of Sganarelle, who snatched a piece of meat from his plate and attempted to hide it in his cheek. When the Statue strides into the room to issue his invitation for the following night, the Don is at last gorging himself on the meat he has denied Sganarelle, too busy with his mouth full of half-masticated matter to pay

tion of the seven lessons, *Elvire Jouvet 40* (Paris: Beba, 1987). Jouvet translated some of the ideas that came to him during the lessons into his own production of *Don Juan* in 1947, one such idea being that Elvire's love for Juan has been metamorphosed into a spiritual, selfless affection.

much attention to the stone visitor, much less show any trepidation. There is something earthy and blatantly antispiritual in the role that extends to a contempt for table manners.

During the journey that comprises the action of the play, some of the secondary figures (Gusman, the peasants, the Poor Man, Don Alonse, Monsieur Dimanche) each make only one necessary appearance. Others briefly and pointedly revisit Juan (Elvire, Don Carlos, Don Louis, the Statue) But Sganarelle is always on hand. I have conjectured that Juan keeps him in his employ for entertainment value, but there is a further reason. Don Juan is an early attempt at the Superman. I believe that Bernard Shaw saw this when he added John Tanner to the growing collection of Don Juans and deduced from Molière that the Superman would have to be first, a naysayer, a smasher of idols, and second, a person of privilege who could assail society near its apex—one of the ruling caste or, as Tanner calls himself, a member of the idle rich class.[17] Tanner has a revolutionary program to publish; his resistance has gone a step beyond Juan's and into a positive alternative, just as Juan's has gone beyond that of Molina's Trickster of Seville. But Juan's defiance of the manners of his time remains negative. A remark spoken (twice) by a character in *The Mountebanks* (1918)[18] could well synopsize Juan's function in the society he inhabits: "Evil purifies good." He transcends the Molière villain while remaining a separate case, a freak, for whom being a master of the house would not begin to suffice. This is a character who could engorge the fictitious worlds of Sicily, if not the world, and for transient pleasure rather than for power. Against his era he wages no reforms and not quite a one-man war; he simply refuses to comply, because he is selfish, even egomaniacal; although at least three times in the play he will risk his life on an impulse, and the third time lose it to the vengeance of a father-in-law, the dehumanized, implacable father that his father could never be. Vilar's sardonic speaking of the Don's lines, in a disinterested drone, removed the character from the realm of reality occupied by the other characters. In keeping Sganarelle by his side, this negative Superman

---

17. If Juan meets defeat by the loss of his life, Tanner is disarmed in a less brutal but efficacious stroke by his marriage to Ann and reabsorption into the social sphere from which he has brashly tried to disengage himself.

18. By Clément Pansaers. Included in *Theatrical Gestures from the Belgium Avant-Garde*, ed. David Willinger (New York: New York Literary Forum, 1988), 37–43.

has taken for his companion an Everyman, an embodiment of those human traits (particularly cowardice, conformity, and unquestioning, superstitious piety) for which he has the highest contempt in order to be constantly reminded of what he must never allow himself to become. He also takes an ornery delight in keeping companionship with a man who has no hope of fathoming him.[19]

In the first act, Sganarelle introduces Gusman and us to his master as the most irredeemable blackguard ever. In the next act, he advises Charlotte and Mathurine to have nothing to do with the Don. In the third act, he stretches his rubbery principles when he urges the Poor Man to swear in order to win the gold coin Juan is holding out; soon after, he runs for cover when Don Alonse and his followers turn up; in hiding, he soils his doctor's gown out of fear. By act IV, he mimics Juan's dismissal of Monsieur Dimanche and he tremblingly acts as Juan's emissary when he invites the Statue to dine. He keeps dropping uncomplimentary asides about his master, but like a clucking, tsk-ing, but inveterate reader of stories about violent crime, he is hooked, cannot give him up. He could never tell himself, as does his successor, Leporello, in *Don Giovanni*, "I'll serve no more *(non voglio più servir)."* Throughout the action, he responds predictably to every situation with pity, shock, horror, whereas Juan continually changes the subject with finality and refuses to respond, as though to say, "Next business." But in his final speech after Juan has gone down in flames, Sganarelle responds as his master might have done if somebody else had died. No pity, no horror, no shock, only "next business": his pay, his future. The sociable Everyman has been affected by the asocial Superman, which is to say, infected by the Don Juan virus. He may never recover.

19. See the *Don Juan* essay in Guicharnaud's *Molière: une aventure théâtrale*, esp. 182–93 and 206–7, for a study of the relationship between Sganarelle and Juan. The essay concludes that Don Juan is "nature stark naked *(la nature toute nue),"* a primitive, a throwback, a jungle appetite that thrives on its momentary satisfactions. Yet if Molière had wanted to depict Juan so unambiguously, he could have shown more of the brute satisfactions being realized, not simply projected and then denied.

The Misanthrope
(*Le Misanthrope*, 1666)

Where is upper society? Wherever it meets. When the titled and entitled in seventeenth-century Paris are not devoting their waking hours to dress and toilet, to penning and receiving letters, love poems, and libelous prose, they kill time. They hang out on the fringes of the court to seek favors and appointments, exchange gossip, wait for a glimpse of a royal personage or a well-connected functionary. The litigious ones pursue lawsuits having to do with the upholding and undermining of reputations. At other moments these rich or pseudo-rich unemployed may drop in on acquaintances or, less often, respond to invitations.

Some women keep open house. One gauges their influence by their popularity. When the number of casual callers falls away, so does their public esteem. But as long as they can count on a throng of visitors, their premises serve as a refuge for idle busybodies, the loose human ends that shift between social groupings called salons—rapidly filled and drained reservoirs of men and women every one of whom has literary pretensions.

Those newcomers to town, Cathos and Magdelon, fiercely hope to convert Gorgibus' home into such a gathering place. Uranie has already done so with her house, and Philaminte means to transform hers into an academy of sorts, although she would restrict the quantity and opinions of her guests. In *The Misanthrope*, Célimène, the weathy young widow, plays hostess to two women (her cousin and an older rival), four suitors who include a couple of marquis, and the hero, Alceste, and Alceste's friend, Philinte. The play doesn't tell us how she came by her property, whether she inherited it from her parents or from her late husband; he must have been considerably older than she, since she is now only twenty; and he must have died some time before, since she neither wears mourning nor mourns nor mentions him. Her role has no early personal history and is untrammeled by the tyrannies of a father or mother. A quartet of suitors means that she attracts men because of her looks, her wealth, her *esprit*, and/or her celebrity, although not one of them is so crass as to speak of her wealth. Of her *esprit* (spirit, wit, quickness, vivacity, intelligence) the play gives abundant proof, and if, as it further suggests, this constitutes her drawing power, it also invites her downfall.

Critics often call *The Misanthrope*, which is one of the most thoroughly chewed-over plays of all time, Molière's *Hamlet*. Possibly. But it is equally his *Much Ado about Nothing*, his *Antony and Cleopatra*, his *Troilus and Cressida*, his *Bérénice*, his *Dance of Death*, and his *Little Eyolf*. The comparison with *Hamlet* is continually raised, in part because many people take *The Misanthrope* to be Molière's most dialectical play,[1] and in part because its hero, like Shakespeare's, has an enigmatic core. Actors can interpret the role with such latitude that one Alceste garnished with the same green ribbons as another, like one Hamlet in the same inky cloak as another, may appear as contrasted, if not opposed, personalities: as a conceited prig and as an admirable champion of straight speaking and social betterment. But so can two versions of Célimène contrast dramatically, for she too is an enigma. Acting can make her lines fit a chilly shrew or a bewitching tease.

Now, Alceste would seem far less enigmatic and engaging if he did not love Célimène, just as the heart of Hamlet's mystery might more easily be plucked out and delivered whole to audiences if the plotting did not declare his love for Ophelia and Gertrude—and Horatio. Hence the comparison with *Much Ado, Antony and Cleopatra, Little Eyolf,* and other plays, including several more by Ibsen and Strindberg, which go well beyond being character studies in order to make us listen to the strange harmonies and discords sounded *between* each male and female principal. Among its other seekings, *The Misanthrope* persistently questions, right up to the last curtain, the nature of Alceste's love for Célimène and asks whether it is reciprocated. Critical writings have generally slighted Célimène. They perceive her as, at most, a symbol,[2] which she is, but that is not all she is. Those writings, particularly the ones with a metaphysical or ethical bias, fasten on to Alceste's verbal tussles with Philinte, Oronte, Arsinoé, and Célimène and look at them from *his* point of view. He certainly occupies center stage through most of the play, but all of the play takes place in her house, and the other characters do speak of Célimène in the first act, before we have met her, and at other times when she is absent.

Molière's plotting uncovers a ripe paradox. Alceste tells Philinte of his disgust at the stratum of society in which he lives; he perceives it as corrupted by its insincere manners and made up of people who are shallow, purposeless, polite backstabbers. But he loves the woman who most successfully embodies

---

1. In *Hamlet*, but not in *The Misanthrope*, some of the finest dialectical arguments are exchanged between the hero and himself.
2. See, e.g., Gossman, chap. 3, 66–99.

that society.[3] Does he hope to convert her, to win her over as an ally or a companion who will share his distaste? Very possibly he does. But as Philinte wonders, if the fellow is bent on a conversion, why doesn't he seek a more convertible candidate? For two probable reasons. First, he would *like* to convert her but doesn't *intend* to, perhaps because he realizes that such a conversion would not be feasible (any more than Arnolphe's attempt to groom and mould Agnès is feasible). Second, someone convertible, a neutral, pliable personality, would not interest him, but Célimène's excessiveness does. Like goes to like and deep calleth unto deep. She is a conquest worthy of him, or would be, if he made a serious attempt to conquer her—as he might be forced to do before he could convert her. The conquest would have to begin by removing her from temptation, this society, and that precisely he will propose shortly before the play ends: a life shared with him in isolation in "my desert," a word variously understood and translated as a literal desert (but which one? the Sahara? the Kalahari?—the world's deserts lie outside France) or as a remote spot yet to be picked or as Alceste's country estate.

Alfred Simon in *Molière par lui-même* notices that *The Misanthrope* resembles *The Nuisances* in providing a rundown of various samples of lapel grabbing and other irritants. But the fault in his contemporaries that incenses Alceste is less importuning than lying for the sake of courtesy. Monsieur A extravagantly flatters the Comte de B to his face but, behind B's back, cuts him to shreds in front of the Marquis de X and Madame Y. He does the same with Y and Z when conversing with P and Q. So does everyone else. No person has a coherent idea of how many close friends are secret foes. Each has to assume that practically everybody has a low opinion of practically everybody else, but the proviso "practically" allows for a narrow margin of hope. Alceste will exploit that margin, but in an Alcestian fashion. He does not care whether others like him, so long as they respect him, so long as they separate him from the herd of others, the hypocrites: "I insist that they acknowledge me as different" (I, 1). He will proclaim his dislikes openly, fearlessly, will become a known quantity by being *and seeming* sincere. Whether or not he is sincere in wishing to seem sincere, he is certainly cruel. He has the characteristic of

---

3. Gutwirth calls her "the flower on this dunghill, ravishing because frivolous" (94). Jasinski believes "Célimène is characterized in one word: she is a flirt" *(Molière et le Misanthrope,* 163). As a result, she is not as "profound" or witty as Alceste is, but she does "incarnate the highest form of feminine lightness" (186). Jasinski's chapter on Célimène, like his other "character analyses," treats this figure as something of a discrete phenomenon, rather than as a dynamic part of a theatrical interplay.

people who like to be candid at others' expense, assuming that candor gives him license to say anything he pleases. He is a variant on the callous truth-teller who announces, "Frankly, you ought not to do this or be that"— as though the "you" could hardly wait to listen to a recital of personal shortcomings.

In adopting this attitude, Alceste deceives himself. It doesn't make him "different," for in a later scene Célimène and Arsinoé will practice more or less what he preaches. And Philinte, to whom he is speaking, soon points out that his corrosive anger has made him not respected but an object of ridicule. No wonder. Alceste's "sincerity" smacks of insincerely strong language, wild overstatement, replete with superlatives. "You ought to die of pure shame," he tells Philinte, who has just returned warm greetings to a man he doesn't know well. "I see you overwhelming him with affection and showing him the most extreme tenderness. . . . / This is something unworthy, cowardly, infamous, debasing yourself to the point of betraying your soul; / and if, by mischance, I'd done that, I'd run right off and hang myself." He assures the incredulous Philinte that "I hate all men," with no exceptions. He spits out these sentiments during the opening scene, while the audience is still assessing him. The plotting here brings us smack up against Alceste's profession of a set of extreme beliefs, which the action will steadily erode, without diminishing the force of his role. They support Philinte's observation that he is making himself ridiculous. Not that Alceste cares; other people are so odious to him, he says, that he would never wish them to consider him wise. Célimène later tries to preach back at him with, "You are, without a lie, a great exaggerator" (*un grand extravagant*, IV, 3), at the same time as she mocks his candor ("without a lie"), but he brushes her charge aside.

Unluckily, it does Alceste no good to hand out straight talk, whether sincere or hyperbolic, if we can judge by the reactions of other characters in the play. A recipient of insulting criticism offered in Molière under the guise of advice from the heart does not swallow it or follow it, only resents it and sometimes retorts in kind. As Alceste moves through the five acts he arouses and confronts a growing hill of indignation. He does not start out on the attack, as Guicharnaud (351–52) observes. (If he enters the play at a run, puffing and blazing, his role has nowhere to go. Alceste isolates himself in, not before, the action.) He justifies his disparagement of Célimène with an astonishing statement: "The more you love someone, the less you should flatter her;/ love shines forth purely when it forgives nothing" (II, 4). As a corollary to this apothegm, it would seem that the stronger and harsher the criticism, the more devotion one is revealing. If Alceste wrote a play, the love scenes would consist of violently antagonistic lines, culminating in a suicide pact. Is this an Alcestian overstatement? Not really, for as the play closes he endeavors to steer his affair with Célimène into a parody of just such an agreement.

Can unsparing honesty be truly a virtue? It was for the early Romans and Spartans and is for a number of Corneille's heroes, those unyielding resuscitations from antiquity. Philinte, as he reminds his friend of "that great rigidity in the virtues of ancient times," which "demanded too much perfection of mortals" (I, 1), lets us see that Molière has set his sights—and not for the first time—on a stern and implacable Cornelian model (Horatius, perhaps?) and speculated on how such a character might fare when transplanted to a modern setting. In seventeenth-century Paris, he will send out shock waves of disbelief and anger; but that very rigidity *(raideur)* that Philinte refers to, and Bergson much later confirms, is also bound to have comic results. Yet, Molière is not, I think, burlesquing Corneille or this hero. Alceste has formidable intellectual and moral prowess. His is not necessarily a personality to admire, although plenty of people have thought of him as virtue personified; but like John Tanner (in many respects his scion), he has an inner force that makes us sit up, listen, and now and then assent to even his most outlandishly expressed views. If he is not altogether right, he is far from being altogether wrong. A society peopled with the witty but phlegmatic Philinte, who does what the others do for the sake of a quiet life (and yet likes the combustible Alceste and remains faithful to him), and the complacent braggart Acaste, who proclaims himself God's gift to everyone, and Oronte, who *must* elicit Alceste's approval of a poem and turns nasty when he doesn't get it, and other figures Alceste comes up against every day—such a society *needs* a scourge. But this scourge will never be a threat, never be more than a mildly chastening influence, a gadfly whose bite leaves bile instead of poison in the wounds he inflicts, unless he goes on to become an active reformer with a potent following. But Alceste would never seek or accept followers. Like Don Juan, he would be a loner by choice.

The author originally added the words "The Melancholic in Love" to his published title, and they are worth keeping in mind. He may have conceived of the character as a fixed disposition, a Jonsonian or Shadwellian "humour." Thus, if Alceste hardly affects the life of Paris as he chants his jeremiads in that wilderness of the spirit before finally saying he will withdraw to his private desert, the society's mocking defenses and counterattacks will make no real counterimpact on him.[4] But why was the subtitle dropped? Because it seemed overexplanatory? Because Alceste is not sure if he *is* in love? Because the *audience* is meant to remain unsure? He does not exactly equivocate when it comes to discussing his feelings, but neither does he soar into theatrical raptures. At the start, he declares he loves Célimène in spite of her flaws, "these vices of the age," which his love will purge from her soul. But when asked by Philinte if he believes she loves *him,* Alceste replies, "Yes, by God! / I wouldn't love her if I didn't believe that" (I, 1). As though to bolster that belief, and so convince himself that he does indeed love her, he tries in his later scenes with her to extract an admission that she loves him and him only. She says he can be happy "to know that you are loved." That is not affirmative enough. Like Don Garcie, from whom he borrows lines and phrases, he suffers from jealousy, not as all-consuming as Garcie's, but noticeable and offensive to Célimène. How can he be assured that she does not tell her other admirers that they, too, are loved? She bridles at that; the skirmish intensifies; and before it is over, he is ready to bless the heavens if he can only break free from this "terrible attachment" (II, 1). In matters of the heart, Alceste seeks 100 percent security. He will never achieve it, because the answer to one doubt breeds another.

The changes in his demeanor, from flat dogmatism in the scene with Philinte to carping and wavering in the scene with Célimène, invite us to question whether Alceste is as rigid as Philinte (and Bergson) say. As it happens, Célimène herself points out to Philinte that Alceste takes so much pleasure in gainsaying what others say that he sometimes "takes up arms against himself" (II, 4). She is correct. Alceste is a mass of contradictions. He wants to win his current lawsuit but will be glad if he loses because the loss will prove there is injustice and that he therefore has the right to hate other men. He allows that "reason doesn't rule love," yet he expects it to rule other emotions and behavior. He means to be different, yet woos the woman wooed by the fops he despises. And to *be* different, he strives to appear imposing, if not forbidding, but when, for example, he declares that, short of

---

4. The word "melancholic," although an accurate translation of the French *atrabilaire* (whose root syllable is connected with bile) does not have quite the same quality of meaning. It is softer, more wistful. Thus, it would be folly to attempt a production of the play in which Alceste was "melancholy," in the English sense, throughout. He would yearn, rather than radiating bilious energy (see "Molière's *Misanthrope:* Melancholy and Society in the Age of the Counterreformation" by Lionel Gossman in *Theatre Journal,* Oct. 1982, 323–43).

an express command from the king, he will always contend that painful poems are bad and that the man responsible for them should be hanged, Clitandre and Acaste laugh, and he has to protest, "Messieurs, I did not think I am so funny" (II, 6). When Arsinoé flatters him, promises to advance his name in court circles, and shows him a warmly worded letter unmistakably written by Célimène, he responds with suitable dignity and distance; but he does read the letter, gets frothed-up over it, and brings it back to Célimène as a challenge. (She defends herself by saying it was written to a woman, not a man.) He is courteous (at first) to Oronte and to Arsinoé but rude and unfeeling to the gentle Éliante, who is fond of him, when he thinks her cousin has betrayed him, and proposes to her in order to take revenge on Célimène (IV, 2).

His most striking contradiction is also his most heartless one. He wishes Célimène had been born penniless and was now unloved, alone, and miserable, so that he might rescue her (IV, 3). His chance arrives in the last scenes, when her cutting comments written about some admirers to others come to light. Each of the men present chastises her brutally and then departs. She is abandoned, except by Alceste. Instead of making good on his word, he lays down preconditions: she must give up everything, go with him to his "desert," and become dependent on him (V, 4). This is no rescue: he merely holds out the bleak prospect of living on literal or metaphorical sand. He will pull her away from the competition. At the same time, he will rescue *himself,* because his servant said in the previous act that Alceste has lost his lawsuit and had better get out of town fast, before he is arrested.[5]

It is not necessary, desirable, or possible to find a way to settle these contradictions without inhibiting the performer. But one clue to Alceste's stage behavior goes back, as clues often do, to the first casting. How old are the principals? Molière was forty-five when he played Alceste; the Philinte, La Thorillière, was about five years younger. If the two characters are roughly forty, we can understand a worry that nags at Alceste as he asks himself what he, a powerful presence and a man of uncommon intellect, has made of his

---

5. The servant's warning may be a false alarm. Alceste subsequently explains that he is being falsely prosecuted for having written a scurrilous book and that Oronte, still smarting from Alceste's refusal to praise his poem, has testified that Alceste is indeed the author of the offensive work. Philinte then counters by saying that Alceste has not been arrested; that there is no hard evidence against him, only an unbelievable rumor; and that Alceste will surely win his other lawsuit. But Philinte is talking to a man who has made up his mind that the world is against him and he must escape from it.

life. Not much. He has been an attitudinizer, playing the misanthrope, perhaps mildly, to amuse others and give himself a substitute for a genuine
vocation. The waste of it! He has achieved only the status of becoming a
laughingstock. But he does not know how to change, does not even want to
change or feel capable of doing so. He retreats into himself, intensifies the
role. Philinte mentions that he and Alceste grew up together. He may well
have known a less acidic Alceste, someone more approachable than the one
portrayed in these five acts (by analogy with Orgon before he met Tartuffe),
and he is attempting to show Alceste the error of his ways and to induce him
to revert to the more likable man he was. If this holds true, the play's action
represents a crisis and a turning point in Alceste's life. By resolving to *be*
someone different and memorable, someone who counts, he succeeds in
painting himself into a corner, that corner proving to be his "desert," because
he feels he must make good on his threat to walk away from this setting, this
society not unlike the one described by Pailleron, two centuries after, as "the
world of boredom" *(le monde où l'on s'ennuie).* The action similarly produces
a crisis for Philinte. He observes his old friend, almost a brother, slipping
away from him and into the ooze of all-out misanthropy.

History, including this chapter, has judged Alceste more harshly than many
of his first audiences evidently did. In this play, for the first time, Molière
appeared onstage "with his face uncovered" and "in elegant court dress."[6]
The Misanthrope had twenty-one consecutive performances "with receipts
that rose to 1,617 livres on the second [showing], and fell only twice below
300 livres," an unusually active box office.[7] According to Adrien de Subligny,
a playwright produced by Molière, "all the court speaks well of" the play,
even one gentleman taken to be its target. "The austere and virtuous M. de
Montausier, deeply angered at the idea of having served as a model for the
character of Alceste, leaves charmed by the performance and declares he
holds it a great honor for a resemblance to be noticed between this honest
man and him."[8] There can be little doubt that Molière, while depicting
Alceste's boorishness, especially in matters that sting his heart, shared some
of his character's feelings and respected the sort of tenacity he shows, rather
as Ibsen seems to sympathize with his boastful and cantankerous social rebel,
Dr. Thomas Stockmann; but a fearlessly honest creation demands to be

6. Chevalley, 237.
7. Ibid., 238. These figures are taken from the *Register* kept by La Grange, of which
Chevalley provides many samples.
8. Ibid., 238.

portrayed with fearless honesty.[9] (In the very naming of his hero, the author may mean to invoke a memory of Euripides' heroine Alcestis, who makes the ultimate gesture of selfless virtue by volunteering to sacrifice her life to preserve her husband's.) Similarly, the role of Philinte, this play's advocate of the contemptible but valuable art of getting along with those one despises, if offered as a bland disciple of moderation, will not become an effective counterpoise to Alceste. Philinte is as vehement as Alceste in putting forward his beliefs ("My phlegm is as much of a philosopher as your bile is," I, 1). Better for him to yell about the need to be reasonable (the play *is* a comedy) than to stroke Alceste with his lines. Alceste puts up with his arguments for the same reason that he woos Célimène: these are his two most worthy opponents.[10]

Célimène is more than twenty years younger than Molière was when he wrote the play (and so, probably, is Éliante). Her other three pursuers in the action—Clitandre, Oronte, and Acaste, who says in his self-complimentary speech that he is young (III, 1)—may not be much older than Célimène. Seeing himself in this youthful company, Alceste must squirm at appearing as simply one more hanger-on. Hence, one motive for making himself different: at his age he ought to have accomplished more, even to be morally *worth* more. He does have his admirers. Philinte sticks by him, despite many rebuffs. Éliante would marry him at first, until he asks her vindictively, in order to spite her cousin. Oronte goes resolutely after Alceste's friendship by seeking an approbatory opinion of his poem (I, 2)—Philinte's eulogy will not suffice. Arsinoé, evidently at least ten years closer to his age than Célimène is, virtually throws herself at him (III, 5). Even Célimène, who believes—rightly, for the time and circumstances—that a man should take the initiative when it comes to marriage, keeps inviting him to propose. But she will not overstep the usual decorum, and her refusal to say outright that she loves him and

9. In his *Letter to M. D'Alembert* (1758), Jean-Jacques Rousseau, that supreme egalitarian, eulogizes *The Misanthrope* as Molière's best comedy but resents the laughs evoked by making this "truly virtuous" figure look ridiculous; he also resents the portrait of Philinte as an exponent of reason that must be restrained to moderate doses, because he believes Philinte to be the author's mouthpiece. Rousseau's interpretation of these two roles has influenced many subsequent writings.

10. For favorable character studies of Philinte, see "Philinte and Éliante" by Merlin Thomas in Howarth and Thomas, 73–92, and Jasinski, ibid., 188–202. The latter interprets Philinte as "the visible expression of [Molière's] ideal" and an "incarnation of Molière's idea of perfect wisdom" (202).

him alone is not committal enough for him: the furthest she will go in the way of an admission is a passive, impersonal statement: "You are loved." Alceste, then, is no boor, but a sparkling, loyal, engaging personality in his best moments and, at other times, a talker who commands attention.

Célimène undoubtedly wants him but seems to fear that if she says so, she may not be able to hold onto him. He pretends to be put off by her having become a creature of fashion or custom. Visitors swarm to her house because other visitors do the same. They praise her lampooning comments but not her person. They each picture themselves as her partner for the social glow they would bask in if she accepted them. Alceste catches her on her own for a brief time during their first encounter in the play (II, 1). He keeps chiding her and telling her how much he is suffering. He suffers further when interrupted. Visitors barge in. Among them is Clitandre. Alceste has shortly before asked what she finds so alluring in this fop—the long nail on his little finger, his blond wig, knee ruffles, overflow of ribbons, bulky pantaloons, manner of laughing, falsetto voice? She replied then that Clitandre has promised to provide assistance in her lawsuit, for she too is a litigant. Alceste now dreads the prospect of another session in which those present will douse one another in compliments and affectation while they cut to pieces those who are absent (as he has just done), a round of dirt scattering in which the participants recite their own faults—which they ascribe to others. He decides to leave. She tells him to stay. Three times she says, "I insist" *(je le veux— je veux* being one of Alceste's favorite sentence openers), and he refuses. But when she impatiently responds in effect, "Suit yourself" *(il vous est tout loisible),* he stays after all. Through that second act, as throughout the action, he behaves contrarily toward her, yields not a centimeter of understanding, only repines about his misery and perplexity.

Stimulated by the backbiting that ensues, Célimène launches into her "portraits" of the salon circle, showing off and revealing the same penchant for malice as Alceste's (II, 4). When he indulges in it, however, he castigates the entire society and people take his wit for moralizing; when she does it, she selects her targets one by one and is applauded as a star turn. Alceste fires salvoes and blunderbuss volleys; Célimène tosses darts. He remains silent as she "paints" eight absentee friends, concluding with a certain Damis who picks holes in everybody else's writings and speech, considers himself superior, and looks down "with folded arms" and "in pity" on whatever others say. Clitandre finds her portraiture "admirable." Then Alceste intervenes; he upbraids the onstage audience for encouraging her. Why does he wait so long? Is he stung by her putdown of Damis, who might from her account as easily be—Alceste? As with Orgon under the table, his bile flows faster when he becomes, or thinks he has become, the subject of unflattering talk.[11] It does not occur to him that her strictures could apply with equal justice to herself.

Éliante's monologue, which follows shortly, gives Alceste further cause for unease and also troubles her cousin. She speaks of the generosity of true love, which sees blemishes as reasons for heightened affection and confers "favorable names" on all flaws. The pale woman becomes "as fair as jasmine," the skinny is "slim," the heavy "majestic," and so on. The speech spurs Alceste, who always speaks churlishly of his beloved, to a protest; but this in turn is cut off by Célimène. Éliante's words, if applied to Célimène herself, could mean either that she does not love Alceste or that he does not love her. She suggests a stroll through the house and asks Clitandre and Acaste whether they are leaving. Troubled by Éliante's speech, she intends to take up the private talk with Alceste that broke off with the arrival of the visitors, whom she is now requesting to go. They do not pick up the hint; they say they have no other pressing business. But Alceste, who misinterprets her tact and their tactlessness, charges her with being "frightened" of losing their company. Like George Dandin, he muffs his chance. She has offered him an initiative; he spurns it, berates her and insists he will stay there as long as the other men do.

A dramatist of high caliber composes a set speech like Éliante's, apart from its intrinsic values as a statement and as a gift to the actor, to let it sound its reverberations.[12] Molière has transcended his earlier solos, duets, and other scenes that show off the prowess of the individuals in the Palais-Royal troupe, raising them to arias and linking recitative, which thunder or croon, bel canto alexandrines with flexible stresses: the ictus, like that in late Shakespeare, falls with natural emphasis on topic words in order to keep the tone conversational. This is poetry designed not for mere declamation but for singing and communicating. It *affects* the onstage listeners, who cannot perforce be numb and dumb bystanders but must become active receivers.

Another set speech that reverberates opens the third act. Spoken by Acaste

11. Guicharnaud has a different explanation of Alceste's outburst at this point: that as a "serious" person he resents the mocking laughter, the frivolity of Célimène and her circle (ibid., 410 ff).

12. Éliante's speech, closely modeled on a passage from Molière's translation of Lucretius and sometimes criticized in the past as plagiarism, is an almost perfect example of an apposite sustained quotation, put to even better use than the original.

to one listener, his fellow marquis, Clitandre, it proclaims the list of reasons why Acaste will be a great catch for some woman, and he means Célimène—his wealth (first), youth, rank, courage, vigor, and other entries in the list of assets, down to his popularity with "the fair sex" and good standing with the monarch. The speech discomfits Clitandre, as it was meant to do. At the same time, its high comedy projects the self-satisfied character that Alceste may once have been but will never be again. It also signifies the sort of talk Célimène hears from the procession of guests as they boost themselves before getting down to the less rewarding performance of tearing into others. When Alceste is present, Célimène's routine varies slightly: she has a guest who attacks *himself,* but on grounds she must find disquieting, for he admits to one fault, his love for her, although he gives no sign of it. Rather than having to listen every day for twelve hours at a stretch to his railing and their bragging, she talks and talks out of self-defense and can glory in earning herself laughter and praise. Her sprightly receptions may not go on for many more years, but for the time being they will do. One can fancy the color of Célimène's soul, like that of Hardy's Eustacia Vye, to be flamelike. On occasion she must match wits with a jealous rival like Arsinoé, yet even doing that is a pleasure. To Arsinoé's veiled suggestion that Célimène is any man's mistress, Célimène can openly answer, "Prude!" If Arsinoé inflicts on her what other people are supposedly saying, she can reply in the same vein and then boomerang back Arsinoé's exact words: "I take you to be too reasonable / Not to heed this useful advice" (III, 4). So confident is she in her power and Arsinoé's weakened hold over men that she cheerfully improvises an excuse to take herself out of the room and leave Alceste with her enemy (III, 5) and the opportunity to compare the two women.

That the enemy will torture him with the ambiguous letter is a trick Célimène had not foreseen. She is deeply immersed in the indecisive present. When Philinte asks Éliante whether Alceste "is loved," she replies that Célimène's heart "is not very sure of what it feels" (IV, 1). Sometimes her cousin is in love without properly knowing; sometimes she believes herself in love when she is not. This description accords with what we witness in the play. Célimène too is contradictory. She complains that Alceste doesn't love her as he should; she expects a firm commitment, as he does, with no clauses attached. But despite her pleasure in her role as queen of the salon community, such a career is short-lived; before long she must dwindle into an Arsinoé and out of the winning combination of youth, beauty, and wit, the loss or decline of the first two leading inevitably to a souring of the third. Visitors will stop coming. She will have to frequent the salons of others, the ones who supplanted her, and proffer introductions and other favors to solicit friendship.

If Célimène doesn't find anything good to say about anyone else, in that respect as well she is Alceste's counterpart. Consciously or not, she has chosen to battle the system by remaining in it and boring at it from within. It is her world; she despises its component parts, the individuals who pass through her home, but she has grown to need them. She sees no alternative. For this reason she is more sincere than he is. He cannot bring himself to admit that he belongs to that society; but she does boldly belong to it, even while she mercilessly criticizes its populace.

There are two misanthropes in this play—three if one counts Arsinoé, more if one includes the visitors who speak ill of their "friends," and more yet if one extends the definition to Philinte and Éliante, who behave with studied toleration toward their world for the sake of a quiet life. Alceste happens to be the most outspoken among them. He has given up hope of effecting improvements; he is too old; the best he can manage is to set a vinegary example. His assaults from without do no harm; he succeeds only in arousing the society's hackles and resistance. Célimène's boring at it and attempting to pull it to bits from within succeed only in shoring up its rickety structure. He, who pities himself for being so sensitive, unable to endure insincerity, never notices that she is his opposite number and just as sensitive.

If he does want her, in the last act he misses his chance more seriously than before, perhaps irreparably. In the play's most painful scenes (V, 2, 3, 4), she is beset by the men who courted her. First, Alceste and Oronte demand that she state outright which of them she loves; she can only reply lamely that she has made her choice, which she considers untimely and embarrassing to reveal.[13] Why does she prevaricate? Perhaps because neither of them has given an unmistakable signal that he loves her. Then the two marquis storm in and read aloud her letters, which they have exchanged, and which contain bitter commentary about the two of them—and also about Oronte and Alceste. Arsinoé stands by and pretends to be scandalized as she sniffs gratefully at the humiliation of her usurper. Philinte and Éliante also watch and listen but do not interfere. Three of the men take themselves off, in more of a huff than when they entered. Arsinoé offers to console Alceste, but in one of his more laudable speeches, he coolly dismisses her. Célimène

---

13. The dramatic triangle, two men asking a woman which of them she loves, is the exact obverse of the triangle in *Don Juan* (II, 4) in which Charlotte and Mathurine ask the same question of Juan, which he answers ambiguously.

does not defend herself. She has been treacherous toward Alceste, she says, and he has cause to hate her.

But does he hate her? Fate, in the form of Molière's plotting, has at last held out its definitive opportunity to him. He can now make good on his desire to rescue her from that isolation in which, not long before, he wished to find her. The competition (by implication, the society at large) has turned away from her. He can exert the almost saintly power of accepting her and bringing her out of disgrace. He makes his proposal, but for her it is a frighteningly limited one. He tells her, as he earlier told Philinte, that he wants to flee the human race and go "into my desert." She may, if willing, accompany him. By so doing, she will be able to repair the bad reputation her letters have given her "in everyone's opinion" *(dans tous les esprits)*. It will then be possible for him to love her again.

Alceste may or may not choose, after the action, to cut himself off from the society he abhors, but he has caught its hypocrisy, which is contagious. Throughout the action, he has protested his indifference to the opinions of others, has even said that he welcomes their disapproval. Now, suddenly, they must have a high opinion of *her* before his love can revive. In such a proposal, there is no glimmer of love, only anxiety over what others think. An air of tragedy, of a self-willed downfall, haunts the final scene, and it is at least as much her tragedy as his. Only moments before, she had been the cynosure of Paris. Abruptly, she finds herself cast aside, owing to her own joking malice. A stage direction has her "withdraw." The words she leaves on are Alceste's: "I hate you . . . Go . . . I am free of your worthless love forever." Yet, Alceste, for all his rage, is still capable of kind words. He turns to Éliante and praises her virtue, beauty, and sincerity. Then, with the announcement that he will now "leave this gulf in which vices are trium-phant,/ And look for a remote place on earth / Where one is free to be a man of honor," he rushes out. The plotting has formally prefigured this exit four times: he leaves the stage at the end of each of the preceding acts. This time, no line tells him to go, at a point only one couplet removed from the end of the play; but the couplet, spoken by Philinte, urges Eliante to come with him to try to dissuade Alceste from his "plan," and when they depart the stage is empty for the last curtain.

Nobody follows Célimène. Alceste has his confidant; Célimène has none; her cousin, who has not one private moment with her through the action, has gone to comfort Alceste. The male rebel wins sympathy for his peremptori-ness, disappointment, grief, or all three. The female rebel receives no solace; she remains alone somewhere in her open house.

In his updating of the play to 1966, during the de Gaulle era, John Dexter drew attention to her ultimate isolation by ignoring the instruction that she withdraw.[14] He kept her visible onstage after the others had departed. She gazed from the window of her luxurious living room away from the auditorium and out at the night lights of a contemporary Paris. This final emphasis on the plight of Célimène, quarantined in her own quarters, was something of a jolt to traditionalists but a salutary reminder that *The Misanthrope* is not a one-character play. It also completed the summation of the play's action, for Célimène's salon, at the center of Parisian society and seething with visitors earlier in the day,[15] goes dark, like the playhouse, shortly after this moment. The crowd has moved on to a new gathering place.

In another antitraditional version, Garland Wright tackled the question of *how* Alceste loves Célimène.[16] He may not love her enough, but how can we

14. Dexter's production, based on an adaptation by the British poet Tony Harrison, starred Alec McCowen as Alceste and Diana Rigg as Célimène. It came to the Kennedy Center and the St. James Theatre on Broadway from the National Theatre.
15. Some well-budgeted directors in the recent past have kept Célimène's home buzzing with extras who play unnamed visitors, as though the play occurs during a party. In an updated version like Michael Simpson's, this sort of staging encourages a succession of distracting bits of business: pouring drinks, drinking them, lighting and puffing of cigarettes, curious bystanders peering through doorways, and oceans of background music—a tame, because formalized, twentieth-century bacchanalia.
16. Because of his selfishness, it is tempting to believe that Alceste loves only himself. Thus, Brian Bedford, who played the role in 1963, in talking to a news reporter: "I think I was misled by the director [Stephen Porter], who saw Alceste as a saint. And of course, he's the absolute opposite of that. This man is to a great extent a monster. Some of what he says is justified and even heroic, but some is monstrously egocentric." The reporter continues: "By lashing out constantly at what the character sees as lack of candor in everybody but himself, 'he puts up terrific smoke screens around himself— because there's nobody there. The man doesn't exist when he's in a room by himself. I think he must be the most unconfident man.' And Mr. Bedford now thinks Alceste is not truly deeply in love with the flirtatious Célimène (Mary Beth Hurt), who embraces the silly values that Alceste despises" (*New York Times*, 22 Feb. 1983, byline: Eleanor Blau).
Bedford's opposition to the notion that Alceste might be played as some sort of saint was a necessary corrective to the director's views, if he was stating them fairly. But his own view implies a character played apart from the rest of the cast, especially his observation that "the man doesn't exist when he's in a room by himself." In no scene of the play does Alceste appear by himself; Bedford, like Jasinski, substitutes individual character analysis for dramatic interpretation.

measure what constitutes enough? By imprisoning himself in the language of self-conscious misanthropy, he prevents himself from wooing her persuasively with the impulsive words of love—which seem to be precisely what she wants from him. Words, his great and overflowing torrent of words, have failed him. Wright did not confine himself to the succession of contacts and misconnections allotted by the text. His Alceste had an uncontrollable, literally physical crush on Célimène, seizing her when he had her momentarily to himself and making anguished (and convincing) love to her. His infatuation was not simply spoken of as the weakness he deplores in his lines but *seen* as a state of helpless infatuation, and his renunciation of her at the end became all the more tormented.[17]

As though to offset that pair's complex *malentendu,* Éliante and Philinte understand each other easily. As lovers, they have both been rejected, he by her after his first tentative proposal, she by Alceste; but they form a partnership that is possible for them because of who they are,[18] whereas her cousin and his friend remain apart because of who *they* are.

If Alceste does go as far as his "desert," he will have deprived himself of even the meager and thankless function he took on in Paris. And Célimène— will she ever be reintroduced to society's good graces, which she loathes but cannot forswear? Alceste has hankered after her looks and wit, yet one cannot help feeling that she drew him toward her because she deserves him, as he does her; she is the one female character in the play capable of standing up to him. But he backs away for what to him ought to be a trivial reason.

Over the end of the dark comedy hangs an aura of tragedy betokened by the separation and futility of two extraordinary lives.

17. *The Misanthrope* at the Guthrie Theater, Minneapolis, June–July 1987, directed by Garland Wright, Daniel Davis as Alceste, Caroline Lagerfelt as Célimène.
18. The partnership of Éliante and Philinte resembles the contented couplings in some of Ibsen's plays, not as an exemplary matching of people with low expectations but rather as a wry pointing-up of the unmatchability of the principals. The paired Ibsen couples include Kristine Linde and Nils Krogstad in *A Doll House,* Thea Elvsted and Jorgen Tesman in *Hedda Gabler,* Fanny Wilton and Erhart Borkman in *John Gabriel Borkman,* and Maja and Ulfhejm in *When We Dead Awaken.*

The Doctor in Spite of Himself
(*Le Médecin malgré lui*, 1666)

Some Molière scholars advance the theory that the Sganarelles who appear in seven of the plays trace a line of development, an evolution; that they have characteristics in common, in addition to being roles the playwright designed for himself. Such a theory, even with careful reservations attached, seems to me misleading, if not harmful when the plays come up for performance. Even the same historical or mythical character moved into another work—Bolingbroke, say, aging as he leaves *Richard II* for the two parts of *Henry IV* or Prince Hal reformed into Henry V or Clytemnestra transposed from vengeful mother and wife to defensive mother and queen—may have certain mannerisms that carry over, but the new situations dictate a new *role*. The seven Sganarelles, however, are not the same, but distinctive figures; they differ from one another in rank, age, personality, and dramatic circumstances. To confuse them or use one as a guide or model to the interpretation of any other is to practice well-meant distortion.

The Sganarelle in *The Doctor in Spite of Himself* spends lonely days as a woodcutter away from his wife and children and evidently not missing them. His preferred companion is a bottle of wine to which he sings a tribute in an early scene (I, 5). Like most of Molière's protagonists, he has a streak—if not a wide stripe—of malice in him. But unlike some other protagonists, who change superficially during the action, this Sganarelle undergoes a personal transformation nearly as drastic as that of a Euripidean principal. The malice does persist as a fluctuating influence on his behavior; he is less than admirable as he figures in an action that boils down to a sequence of farcical and satirical sketches. The sketches, which do not quite correspond to the numbered scenes, are so arranged as to need little linking or expository material between them.

Act I, a forest clearing:

1. Sganarelle quarrels with his wife, Martine. He ends up beating her.

2. A neighbor named Monsieur Robert interferes and regrets his chivalry after being assaulted, first by Martine, then by Sganarelle, for not minding his own business.

3. Valère and Lucas appear looking for a doctor who can cure their master's

daughter of her strange ailment, and Martine improvises some stories to the effect that Sganarelle is really a renowned healer posing as a woodcutter and will not admit to his true identity until somebody thrashes the truth out of him.

4. Valère and Lucas discover Sganarelle who denies that he is a physician until they reluctantly beat him and promise he can name his own fee.

Act II, Géronte's house:

5. Their master, Géronte, argues with Lucas' wife, Jacqueline, the family wetnurse, about his daughter's illness, while Valère and Lucas praise Sganarelle's reputation. Jacqueline (like Lisette in *Doctor Love*) insists that the young woman needs a husband, not medicine.

6. Enter Sganarelle, in a doctor's black gown. He beats his new employer and addresses him as Doctor ("*I* had no other training"), apologizes, and makes advances to the buxom Jacqueline in front of her husband.

7. The daughter, Lucinde, is brought in for a consultation. With the aid of jargon, tautology, Latin, and nonsense, Sganarelle diagnoses her inability to speak as dumbness. He prescribes bread soaked in wine, the "only food you give parrots. . . . They eat that and learn to talk."

8. Insisting that he never medicates for money, Sganarelle accepts a fee from Géronte.

9. He is then approached by Léandre, Lucinde's lover, and repulses him until Léandre produces a purse and reveals that Lucinde is playing ill to avoid a marriage wished on her by her father. Enlisting Sganarelle's aid, he is assured that "the patient shall either croak or be yours."

Act III, outside Géronte's house:

10. To Valère, now dressed as an apothecary, Sganarelle explains how easy and profitable it is to declare oneself a doctor and then, when something goes gravely wrong, to blame the corpse.

11. Sganarelle's fame has spread as a purveyor of miracle remedies. To a peasant who desperately seeks a cure for his very ill wife, Sganarelle gives a morsel of "chayze," cheese that "contains gold, coral, pearls, and many other priceless ingredients," for two gold coins.[1]

12. Sganarelle offers to cure Jacqueline "to high heaven" of a nonexistent

---

1. In France some productions have omitted this scene (III, 2) on the grounds that it amounts to a subplot that is irrelevant (but on the unstated grounds that it depicts Sganarelle—and by implication, any doctor—as a heartless rogue). It is actually the most bitterly written sketch in the play and jibes with the darker side of Sganarelle's personality.

ailment and make a cuckold of her husband—while the husband, Lucas, is listening. When Lucas enters the scene, they take off swiftly.

13. Lucinde recovers her voice on meeting Léandre (disguised as the apothecary) and recognizing him. Once she starts to speak, she can hardly be stopped. Sganarelle distracts her father with medical-sounding gobbledegook while Léandre runs away with her.

14. Géronte congratulates himself on having stopped Léandre from seeing his daughter while Sganarelle keeps him talking. But the trick is discovered: Sganarelle will be indicted for abduction, a capital offense at that time.

15. Martine finds her husband again, waiting to be hanged. She taunts him.

16. Léandre returns with Lucinde, instead of eloping. He has just inherited his uncle's estate. Following this news, Géronte is "favorably impressed by your character" and gives Léandre his daughter. Sganarelle rejoices at the prospect of remaining a doctor for good.

In most of these sketches the economical plotting brings on only the two or three actors needed; when more appear, they form a necessary onstage audience or serve as required witnesses. It will be noticed that there are four sketches in act I, five in act II, and seven in act III, even though the first act is the longest and the last the shortest. As the action accelerates, Molière tightens up the playing time of the sketches.

The story of *The Doctor in Spite of Himself* comes from a number of earlier writings, medieval French, Italian, and Spanish. The *fabliau* called *The Marvelous Peasant (Du Vilain Mire)* is probably the original source of the tale (Molière's first act) of the rich, brutal peasant whose wife takes revenge for his continual beatings of her by telling the king's messengers that he is a gifted doctor who must be manhandled before he will admit to his skills. The peasant later successfully removes a fishbone stuck in the princess's throat. Molière's second-act situation has resemblances to a tale in Rabelais of a dumb wife, cured by a doctor, and then becoming so loquacious that her husband asks to be deafened. (Anatole France reworked this incident in his play *The Man Who Married a Dumb Wife.*) This tale, too, had been variously adapted before Molière took it over. He had already used a woodcutter-turned-doctor in a lost farce called *The Woodcutter;* and in *The Flying Doctor* the earliest Sganarelle, posing as a doctor, "cures" Lucile. In this later play, the woodcutter, established as an addictive wifebeater, reminds Martine in the first scene of his schoolboy prowess at Latin and of his six years of working for a doctor. He comes onto the scene appropriately hardhearted for his mission and equipped with some practical and abstract background for undertaking it, as well as a usefully obfuscating vocabulary: he knows how to misquote and falsely paraphrase Aristotle. The author may have lifted some of these refinements from *The Woodcutter*. In any case, they lend the play a structure that is tighter than that of *The Flying Doctor*. Similarly, his wife has been introduced for structural reasons—to force her tormentor into his new vocation and to make his transition more plausible, instead of having him turn medico simply to please a master. And when Valère and Lucas meet up with her, she has the wit to invent a couple of Sganarelle's instant, barely credible cures. Her role is not a large one but in its bracketing of the play, an actress can do something with it. Originally it was almost surely assigned to Madeleine Béjart.

Given the authoritative manner of many doctors, based on their need to put on a bold front before their anxious and flustered clients, the conventional doctor's presence has always lent itself to impersonation, the essence of theatre, and to its satirical variant, ridicule.[2] In watching Sganarelle's impersonation of a doctor in this play, we do not bother to ask ourselves how he manages to carry it off, because we are delighted to see someone moving with aplomb into that shadowy but spacious area that lies between actual competence and its sound and appearance.

Despite the play's revue structure and neat subdivision into separate sketches, Molière's craftsmanship traces themes through the text and derives variations from them. When Martine resents Monsieur Robert's attempts to protect her she not merely surprises us—the victim turns on her helper—but also signifies her determination to choose her own method of punishing Sganarelle. (Not that Monsieur Robert could have done much on her behalf.) When Sganarelle shocks his client Géronte by beating him on their first encounter and then calling him "Doctor," we are being told that he has accepted his new calling and will gleefully live up to the false reputation Martine has conferred on him. When he begs to be wet-nursed (for a start) by the plumply alluring Jacqueline, while her husband stands by fuming, he shows himself to be an actor who delights in going out to the edges of his role and risking its verisimilitude. (Eminent careers in politics and the loftier professions constantly founder on just such risks.) When the "doctor" reverses the left and right positioning of the heart and liver, the flash of

2. See Gutwirth, 19–21 for reasons why the doctor is a valuable instrument of farce and comedy, in particular the comment that "the doctor, like the music teacher, is a man who has access to a beautiful woman" and is thus "a convenient intermediary."

suspicion evinced by Géronte, followed by Sganarelle's famous retort, "We've changed all that," carry him to the height of his audacity and prepare us for his announcement to Léandre: "Everybody's hell-bent on taking me for the big authority. They're coming at me from all angles" (III, 1).[3] He pretends not to understand the dialect as the peasant describes his sick wife's symptoms, but suddenly everything becomes clear when the peasant's son holds out two gold crowns ("This young man speaks clearly and offers me an intelligible explanation"); and this fleecing of the peasant and his son harks back to his brutality toward Martine.

He takes the largest risk when he enables Léandre to escape with Lucinde, and it looks as if he will have to pay for it. The jig is up. He will be hanged. But not for impersonation and swindling. For abduction. (There is a nice irony in that charge, since Sganarelle was himself abducted to treat Lucinde.) Nobody yet says or realizes that he is not a doctor. Léandre returns with the news of his inheritance, and, since there is no longer any abduction, Sganarelle is reprieved. His final speech, in which we might expect a confession, if not an expiation, goes in the opposite direction as he proclaims that his impersonation of a doctor, far from being over, has just begun. He has successfully sprung from the ranks of the laboring class to the role of an independent entrepreneur, in contrast to the earlier Sganarelle of *The Flying Doctor*, who reverts to being a servant. He has relied on his not-always-reliable wits to carry him from one moment to the next as he breaks the "rules" of medicine and etiquette. In its modest way, this farce is one of its author's pioneering efforts in developing characters who go it alone.

Like Monsieur Jourdain, he takes his leave of us happily immersed in his new condition. The settings have transferred him from the isolated but familiar (and familial) clearing outside his house, a woodsy openness, to the second act in Géronte's bourgeois interiors, and then, in act three, out of doors again when he falls from grace and very nearly swings as a felon, before his final return to power. Behind the homely frolics is a mythlike transformation of a beggar to a king.

As a country play, *The Doctor in Spite of Himself* is also appropriately earthy. Directors constantly look for ways of reimagining it. In 1978, Andrei Serban

---

3. *Dr. Knock* by Jules Romains, one of the hits of the French theatre in the 1920s and 1930s, as interpreted by Louis Jouvet, was also about the leap to popularity of a doctor. He takes over an ailing country practice and converts it into a high-pressure business operation when he convinces the people for miles around that they are all ill.

could not find an English translation of the play that he wanted to stage and decided to turn it into a "dumb show," in which the dialogue consisted of a cryptic, barked-out mix of Russian, Rumanian, smashed English, and gibberish, while the actors of the Yale Repertory Theatre held up title cards with what purported to be translations on them. The bulkily padded costumes and ferocious makeup resulted in performers who looked like versions of Eric Campbell (the women too), that angrily eyebrowed "heavy" from silent film farces. Serban's experiment may launch no new tradition—it would not be easy to imitate—yet it was a salutary effort, for all of its disavowal of the dialogue, in whisking Molière to the other end of the stage spectrum from conventionally dated and stuffy bowings and scrapings.

The Scams of Scapin
(*Les Fourberies de Scapin*, 1671)

When a Confederate army recruiter in *The General* asks the occupation of Johnny Gray, played by Buster Keaton, the young man answers, "Engineer."

The word accurately designates not only the job but also the character of Johnny and the artistry of Buster; it connotes a phenomenal talent for mechanics, as well as the cognate word "ingenuity." In French, *ingénieur* and *ingénieux* differ by only one letter, and in a consideration of *Scapin*, both aptly apply to the playwright as a master of plotting and to the part he chose to enact, for Scapin apparently becomes the author's surrogate—not his message carrier but the playwright within the play—as he engineers the plotting's intricacies and consequences. Molière here wrote himself into his most energetic role at a time when he was ill, less than twenty-one months away from his collapse onstage and his death.

Like "Doctor" Sganarelle, Scapin revels in stretching his appointed task to markers laid impudently beyond its expected limits. He savors his checkered past, in the course of which he has met the law (and lawyers) close up, swindled his master several times, and made himself indispensable. Now he practices, and looks forward to, more of the same. He tells a fellow servant, Silvestre, whom he has taken on as a fearful accomplice, that in the event they are caught, three years, more or less, aboard one of the stinking galleys to which criminals were consigned "are not enough to deter a brave heart" (I, 5). When a young woman sighs that love affairs would be wonderful if nobody interfered, he retorts that a calm love affair is like a calm ocean—flat—and that one needs highs and lows in life. He hurls himself into the teeth of chance and despises timorous people (III, 1).

The setting in Naples and the primary and secondary characters, who hark back to the commedia erudita, to Latin farces and Greek New Comedy, inform us before the action gets under way that the plotting will be recognizably Italian. Two young men *(innamorati)*, one of them Scapin's master, love two young women *(innamorate)* who are taken to be lowbred strangers and therefore will be rejected as wives by two Pantalone figures, the men's tightfisted merchant fathers, although one of the marriages has already taken place. The valets, Scapin and Silvestre, the first daring and mercurial, the second sensible and hesitant, parade characteristics associated with Scapino, Pulcinella, Brighella, and other *zanni,* mostly Neopolitan, from the commedia dell'arte. And a nurse-guardian, a substitute mother-cum-messenger, bobs up in the last act, much as the abbess, Emilia, does in *The Comedy of Errors,* and identifies one of the women as an approvable match. The other *innamorata's* upper-bourgeois breeding will be ascertained from her bracelet, her *gnorísma,* or identification of birth. From the beginning, there is no doubt that a happy ending is on the way as soon as the misunderstandings are wiped out. The questions are not whether Léandre will win Zerbinette and whether Octave will be able to reconcile his father to Hyacinte, his wife of three days, but *how*—that is, which Moliéresque flourishes of ingenuity will drape the familiar bones.

Scapin is a farce about playfulness. It flaunts and mocks its own formulaic situations. In the opening scene, the author makes a mockery of conventional exposition. Octave recites the given circumstances, the unlooked-for return to Naples of his father, Argante, who has settled on a marriage partner for him, while Silvestre wearily confirms and repeats the words, taking the "newsiness" out of them, because, as he says, if they both know what has happened, why bother to review it? After this tip-off to the audience that the action will not take itself seriously, Scapin the undefeatable arrives, presenting himself as a shameless performer who, we soon see, treats every venture as a flight into the fathomless unknown. From then on, the scenes shoot forward, each serving as a solo "turn," a duet, trio, or some other pretext for showing off individual virtuosity or ensemble acting, and each begetting the next, much as the stanzas of a good poem do, according to Joseph Brodsky.[1]

The scenes that draw the greatest displacement of farce pit Scapin against the pair of grudging fathers as he assails them with his favorite instrument, terror. Octave's father, Argante, shouts that he will annul his son's marriage to Hyacinte but is reduced to quivering after the cautious Silvestre (coached by Scapin) puts on a roughneck act by claiming to be her brother, an insanely quick-tempered lout (dredged up, perhaps, from Silvestre's unconscious), who threatens Argante with a sword through the guts unless the old man parts with a bribe of two hundred of his dear pistoles (II, 5, 6).

Scapin then gets Géronte, the other father, alone—the entrapment and

---

1. "A stanza . . . is a self-generating device: the end of one spells the necessity of another." (from Brodsky's exegesis of Auden's poem, "September 1, 1939," in *Less Than One* (New York: Farrar, Straus, 1986), 326.

terrorizing of one victim at a time is essential to the plotting here—and tells him his son has been kidnaped and shipped out into the Mediterranean on a Turkish galley, to be deposited on the shore of North Africa unless Géronte comes up fast with five hundred crowns. The stricken parent moans and temporizes. Can't Scapin sell some worn clothes to pay the ransom? (But the clothes are worth a tiny fraction of the ransom, even supposing someone is willing to buy them.) Can't Scapin take Léandre's place on the galley? (But the Turkish kidnapper will never accept a servant to substitute for a rich man's son.) Can't the law help? (But the law doesn't operate on the high seas.) Scapin has his answers ready and bubbling. This last scene (II, 7), one of the two funniest episodes in the play, is sharpened by Géronte's continual attempts to evade the issue, to think up some way of saving his money rather than his son's life. When he finally produces a purse of gold coins, he cannot seem to let it out of his clutch. Again and again he wails, "What the hell was he going to do aboard that galley?"—a line that, in every performance I have seen, amateur as well as professional, wrings tears of laughter from an audience.

It would appear that Molière cannot top this moment. But he does, in the celebrated sack scene, as Géronte again falls prey to Scapin's wickedness. Pure wickedness, this time. In his two earlier encounters with the fathers, he sought not only money but revenge for having been falsely accused of betraying his master, Géronte's son. As one of the quirks of his role, this swindler takes as much finicky pride in his honor as does the Mascarille of *The Botcher*. He cannot wipe this precious honor clean unless he punishes the person he believes responsible for having sullied it. That person is Géronte. Therefore, he entices Géronte into a sack and pretends to be not one but a succession of Géronte's enemies. They wallop him, Scapin, while he simultaneously plays himself subjected to their blows, which, by no accident, land on the sack and its aged contents (III, 2). The sack-beating incident, in addition to being a nightmare for Géronte, a triumph of multiple role playing for Scapin, and a joy for spectators, undercuts the nobility of personal honor nearly as damagingly as Sganarelle does with his Falstaffian soliloquy in *The Imaginary Cuckold*. The playwright piles on the humiliation for Géronte by following up with a scene in which Zerbinette appears and, having just heard the sack tale from Scapin, keeps breaking into peals of laughter as she (performed originally by the laughing specialist, Mlle Beauval) relates it back to Géronte without knowing who he is, and worse, without knowing him to be the father of her beloved Léandre. The humiliation deepens for both fathers when they learn that the sack incident and Scapin's bilking them of their cash have become common knowledge.

Amid the flurry of recognitions as the young women discover their true
ancestry in the third act, the play ends on a couple of strange notes. Géronte,
who employs Scapin as his son's valet and presumably pays his keep and even
possibly a wage, does not threaten to fire him, but only to punish him without
saying how. Scapin has hedged against this likely outcome. He enters carried
by two men and with bandages covering a wound supposedly incurred by a
hammer that dropped from a building and split his head open.[2] Géronte
forgives him, but only on condition that he dies of the wound. Scapin,
however, in the play's last and most enigmatic line, asks to be carried to the
head of the dinner table, *"en attendant que je meure,"* which could mean "to
await my death" or "until I die" or "in case I die"—which he doesn't seem
willing to do just yet, anyway. Still, the line does plunge the final moment
from reconciliations and settled accounts into uncertainty. Most directors
decline to undercut the fun and good humor, but Scapin's words seem chosen
to end the play on a strange note.

By his scheming and extortions, Scapin apparently governs the action;
hence, the reason for looking on him as the playwright within the play. But
what do his frantic activities amount to? He wheedles the first sum from
Argante and passes it on to the son, Octave, who has been pining to give
some financial relief to his new bride Hyacinte;[3] but after she marries Octave,
she will no longer be impoverished. The five hundred crowns he squeezes
out of Géronte go to ransom not Léandre but Léandre's sweetheart Zerbinette, whom the band of gypsies that raised her would not otherwise set free.
However, his ransoming of Zerbinette and keeping her in Naples could have
been carried out by her father, Argante, as soon as her true identity was
established. Thus, the plotting's ostensible purpose, to unite the two couples
and reconcile each young woman to her future father-in-law, has virtually
nothing to do with Scapin, since the women turn out to be the fathers'

2. Edmond Rostand may have felt a couple of centuries later that this was too provident
an accident to waste on a farce, because his Cyrano also enters in the last act with his
head opened by a log pushed out of a window by one of his enemies. Unlike Scapin,
Cyrano does die, in an atmosphere of pathos and nostalgia, perfumed by yearnings
on the part of Roxane for a love that might have been. The real Cyrano, a contemporary
and friendly acquaintance of Molière, may have already written or collaborated with
Molière on a scene that Molière takes over in *Scapin*. Rostand insists in his play that
Cyrano was the sole, original author of the scene, and that Molière filched it.
3. This is a desire that corresponds almost exactly to that of Cléante in *The Miser* (I,
2), when he tells his sister how badly he wants to give money and aid to Mariane.

respective daughters, and the fathers had already determined on the cross marriage. The unraveling of the conflict-that-is-no-conflict depends on two recognitions, a double anagnorisis, based on coincidence, that takes place independently of Scapin's efforts. I am not suddenly saying that realistic considerations play much, if any, of a part in Molière's plotting, only that the plotting is both an excuse for Scapin's displays of ingenuity and, at the same time, a good-natured twitting of that ingenuity, which all goes to waste. The play's resolution is brought about not by his will power and cleverness but by that inhuman agency, fate, that is, synchronicity. *Scapin* must therefore be read and played as a farce, not a comedy (in case this was not self-evident from its physical high jinks), and staged accordingly, with a high regard for farcical conviction rather than comic plausibility.

A few of the scenes that seem to be comic because they call on verbal, rather than physical, ingenuity, on *burli* and not *lazzi,* trouble directors. How can the farcical momentum be sustained through them? One such scene is Scapin's attempt to persuade Argante that it will be cheaper to surrender the two hundred pistoles to Hyacinte's "brother," the tough character played by Silvestre, than to try to dissolve his son's marriage by resorting to the law. Here Scapin lists the sort of palm greasings that would be required at different levels of the legal hierarchy. The speeches are as caustic and topical as any of the author's tirades against the medical profession, but they are couched in a rhetorical vein that demands for its effectiveness an oral equivalent of slapstick.

But think—what are you letting yourself in for? Look at all the handicaps in the legal system! The circuits! Appeals to lower and higher courts! Exhaustive forms and exhausting interviews! The beasts of prey that maul you as you pass through their claws—sergeants, prosecuting attorneys, defense attorneys, assistants, recorders, judges and their clerks! And every one of 'em can find leaks in your watertight case, and sink you. A police officer will make out a false statement that does you in and you won't even know about it. Your lawyer will gang up with the other side for a hefty consideration. Shortly before they plead your case he'll disappear from the court or, if he's there, he'll shift and shuffle and split hairs and miss the point. The registrar, just to be ornery, will file prejudicial notices and stop-clauses. The recorder's clerk will swipe documents or the recorder himself will fail to record something vital to your argument. And if you take every possible precaution and dodge around all those obstacles, you'll be stunned when the judges are turned against you by religious fanatics or girl friends. If you can, monsieur, if you only can, stay away from that pit of corruption. Going to law is hell on earth. . . . In court you'll need money. Expenses for the summons, for the writs, the registration, presentation, documentation, procuration. Fees for your attorneys' appearances and consultations. The costs of the right to write and rewrite the briefs, the reports and records, copies of provisional decisions by the registrar, sentences, arrests, controls, signatures, clerical messages, not to mention bribes at every turn and a final sweetener for the judges. Give this man the money and you're in the clear. (II, 5)

Jacques Copeau, the most resolutely faithful and scholarly of this century's great directors, thought it not unlikely that Molière performed *Scapin* in masks.[4] The suggestion is tantalizing. We have no firm evidence for masks donned by the Palais-Royal players in "straight" plays after 1666 and *The Misanthrope*, though they almost certainly wore them at times in the *divertissements*, as they did during the years while the troupe was taking its Italian-based plays through provincial France. When Copeau introduced *Scapin* to his own repertoire and played the leading role himself, he masked only one character, Silvestre, and only for the scene in which Silvestre does his impersonation of the ferocious "brother."[5] But that production took place more than twenty years before Copeau put forward his hypothesis; and it may be that if Copeau had eventually reinterpreted the play, he would have had most or all of his actors' faces behind masks, or at least have required each of them to maintain a facial comportment throughout the action as stonily innocent as Buster Keaton's.[6] In either case, he would be emphasizing

4. In Copeau's introduction to two of Molière's farces, *Molière farceur*, vol. 1 (Lyons: I.A.C., 1943), xx–xxi. I am grateful to Eric Bentley for drawing my attention to this edition. Further comments by Copeau on *Scapin* and masking can be found in Guicharnaud, ed. *Molière*, "On *Les Fourberies de Scapin*, 150–54, tr. June Guicharnaud, and in John Rudlin's *Jacques Copeau* (Cambridge: Cambridge University Press, 1986), 71–81.

5. An illustration of this scene, with André Bacqué (Silvestre) masked but with Copeau and Romain Bouquet (as Scapin and Argante) both unmasked, appears on the cover and on p. 75 of Rudlin.

Masks, as Copeau pointed out, were definitely worn in eighteenth-century productions of *Scapin*, probably by Scapin, Argante, and Géronte.

6. Among the silent film comics, Keaton was by no means the only "stone face." Most of them animated their features hardly at all. They might twitch their nostrils and the phony mustaches glued to their upper lips, or they might open their eyes wider and

the play's physicality while taking for granted its disinterest in psychological consistency and complexity. For the roles, at their most expansive, are one-and-a-bit dimensional. With the exception of Scapin, the characters never find time to reflect; they must react to one crisis coming on top of another. The plotting, which consists precisely of the working-out of Scapin's *fourberies*, keeps bearing down on them. Literally down in Copeau's version: To differentiate between Scapin and his dupes and to assert his superiority over them, he played the rascally hero from a raised platform or *tréteau*, while the other actors remained at stage level most of the time. When they found themselves dragged onto the platform, as happened once or twice, they had entered Scapin's world, with its own collection of rules and customs, and could not accommodate themselves to it. This setting, otherwise unadorned, must have made for a refreshing change from the Terentian-Renaissance set generally shown at the Comédie-Française, with its houses and central avenue, much imitated in other French playhouses and in other countries.[7] Copeau had seen, and seized on, the impersonal, stagey nature of the action's precincts, which are more an atmosphere than an environment and match the impersonality of the characters. What Molière himself required in the way of a set we may never know. The terse stage direction at the head of the play says merely, "The stage (scene) is in Naples." In this ambivalent area, Scapin the malign, masked magician has all the freedom in the world to open his sack of tricks, show them off with dazzling rapidity, and dance himself toward a suggestion of death, for there is some pathos in the actor's reminding us that his role is over.

furrow their brows; but they conveyed responses as a rule with body language and costume. Even Chaplin, the most expressive of them, was sparing with his features. He accomplishes his most memorable serious moments by means of a steady, extraordinarily intensive gaze, such as the ones directed at Georgia Hale in *The Gold Rush* and at Virginia Cherrill in *City Lights*.

7. "The stage-setting used at the Comédie-Française represents a street running parallel to the footlights with houses at the back and sides of the stage. In the center of the stage at the back is a broad flight of stone steps leading up a hill between the houses. Over the first steps of this passageway an arch extends to the houses on either side" (from an old textbook, *The Principal Comedies of Molière*, ed. Frederick King Turgeon and Arthur Chew Gilligan [New York: Macmillan, 1935], 782).

Conclusion: Molière's Afterlife

How would the Restoration theatre have got along without Molière? At least eighteen playwrights dived or dipped into at least twenty-four of his thirty-three theatrical works before 1700 to emerge with at least thirty-eight Molière-saturated or Molière-moistened comedies.[1] The plunderer plundered. As of the eighteenth century, translations and other Englishing of the work went on steadily. By 1800, the internationalizing of Molière—or the "Molièrizing" of theatre everywhere—was well under way.[2] Don Juans and Amphitryons multiplied; some of them could have reached back for their origins to Molina or Plautus, but a playwright tackling either figure, the legendary or the mythic, would need to be aware of the stage of evolution it had passed through at the hands of Molière. Even the comedy-ballets inspired new theatrical inventions, most notably from Hofsmannsthal.[3]

By the middle of this century, Molière had leaked, unacknowledged, into American television sitcoms, episode after episode. He still does. But these were, and are, ersatz Molière, little more (and usually less) than his basic

---

1. According to my unscientific, statistically clumsy reckoning, the playwrights include Behn, Betterton, Caryl, Crowne, D'Avenant, Dryden, Etherege, Flecknoe, Lacy, Medbourne, Otway, Penkethman, Ravenscroft, Rawlins, Shadwell, Vanbrugh, Wright, and Wycherley; while their raw Molière material included *The Botcher, The Nuisances, Loving Spite, The School for Husbands, The School for Wives, The Criticism of the School for Wives, Two Precious Maidens Ridiculed, The Doctor in Spite of Himself, George Dandin, The Imaginary Cuckold, Tartuffe, Don Juan, The Miser, The Bourgeois Gentleman, Monsieur de Pourceaugnac, The Misanthrope, The Forced Marriage, The Imaginary Invalid, The Learned Ladies, The Sicilian, Scapin, Amphitryon, Psyche,* and *Doctor Love,* in no particular chronological order.

2. Johnson, Trail, and Neumann contains chapters that trace the productions of Molière plays and their by-products in France, Italy, Spain, England, Scandinavia, Austria, Germany, "Central and Eastern Europe," and "the New World," including Brazil (55–409). See also "The Molière Connection: French dramaturgy in Estonia" by Mardi Valgemae, in *Journal of Baltic Studies,* no.1 (Spring 1984): 10–16.

3. Today the theatre has been shoved toward and into spectacle by the competition from movies. Grandiose mountings abound amid lighting, sound, and scene changing so complex that the word "stage" hardly suffices for the intricate, electronic machinery attendant on plays and shows, and often gives way to the term "acting area." In this neo-baroque era, the time may have come for rejuvenating the comedy-ballets.

situations, minced and then flabbily rewrought. An increasing number of theatre productions are appearing on videotape; most of the ones I have seen were adeptly filmed and are welcome as both entertainment and research tools. Yet, for the muscularity, the range of argumentation and conflict, the never-quite defined roles—for the full experience of their theatrical bounty, we go back to the playhouse to relive them as they happen. And in the playhouse they do not need to be carved up or otherwise mauled; the original works—give or take minor emendations by generations of devoted editors— still seem topical and refreshing.

Behind the unsystematic analyses of them in the preceding chapters lurks a question: Why have these plays survived more lustily than those of most other seventeenth-century playwrights and, indeed, than most other plays written since? Comedy, farce, and satire can date within years, within weeks. I conclude that these plays are anything but static conceptions, and their characters anything but fixed personalities. Rather, the roles keep evolving as they redefine one another through the interactions decreed by the plotting. Molière's characters have sometimes been thought of as a rough equivalent of Jonson's "humours," and the word *the* in some of the titles seems to call for a "humourous" enactment of the characters as ultimate prototypes—the most miserly, most misanthropic, most bourgeoisified, most hypochondriacal, most hypocritical. But actors who sedulously play prototypes must expect to convey a monotony in production that does not occur in the texts.

Doubtless, each play has its faults, and by implication, there might conceivably be alternatives that would improve it, but I have not pursued them. I am grateful that these works are exactly what they are. Detecting supposed flaws and sores by putting oneself on a higher artistic plane than the author is a blood-stirring procedure, but it can lead to the dissection of hypothetical constructions a critic ought to have written, not the actual ones that have been written *about.* For determined hole pickers there never yet was a flawless play. In taking Molière as I find him, I have also refrained from lining the plays up in some order of excellence. Years of experiencing *The Misanthrope, Scapin, Tartuffe, The Miser,* and *Don Juan* do not convince me that any one is better playmaking, "deeper," or more fraught with meaning in Molière's time, or ours, than any of the others. A list of graded preferences has negative value; at its most meretricious, it caters to readers assumed to be unable to decide for themselves. In the theatre, how well the plays come across in relation to one another depends on which artists re-create them, and how.

If Molière's drama contends throughout with closed systems of thought, it is hopeless to reduce the plays themselves to a closed system by urging that directors and others who put them on cease to experiment with the staging—hopeless because no self-respecting theatre artist will heed such recommendations. Certainly, some experiments will prove outlandish, overstated, faddishly updated, garishly futuristic; they may forfeit the plays' principal sources of energy in their scrabbling for embellishment and novelty. But even over-zealous extending of a play's stageworthiness may be helpful in freeing it from what have come to be critical straitjackets, from perpetuations of the polite, unfunny, tedious Molière, who is visited as a dutiful obeisance toward the venerable history of theatre art. Besides, there is no nontotalitarian way to close off the unstruck veins in Molière and hang velvet ropes around them. Holding his work to some historical or theoretical standards is like embalming corpses when the plays' popularity argues that they irrepressibly live.

They do belong to their time and place. Molière ridiculed those seventeenth-century prisoners of extreme attitudes, those exponents of orthodoxy, of institutional loyalty, and of rules who have turned into fanatics. "He exposed everyone: doctors, charlatans, the Church, misers, ignoramuses, and, in so doing, he antagonized them all. The only protector he had was the King. When the latter rejected him, he was completely alone. . . . I am sure that under his outer attitude of respect for the King, Molière was thinking, 'I love you, but you are a real skunk.'" [4] The descendants of those targets are easily enough recognized today; and if Stanislavsky is right, the ambivalence of theatre people toward their "angels" has not changed much, either. Yet, as happens with any works of art that are long-lived, the passage of time (especially its bearing on our understanding of place and space) brings discoveries about what seemed to be hardened specifics in each work. Directors will keep plumbing the specifics for overlooked hints. T. S. Eliot may have had these overlooked hints in mind when he wrote to Ezra Pound, "It's what you do behind the audience's back so to speak that makes your play IMMORTAL for a while."[5] An alert director can bring some of what has remained behind audiences' backs to their fronts, "so to speak"—to some of their fronts, at any rate—and make theatrical capital out of it. At some time in the future, directors may appear to have exhausted the hints, in which case the plays will either be granted a respite—an unlikely circumstance as of this writing—and allowed to settle unperformed, like self-charging batteries, or else they will take on a pall of sameness, as has happened to many recapitula-

4. Nikolai Gorchakov, *Stanislavsky Directs,* tr. Miriam Goldina (1954; reprint, New York: Limelight Editions, 1985), 362.
5. From "Five Points on Dramatic Writing," *The Townsman* no. 1: 10.

tions. We have now advanced too far into the century and the open country of interpretation (as opposed to the fenced-in acreages of reproduction) to call a halt, much less retreat.

As the era of realism fades, we perceive that Molière was less a rationalist than the self-appointed enemy of whomever he found to be impersonal, inhumane; and that the challenges he issued are theatrical as well as being documentary. In his prefatory note to *Doctor Love*, addressed "to the reader," he writes: "It is unnecessary to warn you that there are many things that depend on the performance; plays, as is well known, are made only to be performed." Whether or not he would have approved of the latitude taken by some interpreters of his plays, he himself constantly experimented and defied the "standards" enunciated by members of the French Academy and its mental captives as he sought better laughter-producing and wonder-producing scenes and themes for the shorter plays, new forms for the later plays and the comedy-ballets. The more one studies his variations on the old and broachings of the new, the more one admires the breadth of his intellect, imagination, and courage, but particularly that gigantic, restless, sometimes sardonic intellect, fortified by his gift for deceptive simplifying. Much as he refashioned early plays because he saw the new opportunities that resided in them, so we, as receivers of them, find that in our own lives one play changes shape and casts new shadows. The *Misanthrope* and the *Tartuffe* I knew thirty years ago are not the ones I know today, thanks in large part to critics who could think as directors and directors who could behave as critics.

The Father in *Six Characters in Search of an Author* says that characters live (while their creators die), because those characters remain eternally fixed. Not so. Even an actor who thinks he or she hews faithfully to a traditional conception of a role cannot help putting forward a slightly distinctive reading. Any two different interpretations of the Father's role—any two sequential performances by the same actor—tell us that characters, like people, are what they keep becoming. And what others variously make of them. The Father in Pirandello, protesting that audiences must not identify him on the strength of one disgraceful episode in his background, wants to be everything he *could* be. But he is insisting on a task no single actor can fulfill.

Sometimes we believe we have seen a definitive performance. We enshrine it in our memories as another momentous and precious event in our lives. And so it is definitive for *then*. But forever? Out of the question.

Molière's Characters

Bibliography

Index

Molière's Characters

Short titles will be used for certain plays

Acante (*Mélicerte*); Acaste (*Misanthrope*); Adraste (*Sicilian*); Agénor (prince, *Psyche*); Aglaure (sister of Psyche, *Psyche*); Agnès (*School for Wives*); Alain (*School for Wives*); Albert (*Loving Spite*); Alcandre (*Nuisances*); Alcantor (*Forced Marriage*); Alceste (*Misanthrope*); Alcidas (son of Alcantor, *Forced Marriage*); Alcipe (*Nuisances*); Alcmène (*Amphitryon*); Alonse, Don (*Don Juan*); Alvar (*Don Garcie of Navarre*); Aminte (neighbor, *Doctor Love*); Amphitryon (*Amphitryon*); Anaxarque (*Magnificent Lovers*); Andrée (maid, *Seductive Countess*); Andrès (*Botcher*); Angélique (*George Dandin*); Angélique (*Imaginary Invalid*); Angélique (*Jealous Husband*); Anselme (*Botcher*); Anselme (*Miser*); Apothecary (*Monsieur de Pourceaugnac*); Argan (*Imaginary Invalid*); Argante (*Scams of Scapin*); Argatiphontidas (*Amphitryon*); Ariste (*Learned Ladies*); Ariste (*School for Husbands*); Aristione (*Magnificent Lovers*); Armande (*Learned Ladies*); Arnolphe (*School for Wives*); Arsinoé (*Misanthrope*); Ascagne (*Loving Spite*); Béline (*Imaginary Invalid*); Bélise (*Learned Ladies*); Béjart, Madeleine (*Rehearsal at Versailles*); Béralde (*Imaginary Invalid*); Bonnefoy, Monsieur (*Imaginary Invalid*); Brécourt (*Rehearsal at Versailles*); Caritidès (*Nuisances*); Carlos, Don (*Don Juan*); Cathos (*Two Precious Maidens Ridiculed*); Célie (*Botcher*); Célie (*Imaginary Cuckold*); Célimène (*Misanthrope*); Champagne (*Doctor Love*); Charlotte (*Don Juan*); Chrysalde (*School for Wives*); Chrysale (*Learned Ladies*); Cidippe (sister of Psyche, *Psyche*); Claudine (*George Dandin*); Cléante (*Imaginary Invalid*); Cléante (*Miser*); Cléante (*Seductive Countess*); Cleanthis (*Amphitryon*); Cléomène (prince, *Psyche*); Cléonte (*Bourgeois Gentleman*); Climène (*Criticism of The School for Wives*); Climène (slave, *Sicilian*); Clitandre (*Doctor Love*); Clitandre (*George Dandin*); Clitandre (*Learned Ladies*); Clitandre (*Misanthrope*); Clitidas (*Magnificent Lovers*); Colin (*George Dandin*); Comtesse d'Escarbagnas (*Seductive Countess*); Coridon (*Comic Pastoral*); Covielle (*Bourgeois Gentleman*); Criquet (pageboy, *Seductive Countess*); Cupid (or Love, *Psyche*); Damis (uncle of Ophise, *Nuisances*); Damis (*Tartuffe*); Dance Teacher (*Bourgeois Gentleman*); Daphne (*Mélicerte*); De Brie, Catherine (*Rehearsal at Versailles*); De la Dandinière, Monsieur (Dandin, *George Dandin*); De la Souche, Monsieur (Arnolphe, *School for Wives*); De Sotenville, Madame (*George Dandin*); De Sotenville, Monsieur (*George Dandin*); Diafoirus, Thomas (*Imaginary Invalid*);Diafoirus,Monsieur (*Imaginary Invalid*); Doctor

I (*Monsieur de Pourceaugnac*); Doctor II (*Monsieur de Pourceaugnac*); Dorante (*Bourgeois Gentleman*); Dorante (*Criticism of The School for Wives*); Dorante (*Nuisances*); Dorimène (*Forced Marriage*); Dorimène (*Bourgeois Gentleman*); Dorine (*Tartuffe*); Du Croisy (*Two Precious Maidens Ridiculed*); Éliante (*Misanthrope*); Élise (*Criticism of The School for Wives*); Élise (*Don Garcie of Navarre*); Élise (*Miser*); Elvire, Donna (*Don Garcie of Navarre*); Elvire, Donna (*Don Juan*); Enrique (*School for Wives*); Éraste (*Loving Spite*); Éraste (*Monsieur de Pourceaugnac*); Éraste (*Nuisances*); Ergaste (*Botcher*); Ergaste (*School for Husbands*); Ériphile (*Magnificent Lovers*); Éroxène (*Mélicerte*); Euryale (*Princess of Elis*); Exempt (*Tartuffe*); Fleurant, Monsieur (*Imaginary Invalid*);Flipote (*Tartuffe*); Frosine (*Loving Spite*); Frosine (*Miser*); Garcie, Don (*Don Garcie of Navarre*); Georgette (*School for Wives*); Géronimo (*Jealous Husband*); Géronte (*Doctor in Spite of Himself*); Géronte (*Scams of Scapin*); Gorgibus (*Flying Doctor*); Gorgibus (*Imaginary Cuckold*); Gorgibus (*Jealous Husband*); Gorgibus (*Two Precious Maidens Ridiculed*); Gros-René (*Flying Doctor*); Gros-René (*Imaginary Cuckold*); Gros-René (*Loving Spite*); Guillaume, Monsieur (tapestry merchant, *Doctor Love*); Gusman (*Don Juan*); Hali (*Sicilian*); Harpagon (*Miser*); Harpin, Monsieur (*Seductive Countess*); Henriette (*Learned Ladies*); Hippolyte (*Botcher*); Horace (*School for Wives*); Hyacinte (*Scams of Scapin*); Ignès, Donna (*Don Garcie of Navarre*); Isabelle (*School for Husbands*); Isidore (*Sicilian*); Iris (*Comic Pastoral*); Jacqueline (*Doctor in Spite of Himself*); Jacques, Maître (*Miser*); Jodelet (*Two Precious Maidens Ridiculed*); Juan, Don (*Don Juan*); Julie (*Monsieur de Pourceaugnac*); Josse, Monsieur (jeweler, *Doctor Love*); Jourdain, Madame (*Bourgeois Gentleman*); Jourdain, Monsieur (*Bourgeois Gentleman*); Julie (*Seductive Countess*); Jupiter (*Amphitryon*); Jupiter (*Psyche*); King (*Psyche*); La Grange (*Rehearsal at Versailles*); La Grange (*Rehearsal at Versailles*); La Grange (*Two Precious Maidens Ridiculed*); La Montagne (*Nuisances*); Lawyer (*Flying Doctor*); Léandre (*Botcher*); Léandre (*Doctor in Spite of Himself*); Léandre (*Scams of Scapin*); Le Barbouillé (*Jealous Husband*); Lélie (*Botcher*); Lélie (*Imaginary Cuckold*); Léonor (*School for Husbands*); L'Épine (servant, *Learned Ladies*); L'Espine (*Nuisances*); Lisette (*Doctor Love*); Lisette (*Imaginary Cuckold*); Lisette (*School for Wives*); Lope (*Don Garcie of Navarre*); Louis, Don (*Don Juan*); Louison (*Imaginary Invalid*); Loyal, Monsieur (*Tartuffe*); Lubin 9*George Dandin*); Lucas (*Doctor in Spite of Himself*); Lucette (*Monsieur de Pourceaugnac*); Lucile (*Bourgeois Gentleman*); Lucile (*Flying Doctor*);Lucile (*Loving Spite*); Lucinde (*Doctor in Spite of Himself*); Lucinde (*Doctor Love*); Lucrèce (*Doctor Love*); Lycarsis (*Mélicerte*); Lycas (*Comic Pastoral*); Lysandre (*Nuisances*); Lysidas (*Criticism of The School for Wives*); Lysiscas (*Princess of Elis*); Magdelon (*Two Precious Maidens Ridiculed*); Mariane (*Miser*); Mariane (*Tar-

tuffe); Marinette (*Loving Spite*); Marotte (*Two Precious Maidens Ridiculed*); Marphurius (*Forced Marriage*); Marquis (*Criticism of the School for Wives*); Martine, or Sganarelle's wife (*Doctor in Spite of Himself*); Martine (*Learned Ladies*); Mascarille (*Loving Spite*); Mascarille (*Botcher*); Mascarille (*Two Precious Maidens Ridiculed*); Mathurine (*Don Juan*); Mélicerte (*Mélicerte*); Mercury (*Amphitryon*); Métaphraste (*Loving Spite*);Molière, J.-B. P. (*Rehearsal at Versailles*); Molière, Mlle (*Rehearsal at Versailles*); Mopse (*Mélicerte*); Moron (*Princess of Elis*); Mufti (*Bourgeois Gentleman*); Music Teacher (*Bourgeois Gentleman*); Myrtil (*Mélicerte*); Narcissus (Sganarelle, *Flying Doctor*); Nérine (*Monsieur de Pourceaugnac*); Nérine (*Scams of Scapin*); Nicole (*Bourgeois Gentleman*); Night (*Amphitryon*); notary (*School for Wives*); Octave (*Scams of Scapin*); Orante (*Nuisances*); Orgon (*Tartuffe*); Ormin (*Nuisances*); Oronte (*Misanthrope*); Oronte (*Monsieur de Pourceaugnac*); Oronte (*School for Wives*); Orphise (*Nuisances*); Pancrace (*Forced Marriage*); Pandolphe (*Botcher*); Pèdre, Don (*Sicilian*); Pernelle, Madame (*Tartuffe*); Perrin (peasant's son, *Doctor in Spite of Himself*); Philaminte (*Learned Ladies*); Philinte (*Misanthrope*); Philis (*Princess of Élis*); Philosophy Teacher (*Bourgeois Gentleman*); Pierrot (*Don Juan*); Polichinelle (*Imaginary Invalid*);Polidore (*Loving Spite*); Poor Man (*Don Juan*); Pourceaugnac, Monsieur de (*Monsieur de Pourceaugnac*); Robert, Monsieur (*Doctor in Spite of Himself*); Sabine (*Flying Doctor*); Sbrigani (*Monsieur de Pourceaugnac*); Senator (*Sicilian*); Sganarelle (*Doctor in Spite of Himself*); Sganarelle (*Doctor Love*); Sganarelle (*Don Juan*); Sganarelle (*Flying Doctor*); Sganarelle (*Forced Marriage*); Sganarelle (*Imaginary Cuckold*); Sganarelle (*School for Husbands*); Silvestre (*Scams of Scapin*); Sosie (*Amphitryon*); Sostrate (*Magnificent Lovers*); Sylve, Don (or Don Alphonse, *Don Garcie of Navarre*); Tailor (*Bourgeois Gentleman*); Tailor's Apprentice (*Bourgeois Gentleman*); Tartuffe (*Tartuffe*); Thibaut (*Doctor in Spite of Himself*); Tibaudier, Monsieur (*Seductive Countess*); Tireis (*Princess of Élis*); Toinette (*Imaginary Invalid*); Trissotin (*Learned Ladies*); Truffaldin (*Botcher*); Tyrène (*Mélicerte*); Uranie (*Criticism of the School for Wives*); Vadius (*Learned Ladies*); Valère (*Doctor in Spite of Himself*); Valère (*Flying Doctor*); Valère (*Jealous Husband*); Valère (*Loving Spite*); Valère (*Miser*); Valère (*School for Husbands*); Valère (*Tartuffe*); Venus (*Magnificent Lovers*); Venus (*Psyche*); Villebrequin (*Imaginary Cuckold*); Zerbinette (*Scams of Scapin*).

Bibliography

Complete Editions of Molière

No complete editions of Molière are published in English.

Oeuvres complètes. Ed. René Bray. 8 vols. Paris: Belles Lettres, 1935–52.
Oeuvres complètes. Ed. Gustave Michaut. 11 vols. Paris: Imprimerie Nationale, 1949.
Oeuvres complètes. Ed. René Bray and Jacques Scherer. 3 vols. Paris: Club du Meilleur Livre, 1954–56.
Oeuvres complètes. Ed. Robert Jouanny. Paris: Garnier, 1960, 1962, 1965.
Oeuvres complètes. Ed. Georges Couton. 2 vols. 1971. Reprint. Paris: Gallimard, Bibliothèque de la Pléiade, 1981.

English Translations of the Plays

Please note that some of the titles differ in translation.

Baker, H., and J. Miller, tr. *Molière: Comedies.* London: 1739. Reprint London: Everyman Books, 1929–62. Vol. 1, *The Blunderer, The Amorous Quarrel, The Miser, The Romantic Ladies, The School for Husbands, The School for Wives, The School for Wives Criticised, The Impromptu of Versailles, The Man-Hater, The Mock-Doctor;* vol. 2, *Don John, Love's the Best Doctor, Tartuffe, Squire Lubberly, George Dandin, The Cit Turned Gentleman, The Impertinents, The Learned Ladies, The Cheats of Scapin, The Hypochondriack.*
Bermel, Albert, tr. *One-Act Comedies of Molière.* 2d ed. New York: Crossroads Continuum, 1975. *The Jealous Husband, The Flying Doctor, Two Precious Maidens Ridiculed, Sganarelle, or the Imaginary Cuckold, The Rehearsal at Versailles, The Forced Marriage, The Seductive Countess..*
Bermel, Albert, tr. *The Actor's Molière.* New York: Applause Theatre Book Publishers, 1988. Vol. 1, *George Dandin, The Miser;* vol. 2, *The Doctor in Spite of Himself, The Bourgeois Gentleman;* vol. 3, *The Scams of Scapin, Don Juan.*
Bishop, Morris, tr. *Eight Plays by Molière.* New York: Modern Library, 1957. *The Precious Damsels, The School for Wives, The Critique of the School for Wives, The Versailles Impromptu, Tartuffe, The Misanthrope, The Physician in Spite of Himself, The Would-Be Gentleman.*

Frame, Donald M., tr. *Molière: Tartuffe and Other Plays*, New York: Signet Classic, 1967. *The Ridiculous Précieuses, The School for Husbands, The School for Wives, The Critique of the School for Wives, The Versailles Impromptu, Tartuffe, Don Juan.*

———. *Molière: The Misanthrope and Other Plays.* New York: Signet Classic, 1968. *The Misanthrope, The Doctor in Spite of Himself, The Miser, The Would-Be Gentleman, The Mischievous Machinations of Scapin, The Learned Women, The Imaginary Invalid.*

Graveley, George, tr. *Six Prose Comedies.* London: Oxford University Press, 1968. *Coxcombs in Petticoats, Don Juan, The Reluctant Doctor, The Miser, The Self-Made Gentleman, Scapin the Scamp.*

Gregory, Lady Augusta, adapter. *The Kiltartan Molière.* 1910. Reprint, New York: Benjamin Blom, 1971. *The Miser, The Doctor in Spite of Himself, The Learned Ladies.*

Malleson, Miles, tr. *The Slave of Truth, Tartuffe, The Imaginary Invalid.* New York: Samuel French, 1960.

Marmur, Mildred, tr. *The Imaginary Invalid,* in *The Genius of the French Theater,* ed. Albert Bermel. New York: Mentor Classic, 1961.

Ozell, John, tr. *The Works of Mr. de Molière.* London: 1714. Reprint (3 vols.). New York: Benjamin Blom, 1967. (This is the nearest edition to a complete collection of Molière in English, although some of the plays have been lightly edited or bowdlerized.)

Passage, Charles E., tr. *Amphitryon.* (In a collection of three plays entitled *Amphitryon.*) Chapel Hill: North Carolina University Press, 1974.

Wilbur, Richard, tr. *The Misanthrope.* New York: Harcourt Brace, 1959.

———. *Tartuffe.* New York: Harcourt Brace, 1963.

———. *The School for Wives.* New York: Harcourt Brace, 1971.

———. *The Learned Ladies.* New York: Harcourt Brace, 1978.

Wood, John, tr. *Molière: The Miser and Other Plays.* London: Penguin, 1953 and subsequent printings. *The Would-Be Gentleman, That Scoundrel Scapin, The Miser, Love's the Best Doctor, Don Juan.*

Wood, John, tr. *The Misanthrope and Other Plays.* London: Penguin, 1959 and subsequent printings. *The Misanthrope, The Sicilian, Tartuffe, A Doctor in Spite of Himself, The Imaginary Invalid.*

Criticism and Biography

Adam, Antoine. *Histoire de la littérature française au XVIIème siècle.* Vol. 3. Paris: Domat, 1952.

Arnavon, Jacques. *La Morale de Molière.* 1923. Reprint. Geneva: Slatkine, 1970.

Arnott, Peter. *Ballet of Comedians.* New York: Macmillan, 1971.

Attinger, Gustave. *L'Esprit de la commedia dell'arte dans le théâtre français.* 1950. Reprint. Geneva: Slatkine, 1969.

Audiberti, Jacques. *Molière dramaturge.* Paris: L'Arche, 1954.

Bénichou, Paul. *Morales du grand siècle.* Paris: Gallimard, 1948.

Bentley, Eric. *The Life of the Drama.* New York: Atheneum, 1964.

Bray, René. *Molière, homme de théâtre.* Paris: Mercure de France, 1954.

Bulgakov, Mikhail. *The Life of Monsieur de Molière.* Tr. Mirra Ginsburg. New York: Grove Press, 1970.

Cairncross, John. *Molière bourgeois et libertin.* Paris: Nizet, 1963.

Chevalley, Sylvie. *Molière en son temps.* Paris: 1973.

Defaux, Gérard. *Molière, ou les métamorphoses du comique.* Lexington: University of Kentucky Press, 1980.

Demorest, Jean-Jacques, ed. *Studies in Seventeenth-Century French Literature.* New York: Doubleday Anchor, 1966.

Descotes, Maurice. *Les grands rôles du théâtre de Molière.* Paris: Presses Universitaires, 1960.

Fernandez, Ramon. *Molière: The Man Seen Through the Plays.* New York: Hill and Wang, 1958.

Furetière, Antoine. *Dictionnaire universelle, contenant généralement tous les mots françois, tant vieux que modernes, et les termes de toutes les sciences et des arts.* 3 vols. Rotterdam: 1690.

Gaxotte, Pierre. *Molière fameux comédien.* Paris: Hachette, 1971.

Gossman, Lionel. *Men and Masks: A Study of Molière.* Baltimore: Johns Hopkins University Press, 1963.

Grimarest. *La Vie de M. de Molière,* 1705. Reprint. Paris: Brient, 1955.

Gross, Nathan. *From Gesture to Idea: Esthetics and Ethics in Molière's Comedy.* New York: Columbia University Press, 1982.

Guicharnaud, Jacques. *Molière, une aventure théâtrale.* Paris: Gallimard, 1963.

———, ed. *Molière: A Collection of Critical Essays.* Englewood Cliffs, NJ: Prentice-Hall, 1964.

Gutwirth, Marcel. *Molière, ou l'invention comique.* Paris: Minard, 1966.

Hall, H. Gaston. *Comedy in Context.* Jackson: University of Mississippi Press, 1984.

Herzel, Roger W. *The Original Casting of Molière's Plays.* Ann Arbor, MI: UMI Research Press, 1981.

Heymann, Jerry. "The Comedy of Theatricality: A Study of Molière's Aesthetics." Ph.D. diss. Pittsburgh: Carnegie Mellon University, 1971.

Howarth, W. D. *Molière: A Playwright and His Audience.* London and Cambridge: Cambridge University Press: 1982.

Howarth, W. D., and M. Thomas, eds. *Molière: Stage and Study.* Oxford and London: Oxford University Press, 1973.

Hubert, J. D. *Molière and the Comedy of Intellect.* Berkeley: University of California Press, 1962.

Jaques, Brigitte. *Elvire Jouvet 40.* Paris: Beba, 1986. (A play based on Louis Jouvet's Molière classes and adapted from *Molière et la comédie classique.)*

Jasinski, René. *Molière.* Paris: Hatier, 1969.

————. *Molière et le Misanthrope.* Paris: Nizet, 1951.

Jouvet, Louis. *Molière et la comédie classique.* Paris: Gallimard, 1965.

Johnson, Roger, Jr., Editha S. Neumann, and Guy T. Trail, eds. *Molière and the Commonwealth of Letters.* Jackson: University of Mississippi Press, 1975.

Jurgens, Madeleine, and Elizabeth Maxfield-Miller. *Cent ans de recherches sur Molière, sur sa famille and sur les comédiens de sa troupe.* Paris: Imprimerie Nationale, 1963.

Lancaster, H. Carrington. *A History of French Dramatic Literature in the Seventeenth Century*, pt. 3. Baltimore: Johns Hopkins Press, 1936.

Lanson, Gustave. "Molière and Farce." *Tulane Drama Review* 8, no. 2, (Winter 1963).

Lawrence, Francis L. *Molière: The Comedy of Unreason.* New Orleans: Loyola University Press, 1968.

Mander, Gertrud. *Molière.* New York: Ungar, 1973.

Meyer, Jean. *Molière.* Paris: Perrin, 1963.

Michaut, Gustave. *La Jeunesse de Molière, Les Débuts de Molière à Paris,* and *Les Luttes de Molière.* 1923–25. Reprint. Geneva: Slatkine, 1970.

Mongrédien, Georges. *La Vie privée de Molière.* Paris: Hachette, 1950.

Moore, Will G. *Molière: A New Criticism.* Oxford and London: Oxford University Press, 1949. Reprint. New York: Doubleday Anchor, 1962.

O'Connor, Garry. *French Theatre Today.* London: Pitman, 1975.

Palmer, John. *Molière.* New York: Brewer and Warren, 1930.

Pellisson, Maurice. *Les Comédies-Ballets de Molière.* Paris: Hachette, 1914.

Poulaille, Henri. *Corneille sous le masque de Molière.* Paris: Grasset, 1957.

Romero, Laurence. *Molière: Traditions in Criticism.* Chapel Hill: North Carolina University Press, 1974.

Scherer, Jacques. *Sur le "Dom Juan" de Molière.* Paris: Sedes, 1967.

Simon, Alfred. *Molière par lui-même.* Paris: Éditions du Seuil, 1957.

Szogyi, Alex. *Abstract Molière.* Paris: Nizet, 1985.

Teyssier, Jean-Marie. *Réflexions sur le "Dom Juan" de Molière.* Paris: Nizet, 1970.

Walker, Hallam. *Molière.* New York: Twayne, 1971.

Critical Articles in Journals

These, as well as individual chapters in books, are far too numerous to list. The author and his plays continue to come in for literary, attributive, historical, biographical, theatrical, socialist, feminist, structural (and structuralist), semiotic, deconstructionist, and other forms of dissection, such as psychoanalytical and medical.

Index

Plays and most other artworks are indexed under the name of the artist

Abstract opposites, 14–15, 148, 201

Acting styles: presentational, 19, 44, 74, 153, 154, 169n, 188, 233; realistic, 44, 74, 108, 110, 154, 215

Action: contrast with story, 8–10; defined, 8

Actors Studio, 113–14

Adam, Antoine, 212n

Aeschylus: Agamemnon, 9, *Oresteia*, 251

Alexander (the Great), 227n; in effigy, 78

Alkmena, 198

Allio, René, 158

Antoine, André, 158n

Ariosto, Ludovico: *Orlando Furioso*, 66

Aristophanes, 39, 57n

Aristotle, 1–4, 58n, 104, 105n

Arnold, Viktor, 119

Astrology, 85–86, 87

Auclair, Michel, 158

Audience reactions, 4, 115, 118, 119, 124, 156–57, 159, 172, 179–80, 189, 223n, 226–29, 238

Bacqué, André, 262n

Baker, H., and Miller, J. 25, 219n

Ballet of Ballets, 203

Ballet of the Muses, 75–80

Ballet of the Nations, 174

Baron (Michel Boiron), 75, 90n

Barrault, Jean-Louis, 175n

Beaumarchais, Pierre-Augustin Caron de: *The Barber of Seville*, 79n, 94; *The Marriage of Figaro*, 31

Beauval, Jeanne-Olivier, 7, 174, 183, 259

Beckett, Samuel: *Endgame*, 184; *Krapp's Last Tape*, 184; *Waiting for Godot*, 230

Bedford, Brian, 249n

Béjart, Armande. *See* Molière, Armande

Béjart, Louis, 66n

Béjart, Madeleine, 7, 10n, 37, 58, 66n, 108n, 109, 111, 215, 216, 254

Beltrame (Niccolò Barbieri): *L'Inavertito*, 26n, 29n

Benserade, I. de, 67, 77, 86

Bentley, Eric, 40, 262n

Bérard, Christian, 229n

Bergson, Henri, 239, 240

Bertholet, René, 7, 20–21, 66n

Betterton, Thomas: *The Amorous Widow, or The Wanton Wife*, 116n

Bhava (in Sanskrit theatre), 2

Boccaccio: *Decameron*, 20–21, 116n

Boileau, Nicolas, 72n, 112, 156; *Satires*, 210n

Boisrobert, l'Abbé François de, 155n

Bouquet, Romain, 262n

Bourgogne troupe, Hôtel de, 44, 107–13

Boursault, Edmé, 110; *The Painter Painted*, 107, 110, 113

Bray, René, xiii, 7–8n, 112n

Brécourt (G. Marcoureau), 105, 110

Brennus II, 87

Brissart's engravings, 63n

British pantomime, 174

Brodsky, Joseph, 258

Brook, Peter, 44, 122

Browne, Roscoe Lee, 113

Bulgakov, Mikhail: *Cabal of Hypocrites*, 12; *The Life of Monsieur de Molière*, 188

Butcher, S. H., 4

Challusay, Le Boulanger de: *Élomire hypocondre*, 164

Chambord chateau, 80, 84

Chaplin, Charles, 21n, 110, 263n; *City Lights*, 263n; *Gold Rush*, 263n

Chappuzeau, Samuel, 155n, *The Duped Miser*, 166n

Characters: as dramatic entities, 10–12, 50–51, 212; interactions between, 11, 147–48, 149–52, 167, 171; in pairs, 27–28, 32, 34, 45–46, 53, 83, 88, 89, 90, 147, 196, 205–6, 233–34, 236, 242, 247; personality changes in, 11–12, 23–24, 97–98, 153–54, 162–64, 170, 194–96, 197–99, 240–41, 266

Charpentier, François, 191

Chekhov, Anton, 119

Chevalley, Sylvie, 67n, 242n

Christ figurations, 169–70

Cignonini: *Prince Rodrigue*, 44n

Class distinctions, 84, 85, 118–19, 152n, 173, 176, 177–78, 181, 203, 223; masters and servants, 10–12, 24, 34–35, 43–44, 72, 74, 94, 96, 97–98, 154, 164, 182, 199, 210–11, 215, 221, 233–34, 255, 259, 260

Comédie-Française, 112, 113, 157, 158, 175n, 263n

Comedy, 2, 4, 6, 22, 44, 49, 87–88, 105, 111, 112, 152–53, 171, 182, 193, 208, 210, 220, 243

Comedy of character, 43, 44, 154

Comedy of intrigue, 51, 78–79, 93

Comic accents, 83, 253

Comic *récits*, 43; compared with tragic *tirades*, 174, 183, 245–46

Commedia dell'arte (and its masked players), 19, 25–26n, 32, 39, 41n, 64n, 75, 81n, 149, 154n, 155, 175, 191–92, 198, 207, 257–58

Commedia erudita, 155, 257

Compagnie du Saint-Sacrament, 66

Conti, prince de, 169n, 220n

Copeau, Jacques, 16n, 231, 262–63

Corneille, Pierre, 12n, 33, 47, 48, 58n, 104n, 108, 214n, 239; *Cid*, 197; *Don Sanche of Aragon*, 44n, 86n; *Horatius*, 239; *The Liar*, 198n; *Psyche*, 87, 90; *Sertorius*, 97

Corneille, Thomas, 104n, 220n

Court, the. *See* Louis XIV: court of

Couton, Georges, xiii, 19, 23n, 24n, 37n, 38–39, 62n, 72n, 73, 76n, 86n, 104n, 227n

Crow, Joan, 116n

Cuckoldry, real and imagined, 20, 42–43, 45–48, 50–52, 62–64, 78–79, 90, 94–95, 100–101, 115–18, 148–49, 160–61, 168–69, 196–97

Cyrano de Bergerac, Hector Savinien, 260n

Darkness: dramatic convention, 31, 51, 124

d'Aubignac, abbé, 104n

Davis, Daniel, 250n

De Brie (Edmé Villequin), 22n

De Brie, Mlle (Catherine Leclerc), 7, 22n, 37, 66n, 66, 77, 109, 183n, 212, 213, 214n

Delamare, Lisa, 166

De Visé, Donneau, 44n, 104n

Dexter, John, 249

Dickens, Charles: *A Christmas Carol*, 150n; *David Copperfield*, 168

Directors and directing, 3, 6, 11, 16,

110, 153, 154, 155, 158–59, 249–
  50, 255–56, 260, 262–63, 266–68
Doolittle, James, 29 1n, 22 1n, 225
Double-entendres, 51, 93, 97, 105,
  121–22, 153, 202
"Drinkable gold," 73n
Dryden, John: *Sir Martin Mar-All,* 25
Du Croisy (Marie Claveau), 37n
Du Croisy (P. Gassot), 7, 37n, 66n
Dueling, 60, 61, 62
Du Parc (Gros-René). *See* Berthelot,
  René
Du Parc, Mlle (Marquise-Thérèse de
  Gorla) 66n, 67, 111
Duse, Eleonora, 112

Eliot, T. S., 267
Else, Gerald F., 4
Empson, William, 70
Epic (dramatic form), 7, 221, 233
Ernst, Earle, 216n
Euphuism, 36, 206
Euripides, 251; *Alcestis,* 163, 243;
  Electra, 163; Hippolytus, 9, 15n; *Ion,*
  170
Exposition and story, 8–9, 155

Fabulae atellanae, 39
Farce, 19, 22, 24, 38–39, 84, 96, 152–
  53, 162, 165n, 171, 175, 178, 182,
  189, 190, 193, 195, 208, 209, 210,
  211, 220, 251, 257–58, 261–62
Feminist criticism, 205
Fernandez, Ramon, 149
Feuillade, duc de la, 220n
Fielding, Henry: *The Miser,* 156
Films, 15, 49; framing in, 3, 48
Foucquet, Jean, 58, 61n
Frame, Donald M., 219n
France, Anatole: *The Man Who Married
  a Dumb Wife,* 253
French Academy, 35, 268

Freud, Sigmund, 170
Fronde rebellions, 162n

Gallican church, 14, 162, 219–20, 225
Gargi, Balwant, 2n
Gassendi, Pierre, 2n
Gay, John: *Acis and Galatea,* 102n
Gilbert, Sir W. S.: *Pygmalion and
  Galatea,* 102n
Goldsmith, Oliver, 33
Gorchakov, Nikolai, 267n
Gossman, Lionel, 118, 121, 169–70,
  201n, 236n, 240n
Gozzi, Count Carlo, 26n; *Turandot,* 68
Grebanier, Bernard D. N., 10n
Gros-Guillaume, 21n
Gros-René. *See* Berthelot, René
Gross, Nathan, 75n, 169–70, 178n
Guicharnaud, Jacques, xiii, 66n, 159n,
  168n, 171n, 234n, 238, 245
Gutwirth, Marcel, xiii, 26n, 29, 237n,
  254n

Harned, Arthur R., 74n
Harrison, Tony, 249n
Harvey, John, 185
Hawthorne, Nigel, 154
Hebbel, Friedrich, 107
Hercules (Heracles), 70, 231
Hitchcock, Alfred, 23; *To Catch a Thief,*
  196n
Hofmannsthal, Hugo von, 265
Homosexuality: in seventeenth-century
  France, 159
Horace (Quintus Horatius Flaccus),
  58n
Howarth, W. D., xiii, 28n, 108n, 169,
  211n
Hubert, André, 7, 66n, 165n, 174, 215
Hubert, J. D., 44n, 98–99n, 100, 118,
  148, 196, 230
Huguenots, persecution of, 162n

Hurt, Mary Beth, 249n

Ibsen, Henrik, 236; *A Doll House*, 250n; *Enemy of the People*, 242; *Ghosts*, 124; *Hedda Gabler*, 124, 250n; *John Gabriel Borkman*, 250; *Little Eyolf*, 236; *Master Builder*, 101; *When We Dead Awaken*, 250n
Incestuous attraction, 27, 45
Interlocutors, 12n, 95–96, 163–64, 182, 187, 243; defined: 95–96
Interludes, 58, 59, 62, 65, 66–67, 74–75, 80, 86–87, 88, 89, 117, 174, 186, 190–92
Intrigue, 23, 26–27, 51–52, 78, 81–83, 93, 97–98, 99–100, 151, 175, 186, 190, 194–95, 203, 228, 258–59, 260–61

Jacobean drama, 222
Jacques, Brigitte: *Elvire Jouvet 40*, 231–32n
Jasinski, René, 13n, 19, 237n, 243n, 249n
Jodelet (Julien Bedeau), 7, 37n, 38
Jonson, Ben, 239, 266; *Volpone*, 148, 183
Jouvet, Louis, 229, 230, 231, 232n
Joyce, James: *Dubliners*, 220n
Jung, Carl, 40

Kabuki actors: *kumadori* makeup for 216n
Kazan, Elia, 113–14
Kearful, Frank J., 156n
Keaton, Buster, 262; *The General*, 257
King, the. *See* Louis XIV
Knapp, Bettina, 229n
Kosteroski-Kadish, Emilie, 209n
Kurosawa, Ikira: *Rashomon*, 10

Labiche, Eugène, 211n

La Fayette, Mlle de: *The Princess of Clèves*, 36
La Fontaine, Jean de, 58
Lagerfeld, Caroline, 250n
La Grange, Charles de, 7, 37n, 39n, 66n, 77, 110, 196, 230, 242n
Lancaster, H. Carrington, 30n
La Thorillière (F. Le Noir), 66n, 108, 109, 196, 241
Lathullère, R., 36n
La Vallière, Louise de, 65
Le Brun, Charles, 58
Ledoux, Fernand, 168
Legal profession, mockery of, 14, 235, 261–62
Le Nôtre, André, 58
L'Espy (François Bedeau), 37n
Lewis, W. H., 93n
Lope de Vega: *The Sheep Well (Fuente Ovejuna)*, 47
Louis XIV, 12, 58, 61, 64, 65, 66, 75, 89n, 90, 108–9, 113, 114, 171, 176, 193, 199, 210, 267; court of, 12, 13, 57, 59–60, 66, 119, 162, 176, 193, 209, 227, 235, 241, 242
Lowndes, M. E., 93n
Lucretius: *On the Nature of Things*, 245n
Ludlam, Charles, 181
Lully, Jean-Baptiste, 57, 58, 62, 66, 69, 74n, 78, 80, 82n

McCowen, Alec, 249n
Maintenon, marquise de, 216
Mander, Gertrud, 151n
Marivaux, Pierre Carlet de Chamblain de, 33n
Marlowe, Christopher: *Tamburlaine*, 229
Marvelous Peasant (anon.), 253
Masks, 19, 28, 31, 72, 83, 154, 262–63

Massinger, Philip: *New Way to Pay Old Debts*, 148

Mauvillain, Dr., 191n

May, Gita, 205n

Medical faculty, University of Paris, 190

Medical profession: mockery of, 22–25, 71–73, 82, 84, 182–92, 251–56

Medieval theatre, 19

Medieval Vice, 13

Melodrama, 51n, 154, 162

Ménage, Gilles, 13

Mesnard, Paul, 191n

Messenger speeches: in Greek tragedy, 9

Michaut, Gustave, 30n, 66n

Misunderstandings, 30–31, 32, 39–40, 41–43, 46, 47, 48, 79, 83, 202, 250, 258

Mnouchkine, Ariane, 188

Molière, Armande, 10n, 66n, 67–68, 75, 76, 90, 108n, 111, 121n, 167n, 183n, 212, 214n, 217

Molière, Esprit-Madeleine, 90n

Molière (Jean-Baptiste Poquelin): as actor, 7, 10, 31n, 37n, 59, 66n, 67, 68, 76, 77, 79, 84, 87, 90, 105, 108–13, 121, 167n, 182, 195–96, 199–200, 207, 230, 241, 257; as social critic: 13–14, 33, 62, 71–73, 82, 84, 193–94, 225, 235, 244, 247, 248, 252, 267. Works: *Amphitryon*, 12, 193–202; *The Botcher, or The Setbacks*, 13, 23, 25–29, 31n, 39n, 45, 83n, 94, 109n, 259; *The Bourgeois Gentleman*, 5, 15, 23, 34n, 39, 44, 87, 90, 95, 96n, 152, 155, 169, 173–81, 183, 184, 192, 203, 204, 215, 223n, 255; *Comic Pastoral*, 75, 77–78, 90; *Criticism of The School for Wives*, xi, 2n, 103–6, 107, 109, 111, 112, 178n, 180n, 235; *The Doctor in Spite of Himself*, xi, 1, 2, 10, 12, 28, 78n, 83n, 251–56; *Doctor Love*, xii, 70–75, 79n, 84, 96n, 182, 268; *Don Garcie of Navarre, or The Jealous Prince*, 43, 44–49, 60, 93, 215, 240; *Don Juan*, 6, 8, 11, 15, 23, 28, 45n, 73n, 83n, 90, 105n, 115, 148, 156, 189, 219–34, 239, 247n, 266; *The Flying Doctor*, xi, 22–25, 28, 41, 57, 109n, 152, 253, 254, 255; *The Forced Marriage*, 2n, 23, 62–65, 79, 178n, 183, 193; *George Dandin, or The Confounded Husband*, xi, xii, 5, 6, 11, 21, 23, 24n, 80n, 95, 96n, 115–24, 148, 155, 173, 176, 193, 202, 204, 214, 215, 222, 229; *Le grand Divertissement royal de Versailles*, 117; *The Imaginary Cuckold*, xi, 12, 15, 63n, 79n, 87, 95, 96n, 165, 169, 182–92, 204 (see also *Sganarelle, or The Imaginary Invalid*); *The Jealous Husband*, xi, 2n, 19–22, 33, 41, 79, 116, 121, 193; *The Learned Ladies*, xii, 13, 15, 23, 39, 96n, 189, 204, 205–17, 235; *Loving Spite*, 23, 28, 30–34, 39n; *The Magnificent Lovers*, 84–87, 90; *Mélicerte*, 75–77, 84, 90; *The Misanthrope*, 10n, 12, 15, 23, 39, 95, 105n, 111, 115, 121n, 148, 193, 214, 222, 235–50, 266, 268; *The Miser*, xii, 5, 6, 10, 15, 23, 51, 63n, 74, 79, 81n, 95, 105n, 147–57, 169, 173, 182n, 183, 189, 208, 215, 222, 229, 260n, 266; *Monsieur de Pourceaugnac*, 39, 72n, 80–84, 176, 204; *The Nuisances*, 8, 57–62; *The Pleasures of the Enchanted Isle*, 65–70, 75; *The Princess of Elis*, 65–70, 192; *Psyche*, 57, 87–90; *The Rehearsal at Versailles*, xi, 12, 107–14; *The Scams of Scapin*, 8, 15, 23, 24n, 28, 29, 79, 83, 94, 108n, 109n, 150, 182n, 189, 257–

63, 266; *The School for Husbands,*
15n, 49–53, 63n, 79n, 93, 94, 95,
96, 100, 101, 124, 183, 207n, 222;
The School for Wives, 10n, 12, 15, 23,
63n, 74, 79n, 93–106, 107, 115,
116, 121n, 148, 152, 164, 183, 189,
193, 210n, 214, 221n, 222, 229; *The
Seductive Countess,* 23, 39, 203–4;
Sganarelle, or The Imaginary Invalid,
22n, 23, 39–44, 47, 193, 259; *The
Sicilian, or Love the Painter,* 75, 220;
Tartuffe, or The Imposter, 5, 6, 12, 13,
14n, 23, 28, 63n, 65, 66, 73n, 74,
95, 96n, 105n, 115, 154, 158–72,
176, 182n, 183, 189, 214, 215,
220n, 222, 229, 268; *Two Precious
Maidens Ridiculed,* xii, 28, 34–39, 41,
51, 181, 204, 208–9, 213, 235.
Works lost, attributed to: *The Doctor
in Love,* 19n; *The Fine Blockhead,*
19n; *Gorgibus in the Sack,* 19n; *The Pedantic Doctor,* 19n; *The Three Rival Doctors,* 19n, *The Woodcutter,* 19n, 253,
254
Molina, Tirso de: *The Man Condemned
for Being Faithless,* 221n; *The Trickster
of Seville and the Stone Guest,* 219,
229, 265
"Monsieur" (Louis XIV's brother), 38,
159n
Montausier, M. de, 242
Moore, W. G., xiii, 112n
Moreto, Augustin: *Disdain Conquers Disdain,* 67n
Mrozek, Slawomir: *Tango,* 53
Mozart-Da Ponte: *Don Giovanni,* 231,
234
Muni, Bharata: *The Natyashastra,* 2n
Mythical sources, 90, 101–2, 194

Nabokov, Vladimir: *Lolita,* 101
Naples, 79, 257, 263

Neoclassical play conventions, 7, 32,
93, 147, 156, 159n, 200, 206, 222
Newcastle, the duke of, 25n
New Comedy (Greek), 25, 257

O'Neill, Eugene: *Days Without End,* 49;
Strange Interlude, 49
Oreviétan, 73, 75
Ovid (Publius Ovidius Naso): *The Meta-
morphoses,* 102n
Ozell, John, 45

Pailleron, Édouard: *The World of Bore-
dom,* 242
Palais-Royal, theatre of the, 80, 108,
262
Palmer, John, xiii, 66n, 205n
Pansaers, Clément: *Mountebanks,* 233
Pastoral literature, 69–70
Pedants in Molière's plays, 14, 19, 20,
22, 24, 32–33, 63–64, 205–6, 216,
252, 254
Pellisson, Maurice, 57n
Pellisson, Paul, 58n
Pepys, Samuel, 25n
Péréfixe, Hardouin de, 66
Petit-Bourbon Theatre, 38
Pintilié, Lucian, 171n
Pirandello, Luigi: *Six Characters in
Search of an Author,* 268
Planchon, Roger, 119–20, 158–59,
160n, 167, 171
Plato, *The Republic,* 214
Plautus, Titus Maccius, 14, 19, 25, 39,
57n, 151, 198n, 199, 265;
Amphitruo, 194, 195, 196; *Miles Glorio-
sus,* 63n; *The Pot of Gold,* 151n, 155–
56; *Pseudolus,* 63n
Playwright-within-the-play, 26–27, 82–
83, 93–95, 99, 190, 208
Plot: meanings in Aristotle and later, 4
Plotting: defined, 5; in the plays, 5–6,

11, 20, 22–23, 25–26, 30–32, 34–
35, 37–39, 40–43, 44–47, 49–52,
59–61, 62–64, 67–69, 70–72, 73–
74, 76–77, 80–83, 84–86, 88–09,
93–99, 103–6, 108–10, 115–23,
147–48, 159–62, 163, 165–67, 173–
75, 182–87, 190–92, 193–99, 206–
15, 222–25, 235–47, 248, 251–53,
255, 257–60, 261
Porter, Stephen, 249n
Potts, D. C., 226n
Préciosité, 35–37, 103

Quinault, Philippe, 87, 89n

Rabelais, François: *Gargantua and Panta-
gruel*, 62, 64n, 104n, 117n, 253
Racine, Jean: 33, 89n; *Andromache*
214n, 222n; *Bérénice*, 95, 214n, 236;
The Litigants, 117n; Phèdre's *death*,
22n
Rageneau, Marie, 203
Raisonneurs. See Interlocutors
Rambouillet, marquise de, 35, 37, 216
Ranson, John Crowe, 4
Rasa (in Sanskrit theatre), 2n
Reinhardt, Max, 16n, 119–20
Renaissance French theatre, 19
Restoration playwrights, 90; Molière's in-
fluence on, 265
Revue format, 7–8, 59, 65, 162, 174,
252–53, 254, 258
Richelieu, Cardinal de, 35
Rigg, Diana, 249n
Robinet (court gazetteer), 156
Robinson, David, 184n
Roles: vis-à-vis characters, 10–12, 43–
44, 212
Romains, Jules: *Knock, or The Triumph
of Medicine*, 255n
Rostand, Edmond: *Cyrano de Bergerac*,
260n

Roth, Philip: *The Counterlife*, 260n
Rotrou, Jean de, *The Sosies*, 194
Rousseau, Jean-Jacques: *Letter to M.
D'Alembert*, 243n
Rudlin, John, 262n

Saint-Aignan, duc de, 65–66
Saint-Évremond, sieur de: *Le Cercle*,
37n
Saint-Germain-en-Laye chateau, 75
Saint-Sorlin, Desmarets de: *The Vision-
aries*, 211n
Salons, literary, 35–36, 216, 235, 246
Sanders, James B., 158n
Scherer, Jacques, 15n, 229, 230
Scudéry, Madeleine de: 36, 37, 58n,
216; *Clélie*, 36, 41n; *The Great Cyrus*,
36, 37, 76; "Map of the Lovescape,"
37–38
Secchi, Nicolo: *L'Interesse*, 30n
Segrais, Jean, 36
Seigner, Françoise, 167
Seigner, Louis, 158, 168, 172
Seneca, 222
Serban, Andrei, 255–56
Settings, 19, 23, 37, 42, 45, 49–50, 58,
59, 62–63, 67, 76, 78, 80, 84, 87–
88, 94, 99, 103, 108, 116, 158, 192,
194, 195, 203, 206, 221, 232, 236,
249, 255, 262; impact on dramatic
structure, 2, 15–16
Shakespeare, William, 7, 30n; *Antony
and Cleopatra*, 236; *The Comedy of Er-
rors*, 258; *Hamlet*, 110, 236; *Henry
IV, Part I*, 9, 69, 251; *Henry IV, Part
II*, 251; *Henry V*, 69, 251; *King Lear*,
122; *Macbeth*, 229; *The Merchant of
Venice*, 148; *A Midsummer Night's
Dream*, 194; *Much Ado about Nothing*,
236; *Richard II*, 251; *Richard III*,
229; *Troilus and Cressida*, 236;
Twelfth Night, 192

Shaw, Bernard, 112, 124; *Back to Methuselah*, 101–102n; *Candida*, 101n; *Man and Superman*, 226, 233, 239; *Pygmalion*, 101
Sheridan, Richard: *The School for Scandal*, 122, 209
Shostakovitch, Dmitry, 12
Sicily, 79–80, 220, 232
Silvestre's engravings, 67
Simon, Alfred, 170
Simpson, Michael, 154, 249n
Somerville, Paul, 155
Somi, Leone di, 58
Sophocles: Ajax, 9
Spanish theatre, 44, 48, 219, 220, 232
Stage design. *See* settings
Stalin, Josef, 12
Stanislavsky, Constantin, 155, 267
Stendhal (M.-H. Beyle de), 205
Stewart, Fred, 113–14
Sting, 40n
Strasberg, Lee, 113–14
Strindberg, August, 236; *Dance of Death*, 236; *Miss Julie*, 173
Sturges, Preston, 7
Subligny, Adrien de, 242
Suzman, Janet, 154
Swain, Mack, 21n
Synchronicity (and coincidence), 40–44, 47, 48, 86, 99, 152, 171, 260–62

Television, 3, 48; evangelists on, 168; Molière's influence on, 265–66
Tempters: characters as, 151, 158, 160, 161, 167–68, 174, 177, 199, 209, 225, 231
Terence (Publius Terentius Afer, 19, 57n; *Adelphi*, 51n

Teyssier, Jean-Marie, 224n
Theatricalism, 19, 106, 107–13, 174–75, 180, 187, 190–91
Theocritus, 69
Theseus, 70, 231
Thomas, Merlin, 243n
Thought (Aristotle), 2, 12
Toliver, Harold E., 70n
Torelli, Giacomo, 58, 67
Tragedy, 2, 4, 6, 49, 87–88, 102, 105, 111, 112, 152, 248, 250
Transvestite roles, 30–31, 47, 64, 83, 164–65, 174, 176, 186–87, 215–16
Tuileries, 87–88
"Turkishness," 78, 174–75, 176, 179, 259
Typecasting (and casting against type), in Molière's company, 7–8, 58–59

Valgemae, Mardi, 265n
Vaux-le-Vicomte chateau, 58, 61n
Versailles chateau, 65–66, 108, 119
Verse, in Molière's plays, 25, 29, 32–33, 41, 43–44, 45, 58, 78, 86, 183, 206, 245
Vigarani, Carlo, 66–67
Vilar, Jean, 229, 233
Villains, knaves, *fourbes*, 13–14, 27–29, 35, 52–53, 81, 82–83, 84, 158, 170, 189–90, 199, 202, 223–24, 225, 233, 251, 252n, 255, 257
Villiers, André, 230
Virgil, 69
Voltaire, 209n

Wadsworth, Philip A., 155n
Wilbur, Richard, 100, 215
Wood, John, 78n, 219n
Wright, Garland, 249, 250

Albert Bermel, Professor of Theatre at Lehman College and the Graduate Center of the City University of New York, writes plays, translations, criticism, and, on occasion, capsule autobiographies. He has sat through uncounted productions of plays by Molière and, between the sittings and teaching, has published several hundred articles and reviews on theatre, film, education, life, garlic, and related and unrelated topics, as well as a number of books, including *Contradictory Characters: An Interpretation of the Modern Theatre, One-Act Comedies of Molière, Artaud's Theatre of Cruelty, Farce: A History from Aristophanes to Woody Allen, The Actor's Molière* (three volumes), *Six One-Act Farces*, and *Carlo Gozzi: Five Tales for the Theatre* (in collaboration with Professor Ted A. Emery).